The Threshold of the Visible World

The Threshold of the Visible World

KAJA SILVERMAN

Routledge
New York and London

Published in 1996 by

Routledge
29 West 35th Street
New York, NY 10001

Published in Great Britain by
Routledge
11 New Fetter Lane
London EC4P 4EE

The author gratefully acknowledges permission to reprint the following:

Isaac Julien, production still from *Looking for Langston*, reproduced by permission of the artist Sunil Gupta, London.

Marcel Duchamps, *Etant Donnés*, view through the door, reproduced by permission of ARS, New York.

Hans Holbein, *The Ambassadors*, reproduced by permission of the National Gallery, London.

Cindy Sherman, *Untitled Film Stills*, #2, 3, 34, 50, 35, 11, 15, 37, 43, reproduced by permission of Metro Pictures, New York.

An earlier version of Chapter 4 appeared in *Discourse*, vol. 15, no. 3 (1993), under the title "What Is a Camera?, or History in the Field of Vision."

Design: David Thorne
Printed in the United States of America on acid-free paper.

Library of Congress Cataloging-in-Publication Data
Silverman, Kaja
The threshold of the visible world / Kaja Silverman.
     p.   cm.
Includes bibliographical references and index.
ISBN 0-415-91038-2 (cl) — ISBN 0-415-91039-0(pb)

     1. Love.   2. Vision.   3. Psychoanalysis and philosophy.
     I. Title.
BD436.S49   1995   95-42297
150—dc20   CIP

FOR HARUN AND HIS PRODUCTIVE LOOK

Contents

Acknowledgments

Most of this book was written in Berlin, which is for me the city of love. When I live there, my subway station is even called "Blisse Strasse," which signifies nothing in German, but which yields a deep, private meaning for me. So my first thanks go to Berlin and my German friends for creating an atmosphere in which I could, as Lemmy Caution says in Godard's *Alphaville*, move "perpetually into the light."

A number of American friends read parts or all of this book, and helped me to make it better. I am enormously indebted to Amy Zilliax, my research assistant and right-hand woman, who helped at every stage in its production. Hayden White, Greg Forter, Judy Butler, and David Eng were meticulous and brilliant readers of these pages, and offered invaluable criticism and suggestions for improvement. Leo Bersani intervened at a crucial moment with a felicitous mixture of enthusiasm and sound advice, and Brian Wallis was a wonderful copy-editor. I must also thank Mary Russo for her sustaining friendship, and Carol Clover for always staying in touch, even when I was away from Berkeley for months at a time. Eric Zinner became editorially involved in this project at a late stage, but was enormously helpful.

I owe more than I can possibly acknowledge to Mieke Bal, a dear friend who is neither German nor American, but who moves gracefully in and out of many cultures. She subjected every word of this book to a microscopic scrutiny, and wrote pages of astute suggestions about ways to strengthen and clarify its arguments.

But it is to Harun Farocki that I am finally most indebted. He read this book in every draft, with an unerring eye for formal problems. Through him, I also gained a new access to the visual texts discussed here. Most importantly, he made it possible for me to conceive of the larger, theoretical argument of this book by teaching me to believe in the possibility of moving beyond the "either you or me" to a "you and me." He put the "bliss" in "Blisse Strasse."

In the spring of 1992, in a graduate seminar on Freud, one of my students asked, "Does psychoanalysis have a theory of love?" Almost automatically, I began to answer in the affirmative; psychoanalysis is, after all, the theory par excellence of the affective. However, after a moment's reflection, I was no longer so sure. Sexuality, desire, and aggressivity have all been much discussed, both within psychoanalysis proper, and within the many debates which have drawn upon it in recent years. But love has not figured prominently within either context. It has always seemed to lack respectability as an object of intellectual inquiry—to represent the very quintessence of kitsch.

Contemporaneous developments in my life gave both personal and theoretical urgency to the student's question, and the class spent the remainder of the seminar looking for an answer. We found many suggestive passages, but no definitive model for conceptualizing love. All that emerged with absolute clarity from the pages of Freud's writings was that love is intimately bound up with the function of idealization. However, as time went by, I became more and more convinced of the importance of our search. Love began to seem as indispensable in the political domain as in the psychic realm.

At the end of the semester, I began writing *The Threshold of the Visible World*. In a text which provided the basis for what would later become Chapters 1 and 3—and which I believed to be far removed from the concerns of my Freud seminar—I challenged the popular notion of the mobile subject, open to an infinitude of contradictory identifications. I argued that while most of us are, in fact, quite peripatetic when it comes to narrative and structural positionalities, we are considerably less tractable when confronted with the possibility of bodily reconfiguration, especially when it would involve an identificatory alignment with what is socially disprized. Generally, we either cling to our own corporeal coordinates, or aspire to assume ones which are more socially valorized. I sought to articulate the psychic and aesthetic conditions under which we might be carried away from both ideality and the self, and situated in an identificatory relation to despised bodies.

It was not until I began composing Chapter 2 of *The Threshold of the Visible World* that love emerged as the central category of the first half of the book. I realized then that those of us writing deconstructively about gender, race, class, and other forms of "difference"[1] have made a serious strategic mistake. We have consistently argued against idealization, that psychic activity at the heart of love, rather than imagining the new uses to which it might be put. In so doing, we have left the existing system of ideals unchallenged, and overlooked a crucial component within the identificatory process.

I subsequently came to argue in Chapters 1, 2, and 3 of this book that ideality is the single most powerful inducement for identification; we cannot idealize something without at the same time identifying with it. Idealization is therefore a crucial political tool, which can give us access to a whole range of new psychic relations. However, we cannot decide that we will henceforth idealize differently; that activity is primarily unconscious, and for the most part textually steered. We consequently need aesthetic works which will make it possible for us to idealize, and, so, to identify with bodies we would otherwise repudiate.

But it is not enough that we be textually enabled to identify with what is culturally disprized. It is crucial that this identification conform to an externalizing rather than an internalizing logic—that we identify excorporatively rather than incorporatively, and, thereby, respect the otherness of the newly illuminated bodies. It is equally vital that we be brought to a conscious knowledge that we have been the agents of that illumination, so that the newly created ideal does not congeal into a tyrannizing essence. The aesthetic work to which I give paradigmatic status in the first half of *The Threshold of the Visible World* is, therefore, one which resists our attempts to assimilate the ideal image. That work also maintains the gift of love in the form of a provisional bequest, and, thus, engages us in an active rather than a passive form of idealization.

So far, I have not made clear that the representational practices which concern me here are, above all, *visual*. Indeed, the larger project of this book is to offer an ethics of the field of vision, and a psychoanalytic politics of visual representation. In his *Écrits,* Lacan writes that "the mirror-image would seem to be the threshold of the visible world."[2] He thereby suggests not only that all visual transactions are inflected by narcissism, but also that it is only by moving through the mirror stage that one enters the scopic domain. *The Threshold of the Visible World* derives its organizational logic from this suggestive remark. It approaches the field of vision through the mirror stage.

The first half of this book addresses those concepts which are at the heart of that "event": bodily ego, idealization, and identification. The second half focuses on the three categories which are together constitutive of the visual domain: gaze, look, and screen (or cultural image-repertoire). And, whereas the chapters comprising the "Threshold" section seek to articulate the social and psychic constraints hemming in our bodily identifications, as well as the conditions under which we might circumvent those constraints, those comprising "The Visible World" are concerned more with the social and psychic forces regulating the look, and the circumstances under which we nonetheless manage at times to see productively or transformatively.

In the second half of *The Threshold of the Visible World*, I maintain that the look is under cultural pressure to apprehend the world from a preassigned viewing position, and under psychic pressure to see it in ways that protect the ego. The look is exhorted from many sides to perceive and affirm only what generally passes for "reality." Its objectivity is further undermined by all of those forms of misrecognition through which the *moi* is created and consolidated. The look consistently attributes to the self what is exterior and other, and projects onto the other what belongs to the self.

Even before we become conscious of having seen something, that perception has been processed in all kinds of classificatory ways, which help to determine what value it will assume. The visual object may also have been narcissistically appropriated, or freighted with the unwanted detritus of the self, and, so, repudiated. However, we do not ever look once and for all, but within time.

This "time" has two dimensions, one conscious and one unconscious. Although we cannot control what happens to a perception before we become aware of it, we can retroactively revise the value which it assumes for us at a conscious level. We can look at an object a second time, through different representational parameters, and painstakingly reverse the processes through which we have arrogated to ourselves what does not belong to us, or displaced onto another what we do not want to recognize in ourselves. Although such a re-viewing can have only a very limited efficacy, and must be repeated with each new visual perception, it is a necessary step in the coming of the subject to an ethical or nonviolent relation to the other.

The unconscious "time" of any given perception can last as long as a life span, and bring about a much more radical transmutation of values than can its conscious revision. To look is to embed an image within a constantly shifting matrix of unconscious memories, which can render a culturally insignificant object libidinally resonant, or a culturally significant object worthless. When a new perception is brought into the vicinity of those memories which matter most to us at an unconscious level, it too is "lit up" or irradiated, regardless of its status within normative representation. Excluded from that privileged field, value will drain out of it.

One cannot characterize this motility of the look as "agency," since it resists our conscious attempts to direct it. Here again, we need the assistance of aesthetic texts, which can intervene where we cannot. Such texts abound in visual and rhetorical images which, even before being psychically worked over, have the formal and libidinal properties of highly charged unconscious memories. They are consequently capable of moving immediately to a privileged site within the unconscious. At the same time, they are available to conscious scrutiny and interrogation.

For the most part, representational practice works through such mnemic "implants" to confirm dominant values. However, implicit in their exterior derivation is the possibility for each of us of having psychic access to what does not "belong" to us—of "remembering" other people's memories. And through these borrowed memories, we can accede psychically to pains, pleasures, and struggles which are far removed not only from our own, but from what normative representation validates, as well.

In Chapter 2 of *The Threshold of the Visible World,* I argue at length that all of our attempts personally to approximate the ideal end in failure, and leave us in a relation of fatal aggressivity toward others. I oppose to this vain narcissistic quest the active gift of love, or the provisional conferral of ideality upon socially devalued bodies. However, I do not indicate in that chapter how the subject is psychically to negotiate his or her resulting apprehension of lack or distance from the ideal.

It might seem that the only alternative to self-idealization is a determined self-revulsion. However, in the closing pages of this book, I am led by a series of important images toward a concept with which it would seem possible to dismantle the binary opposition of ideality and abjection—the notion of the "good enough." In so doing, I return to the topic with which I began: love. However, whereas I am initially concerned with the terms under which we might idealize and so identify with bodies which we would otherwise reject, I am by the end more concerned with the conditions under which we might ethically love ourselves.

The "good enough" is a paradigm through which ideals can be simultaneously lived and deconstructed. To live an ideal in the mode of the "good enough" is, first of all, to dissolve it into its tropes—to grasp its fundamentally figural status. Equally important, it is to understand that those tropes are only ever partially fulfillable. Finally, to embrace the principle of the "good enough" is to realize that one's partial and tropological approximation of the ideal counts most when circumstances most conspire against it. Once again, these are lessons that we can perhaps only learn from visual texts, since they have the power to reeducate the look. We can only accede narcissistically to the principle of the "good enough" after we have been taught to exercise it in relation to other bodies, and here the image is all-important.

As in the first half of *The Threshold of the Visible World,* I thus insist throughout the second half that the aesthetic text can help us to do something collectively which exceeds the capacity of the individual subject to effect alone. Although none of us is released from the imperative of looking ethically by the fundamental impossibility of that task, nevertheless, consciousness by itself cannot do much to combat the violence of either the self or dominant representation. For that purpose, we need more texts of the sort featured in this book.

Because the films and photographs which instanciate my notion of a psychoanalytic politics of representation so enormously expand our libidinal capacities, they assume an unconventional position in these pages. Those texts—Ulrike Ottinger's *Bildnis einer Trinkerin,* Isaac Julien's *Looking for Langston,* Harun Farocki's *Bilder der Welt und Inschrift des Krieges,* Chris Marker's *Sans Soleil,* and Cindy Sherman's *Untitled Film Stills*—figure here less as objects which I interpret from a position of greater theoretical knowledge, than as the guides which, like Socrates' Diotima, have instructed me in the arts of love and productive looking.

The Threshold

1

The Bodily Ego

In *The Ego and the Id,* Freud maintains that the ego is "first and foremost, a bodily ego; it is not merely a surface entity, but is itself the projection of a surface."[1] Although he does not define any of the terms through which he characterizes the psychic entity which is the primary concern of this often-quoted sentence, one thing emerges from it with absolute clarity: our experience of "self" is always circumscribed by and derived from the body.

On the face of it, this is a puzzling assertion, since the body ostensibly lies outside the domain of psychoanalysis. In "Instincts and Their Vicissitudes," Freud stresses that drives communicate with the unconscious only via an ideational representative.[2] And in *The Interpretation of Dreams,* he refuses to specify a physical location for psychical reality.[3] Moreover, in his account of hysteria, the one neurosis within which the body would seem to occupy pride of place, Freud makes clear that it does so only as a network of denatured signifiers.[4] Lacan insists even more emphatically upon a disjunctive relationship between body and psyche; identity and desire are inaugurated only through a series of ruptures or splittings, which place the subject at an ever-greater remove from need and other indices of the strictly biological.[5]

How then are we to understand Freud's claim that, from the very beginning and in its most profound sense, the ego is corporeal in nature? In this chapter I will attempt to provide a rather different answer to this question than that which is usually proffered. Since my ultimate goal is to clarify how gender, race, sexual preference, and other culturally constructed and enforced distinctions come into play at the level of the bodily ego, I will be concerned not only with the mirror image, but also with the gaze and the cultural "screen," or image repertoire; not only with idealizing identifications, but also with their deidealizing equivalents; and not only with the alterity of the ego, but also with its conventional insistence upon "self-sameness."

The Visual Imago

Lacan's account of the mirror stage has generally been read as a fuller elaboration of Freud's tantalizingly brief description of the ego—as an explanation, in particular, of Freud's insistence upon the ego as the "projection" of a "surface." Lacan proposes that the ego comes into existence at the moment when the infant subject first apprehends the image of its body within a reflective surface, and is itself a mental refraction of that image. Thus, the ego is the representation of a corporeal representation.[6] Significantly, both of these representations have an emphatically visual status. Not only is the "surface" of which the ego is a "projection" specular, but the cerebral cortex itself also "functions like a mirror," a "site" where "images are integrated."[7]

Lacan insists on the fictiveness and exteriority of the image which founds the ego. He also characterizes the psychic process which the ego sets in motion as the first of many structuring identifications (often involving not only exterior representations but other subjects). This has encouraged some commentators to insist that the mirror stage should be understood metaphorically rather than literally. Laplanche, for instance, suggests that the mirror stage be grasped simply as the child's "recognition of the form of another human and the concomitant precipitation within [it] of a first outline of that form."[8] Lacan's discussion of pigeons and locusts in his mirror stage essay might even seem to support such a reading. In the passage in question, normal development once again depends upon the introduction of an image (3). That image need not be a mirror reflection; the simple appearance of another member of the same species, of either sex, is all that is necessary, since what is at stake here is merely species identification.

However, in *Seminar I,* Lacan stresses that things rarely proceed as smoothly with human subjects as they do in the rest of the animal world. With humans, there is an extra term, one that would seem to coincide precisely with what might be called the "*moi*" or "belong-to-me" aspect of the ego, as opposed to those that would be exhausted by the subject's mere recognition of him or herself as a member of a species.[9] And in his account of the mirror stage, Lacan paradoxically insists on both the "otherness" and the "sameness" of the image within which the child first finds its "self." On the one hand, the mirror stage represents a *méconnaissance,* because the subject identifies with what he or she is not. On the other hand, what he or she sees when looking into the mirror is literally his or her own image.

Lacan attributes to this literal reflection both a decisive role in the initial formation of the ego, and a determinative influence over the ego's subsequent development. In *Seminar I,* he characterizes the literal reflection as the "*Urbild,*" or specular prototype of the ego (74), and in the mirror stage essay, he describes it as "the threshold of the visible world" (3). With this threshold metaphor, whose many meanings this book will explore, Lacan suggests that the subject's corporeal reflection constitutes the limit or boundary within which identification may occur.

Seminar I provides an extended discussion of an optical experiment, the experiment of the inverted bouquet, which helps to clarify the notion of the mirror image as a threshold or limit. In this experiment, a stand with an upright vase faces a spherical mirror. An inverted bouquet of flowers is suspended from the bottom of the stand. When a spectator occupies a particular position in relation to the stand and the spherical mirror, a real image of the flowers (i.e., one capable of being reflected in a plane mirror) is projected into the vase, so that it seems to contain them. In Lacan's revision of the experiment, the relative positions of the vase and the flowers are reversed, so that it is an image of the vase rather than the flowers (or, to state the case in terms more directly germane to the present discussion, the container rather than what is contained) that is produced as a mirage on the top of the stand. In Lacan's theoretical appropriation of the experiment, the imaginary vase represents the body's image, which—although fictive—effectively works to structure and contain.

Lacan implies at one point in *Seminar I* that the bodily image plays this including and excluding role with respect to other images, specifying those which are acceptable loci of identification, and those which are not (145). In *Seminar VII,* he makes this axiom explicit, suggesting that the mirror image fulfills "a role as limit"— "it is that which cannot be crossed."[10] Thus, at the heart of Lacan's theory of the mirror stage there would seem to be something which has gone largely unremarked, something which calls into question the currently fashionable notion of a perpetually mobile subject, capable of a wide range of contradictory bodily identifications: the principle of the self-same body. It will be the primary task of this chapter both to elaborate and problematize this principle, which, unfortunately, never comes into sharp focus within the pages of Lacan's *Seminars* or *Écrits.*

Laplanche also says that the identification which first conjures the ego into existence implies the articulation of bodily boundaries. "We are…led to admit the existence of an identification that is both early and probably also extremely sketchy in its initial phase," he writes in *Life and Death in Psychoanalysis,* "an identification with a form conceived of as a limit, or a sack: a sack of skin" (81).

Although here "limit" would seem to signify the dividing line between "self" and "world," through its conceptual proximity to "sack," it also signifies a container whose shape determines in advance the imaginary "contents" which can be put into it. In other words, like Lacan, Laplanche suggests that, far from being wide open to any corporeal imago, the normative ego allows only those identifications which are congruent with its form. As I have already indicated, however, a moment later Laplanche goes on to disassociate the articulation of this bodily container from the subject's own reflection by attributing a metaphoric status to the mirror stage. The *moi* or "belong-to-me" component of the ego makes its appearance from another direction—from the direction of the "sensational" body.

A note added by James Strachey in his translation of *The Ego and the Id,* and approved by Freud, proposes a very different explanation of the bodily ego than that advanced by Lacan in the *Écrits* and early *Seminars.* "The ego is ultimately derived from bodily sensations," this note reads, "chiefly from those springing from the surface of the body. It may thus be regarded as a mental projection of the surface of the body...." (26n). Laplanche draws upon this note from *The Ego and the Id* as well as on Lacan's essay on the mirror stage for his own account of the subject's primordial identification. On the one hand, he explains, the specular image allows "an apprehension of the body as 'a separate object.'" On the other hand, the body is apprehended by the subject as its "own" via the tactile exploration of its "cutaneous surface" (81–82). In a subsequent discussion of physical pain and its role in defining the limits of the corporeal ego, Laplanche once again stresses the crucial part played by the sensational body within the constitution of the ego (82).[11] He thereby accounts more satisfactorily than Lacan for how the ego can be predicated upon both "sameness" and "otherness." However, Laplanche does not elaborate any further on either the nature of the sensational body, or its relation to the visual image. For such an elaboration, we must turn to the work of Paul Schilder and Henri Wallon.

Sensation and the Bodily Ego

It might seem difficult to account for the ego as a projection of bodily sensation without somehow naturalizing that psychic entity. However, in an extraordinary book first published in 1935, *The Image and Appearance of the Human Body,* Viennese neurologist and psychoanalyst Paul Schilder elaborates a radically deessentializing theory of the part played by sensation in the production of the corporeal ego, and one whose emphases are often surprisingly congruent with Lacan's essay on the mirror stage. While Schilder readily grants the importance of images of the body in the formation of the "self," he argues that they represent only one of that entity's components. The "postural model of the body" or "image of the body," the two terms which Schilder uses to refer to the corporeal ego, also include all tactile, cutaneous, and kinaesthetic sensations.[12] Through synesthesia, these sensations are experienced as referring to one body, occupying a single point in space:

> The image of the human body means the picture of our own body which we form in our mind, that is to say, the way in which the body appears to ourselves. There are sensations which are given to us. We see parts of the body-surface. We have tactile, thermal, pain impressions. There are [also] mental pictures and representations.[13]

Far from being a biological given, the postural model of the body must be painstakingly built up. Moreover, this process of construction must be endlessly repeated, since—lacking any stable referent—it undergoes repeated disintegration and transformation. This can be demonstrated most dramatically through that element in the postural model of the body which would seem to evade psychic mediation, and to refer back to Freud: cutaneous sensation. Like the specular image, which forms the basis of the Lacanian ego, cutaneous sensation is conferred upon the subject from outside. Without social exchange, Schilder insists, it would never come into existence, since it can be defined only through the relationship between the body and the world of objects. Without such contact, the cutaneous surface of the body has neither form nor decisive boundaries: "The outline of the skin is not felt as a smooth and straight surface," he writes. "This outline is blurred. There are no sharp borderlines between the outside world and the body. The surface of the body can be compared in its indistinctness of feeling with the indistinctness of Katz's so-called space color" (85).

Schilder later suggests that it is only when the surface of our body comes into contact with other surfaces that we are even able to perceive it (86). This formulation stresses the crucial role played by one's surroundings, but not necessarily by social exchange, in the construction of the body. However, still later in the book, Schilder formulates his view of the relation between the subject's bodily ego and the larger environment in more insistently cultural terms. He remarks that "the touches of others, the interest others take in the different parts of our body, will be of an enormous importance in the development of the postural image of the body" (126). In this way, he indicates that the body is not the simple product of physical contact, but that it is also profoundly shaped by the desires which are addressed to it, and by the values which are imprinted on it through touch.

Elsewhere in *The Image and Appearance of the Human Body*, Schilder indicates that the shape of the body also shifts with the desires of the subject, desires which position him or her once again in a structuring relation to the Other. "Every emotion...changes the body-image," he observes. "The body contracts when we hate, it becomes firmer, and its outlines towards the world are more strongly marked. This is connected with the beginning of action in the voluntary muscles.... We expand the body when we feel friendly and loving...and the borderlines of the body-image lose their distinct character" (210).

For Schilder, bodily openings are particularly important to the postural model, because it is "by these openings that we come in closest contact with the world" (124–25). Consequently, physical desire is most classically localized there. Although Schilder does not actually suggest that erotogenic zones are mapped onto the child's body through the parental touch, that argument would be consistent with his insistence on both the constructed nature of the postural model of the body, and the importance of corporeal openings. Laplanche, who later proposed such a reading of the erotogenic zones, maintains that bodily openings enjoy their powerful status because they represent the points at which fantasy is introduced into the child. Within this formulation, erotic sensation is initially produced not only through parental touch, but also through parental desire (44–47), and hence, it emerges as a privileged site for the articulation of cultural differences.

What I am trying to suggest is that when Schilder is read through Laplanche in this way, it becomes possible to see more clearly than usual that, in addition to being a sexual component, an erotogenic zone is a feature of the bodily ego. Therefore, it would seem that one's apprehension of self is keyed both to a visual image or constellation of visual images, and to certain bodily feelings, whose determinant is less physiological than social. Seen in this light, Freud's *Three Essays on a Theory of Sexuality*, with its emphasis on the erotic value which attaches first to one and then to another bodily zone during the early years of subjectivity, is as much a history of how the bodily ego is normatively constructed and gendered as it is a history of sexuality.[14]

I may seem to be belaboring the obvious here; we all know that the areas of the body in which someone experiences sexual pleasure have a lot to do with his or her identity. However, Lacanian psychoanalysis, with its emphasis on the ego as a product of specular relations, has made it extremely difficult to theorize the role played there by bodily sensation. This represents a crucial task if we are to account for both the ego's "otherness" and its peculiar insistence—in its most conventional and murderous forms—on "self-sameness."

Identity-at-a-Distance

Although Schilder suggests that the bodily ego has a sensational as well as a visual dimension, he insists that these different aspects are so closely integrated with one another as to give rise to a unified sense of self. However, in *Les Origines du caractère chez l'enfant*, a text dating from 1934, French psychoanalyst Henri Wallon maintains that the visual imago, or "exteroceptive ego," is initially disjunctive from what he calls the "proprioceptive ego," and that the unity which they subsequently form is at best tenuous.

Wallon advances a theory of the mirror stage which differs in certain key respects from the one to which we have grown accustomed. In his essay on primary identification, Lacan refers to the period extending from the infant's sixth to its eighteenth month as a mirror stage, but he also describes the infant's encounter with its specular reflection as more of a punctual event than an ongoing process, "Unable as yet to walk, or even to stand up, and held tightly as he is by some support, human or artificial," Lacan's hypothetical child "nevertheless overcomes, in a flutter of jubilant activity, the obstructions of his support and, fixing his attitude in a slightly leaning-forward position…brings back an *instantaneous* aspect of the image [my emphasis]."[15] At this moment, says Lacan, the image is imaginarily assumed or put on by the child. According to Wallon, on the other hand, a lengthy period intervenes between the child's first exposure to a mirror and the moment at which the reflected image is psychically incorporated. During this period, the mirror image remains stubbornly exterior.

In contrast to the scene of jubilant *méconnaissance* which provides the centerpiece to Lacan's essay on the mirror stage, Wallon describes the infant embracing its reflection as a love object at the age of twenty weeks, and still playing with it as a double or rival eleven weeks later.[16] Another of his exemplary children reaches with "ardor" toward its specular image in its eighth month, and is astonished when its hand contacts cold glass instead of warm flesh (197–98). In its fifteenth month, the same child "touches, licks and strikes its reflection, and enlists it as an ally"(204). And upon hearing its name called, another of the infants cited by Wallon looks to its mirror image rather than responding itself (198).

Les Origines du caractère chez l'enfant thus suggests much more forcefully than Laplanche that the infant initially responds to the reflection of its body as a separate thing, like its mother or father. At the same time, as is indicated by the example of the child who looks to the mirror when hearing its name called, that reflection provides an image in relation to which it somehow orients itself. The reflection offers what, for lack of a better expression, I will call "identity-at-a-distance." Such an identity is, of course, inimical to the very concept implied by that word, which literally means "the condition or quality of being the same" (OED, 881). Identity-at-a-distance entails precisely the opposite state of affairs—the condition or quality of being "other."

This is not the only significant way in which Wallon's account of the mirror stage diverges from Lacan's. In Lacan's narrative, the mirror image is sufficient to induce an apprehension of "self" in the child. In Wallon's, two components must be brought together in order for that to happen: the mirror image or "exteroceptive" ego, and the "proprioceptive" ego. It is in relation to the proprioceptive ego that we perceive things as exterior to us, and, so, that the specular image might be said to be "outside."[17]

Proprioceptivity, which is as central to the formation of the corporeal ego as is the visual imago, derives etymologically from *proprius,* which includes among its central meanings "personal," "individual," "characteristic," and "belonging to"; and *capere,* which means "to grasp," "to conceive," and "to catch." It thus signifies something like "the apprehension on the part of the subject of his or her 'ownness.'" This notion must be distinguished from identity, which, at least in the case of the visually unimpaired subject, depends upon the image. Proprioceptivity can best be understood as that egoic component to which concepts like "here," "there," and "my" are keyed. It encompasses the muscular system "in its totality," including those muscles which effect the "shifting of the body and its members in space" (30–31). Indeed, proprioceptivity would seem to be intimately bound up with the body's sensation of occupying a point in space, and with the terms under which it does so. It thus involves a nonvisual mapping of the body's form. It also provides something which the specular imago alone could never provide—something which Wallon elsewhere, in an unfortunate choice of words, designates "presence."[18]

I have put quotation marks around this last word not only to indicate that it derives from another text, but as a way of subjecting it to an implicit deconstruction. For to attribute the experience of "presence" to proprioceptivity is not only to wrench it away from the body in its manifold complexity, but to identify it with a corporeal feature which is singularly vulnerable to cultural interference. By musculature, Wallon means in part the "postural function" (31). I will take the liberty of defining the latter as the deployment of the body's muscles for the purpose of fitting it smoothly within an imagined spatial envelope.

Posture is, of course, hardly an integral feature of the human body. Foucault writes at length in *Discipline and Punish* about the postural coercions induced on behalf of work and education.[19] To those, one would have to add the equally culturally significant bodily manipulations which every child experiences in the process of learning to sit, stand, walk, etc. Thus, in associating proprioceptivity with the postural function, Wallon suggests that—fully as much as Schilder's sensational ego—it is the product of interactions between the body and its cultural environment.

But proprioceptivity implies even more than the postural deployment of musculature. It would seem to be the result of the "gathering together and unification of otherwise disparate and scattered sensations provided by the various sense organs, in all their different spaces and registers."[20] Presumably the concept of proprioceptivity can then be extended to include all of the effects of those physical interactions between the young body and the parental environment whereby the subject comes to have a body that is sensationally marked by gender, race, and sexual preference.[21] Nevertheless, along with muscular sensation, cutaneous sensation would seem to play a particularly privileged proprioceptive role, since together these two things are primarily responsible for the production of a nonvisual corporeal *Gestalt,* and, so, for the subject's sense of him- or herself as a body extended in space.[22] It is in this expanded capacity—implying bodily sensation in general, but particularly muscular and cutaneous sensation—that I will henceforth refer, interchangeably, to the "sensational" or "proprioceptive" ego.

This would seem the moment to note that, even more than the visual imago, the sensational ego is not easily distinguished from its corporeal equivalent. Freud maintains that the sensational ego is a mental projection of the surface of the body, but "mental" may not be quite the right word. The sensational ego is at the same time psychic and corporeal.[23] It includes both physical feeling, and the subject's simultaneous mental registration, on the basis of that feeling, of a "hereness" and an "ownness." In the pages that follow, I will not distinguish between the sensational or proprioceptive ego and its more strictly corporeal equivalent, since I do not believe this distinction can be sustained. Instead, in this context, "ego" and "body" will be considered interchangeable terms.

Even while I stress the constructed nature of the "presence" that Wallon associates with proprioceptivity, I want to propose that there may be a compelling reason why he uses that particular noun. As I have already suggested, the visual imago cannot by itself induce in the subject that *méconnaissance* about which Lacan writes. The experience which each of us at times has of being "ourselves"—the triumph of what I have been designating the *moi* part of the bodily ego—depends on the smooth integration of the visual imago with the proprioceptive or sensational ego. When the former seems unified with the latter, the subject experiences that mode of "altogetherness" generally synonymous with "presence." When these two bodies come apart, that "presence" is lost. Although Lacan never acknowledges that the child's jubilant self-misrecognition depends on the integration of the exteroceptive and proprioceptive bodies, his curious reliance in his account of the mirror stage on a tableau in which the visual image seems a direct extension of the physical body of the child—upon a tableau, that is, in which the two bodies which contribute to the ego somehow converge—implies as much.

The "gender-bending" of recent years has alerted us to the fact that the proprioceptive ego may not always be compatible with what the reflecting surface shows. But Wallon's account of the mirror stage indicates that the proprioceptive ego is *always* initially disjunctive with the visual image, and that a unified bodily ego comes into existence only as the result of a laborious stitching together of disparate parts. Prior to that moment, Wallon suggests in *Les Origines du caractère chez l'enfant,* the child experiences "neither embarassment nor incoherence in perceiving its exteroceptive *moi* in front of it as a complement and natural figuration of its interior and active *moi*" (198). Wallon suggests that this identity-at-a-distance may not be entirely alien to adult subjectivity, either; in "Kinesthesia and the Visual Body Image in the Child," he speaks about the phenomenon of "appartenance," which he defines as "the extension of our feeling of material or bodily existence to objects, whether these be near or far away" (125). Once again, the disalignment of the image and the sensational ego does not seem to produce pathological effects.

Gaze and Screen

The disjunctive relation between the visual imago and sensational body becomes even more evident when we substitute for the mirror another Lacanian category, one which will prove increasingly indispensable as this book progresses. That category, the "screen," derives from *Seminar XI*, and is always conceptualized in relation to a second term, the "gaze." In this text, Lacan suggests, once again, that the subject relies for his or her visual identity on an external representation. However, he refers to this representation as a "screen" rather than a mirror reflection. Moreover, rather than simply misrecognizing him- or herself within the screen, the subject is now assumed to rely for his or her structuring access to it on an "unapprehensible"[24] and unlocalizable gaze, which for over 150 years now has found its most influential metaphor in the camera.[25] In order to emerge within the field of vision, the subject must not only align him- or herself identificatorily with the screen, but must also be apprehended in that guise by the gaze. To state the case in terms closer to those of "The Mirror Stage," the subject can only successfully misrecognize him- or herself within that image or cluster of images through which he or she is culturally apprehended. If it is to be even momentarily "captating," identification must be a three-way rather than a two-way transaction, requiring a symbolic "ratification."

It is perhaps for this reason that when we attempt to understand the mirror stage we so often imagine the mother present, not merely holding the child up to its reflection, but facilitating the imaginary alignment of the child with the reflection. In such an elaboration of this specular drama, the mother's look stands in for what no look can actually approximate: the gaze. It superimposes the structuring reflection upon the child, and so makes possible the child's identification with what it can never "be."[26]

Although I have just attempted to integrate the metaphor through which Lacan initially conceptualized identification with those through which he subsequently elaborated the field of vision, there are limits to how fully even this modified account of the mirror stage can be conflated with *Seminar XI*. In spite of Lacan's insistence on the alterity and fictiveness of the image with which the child identifies, there is both an iconic and an indexical relationship between the image and the child.[27] To state the matter a bit less technically, the mirror reflection resembles the child, and attests to the child's simultaneous spatial contiguity. The concept of the screen implies no such iconic or indexical motivation. Lacan characterizes it as "opaque" (96) or nonreflecting. There is no existential connection between it and the subject who is defined through it, and no necessary analogical link.

The visual paradigm elaborated in *Four Fundamental Concepts* is also calculated to underscore the often-involuntary nature of the imaginary connection between subject and external image. Lacan sharply differentiates the gaze from the subject's look, conferring visual authority not on the look but on the gaze. He thereby suggests that what is determinative for each of us is not how we see or would like to see ourselves, but how we are perceived by the cultural gaze. In the diagrams he uses to illustrate the field of vision, Lacan also places the screen at a distinct remove from the subject, thereby indicating that the screen exceeds the body "photographed" through it (91, 106). All of this suggests that we cannot simply "choose" how we are seen. Nor can we in any simple way conjure a new screen into place. We can struggle at a collective level to transform the existing one. Alternately, we can try at an individual level to substitute another image for the one through which we are conventionally seen, or, to deform or resemanticize the normative image. All three of these options imply a preliminary acknowledgment of both the exteriority and the cultural constructedness of the images through which the subject assumes a visual identity.

By severing the gaze from the look and denaturalizing the relation of subject and screen, *Seminar XI* makes it possible to see that *méconnaissance* may induce a very different affective response than the jubilation attributed to the child in "The Mirror Stage"—in other words, it does not invariably involve an identification with ideality. However, the precondition for such a theoretical apprehension is a culturally specific definition of the screen.

In *Male Subjectivity at the Margins*, I attempted to provide such a definition. I suggested that the visual model elaborated in *Four Fundamental Concepts* can be put to the service of a more emphatically political analysis than that text itself provides. I argued that this is possible if we think of the screen as the repertoire of representations by means of which our culture figures all of those many varieties of "difference" through which social identity is inscribed (150). It now seems crucial to add that since every idealizing attribution—e.g., "whiteness," "masculinity," "heterosexuality"—at present implies its opposite, and since the imposition of all of these forms of difference depends upon the imaginary alignment of certain subjects with what is negative rather than ideal, the images through which the subject is culturally apprehended do not always facilitate the production of a lovable bodily ego. Later in this chapter, we will use Freud's account of (white) femininity and Fanon's analysis of black masculinity to consider what it means for a subject to be held by the gaze to an unpleasurable identification.

The Fantasy of the Body in Bits and Pieces

Perhaps because Lacan's jubilant infant is implicitly gendered masculine, and because other "differences" simply do not figure in his theoretical paradigm, the author of the essay on the mirror stage never suggests that there might be situations in which identification fails to provide narcissistic gratification. However, he does speak eloquently about the impossibility of indefinitely sustaining an identification with ideality. Significantly, the collapse of such an imaginary alignment leads to the experience of bodily fragmentation and disintegration, or what in "Some Reflections on the Ego" he calls the fantasy of the "body in bits and pieces" (13). In the same text, Lacan indicates that this fantasy often surfaces in dreams, which typically show "the body of the mother as having a mosaic structure like that of a stained-glass window" or "a jig-saw puzzle, with the separate parts of the body of a man or an animal in disorderly array." Lacan goes on to enumerate other conjurations of the body in bits and pieces: "the incongruous images in which disjointed limbs are rearranged as strange trophies; trunks [are] cut up in slices and stuffed with the most unlikely fillings, [and] strange appendages [are shown] in eccentric positions" (13).

Whereas the impossibility of approximating an ideal image is apprehended by the subject through the fantasy of bodily disintegration, the successful imaginary alignment with an image evokes values like "wholeness" and "unity." These latter values Lacan imputes to the compositional coherence of the reflected image, which contrasts dramatically with the motor incapacity of the child who stands in front of or is held up to the mirror.[28] However, I would like to propose that when the subject jubilantly experiences "wholeness" and "unity" in identifying with a given representation, that has more to do with the temporary integration of the visual imago with the sensational ego than with the frame around the real or metaphoric mirror. I would also like to suggest that such an integration is imaginable not only when it is sustained by the gaze, but when the visual imago is perceived as lovable, i.e., when it seems to radiate ideality.

It is not possible, as we will see, to be completely "inside" any other kind of image, even momentarily. When held by the cultural gaze to an identification with a deidealizing image, the subject often experiences it as an external imposition. At the very least, he or she refuses to invest narcissistically in the image (unless it can be somehow oppositionally "redeemed"), and attempts in all kinds of ways to maintain his or her distance from it.

Finally, it seems important to note that the fantasy of the body in bits and pieces is only one way of apprehending the heterogeneity of the corporeal ego, and one which is inextricably tied to the aspiration toward "wholeness" and "unity." Lacan suggests that it is "organic disturbance and discord" which prompts the child to seek out the form of the "whole body-image."[29] However, it seems to me that the reverse is actually true: it is the cultural premium placed on the notion of a coherent bodily ego which results in such a dystopic apprehension of corporeal multiplicity.

Wallon and Schilder also stress the discrete nature of the elements which make up the bodily ego, but neither of them regard that heterogeneity as being as problematic as it is for the subject Lacan describes. Wallon stresses that, since it is comprised of disparate elements, the coherence of this ego is always precarious. He describes the breaking away of the visual imago from the proprioceptive body with which it has been aligned in dreams and states of confusion. On such occasions, he writes, the components of the bodily ego "revert to their respective perceptual origins. The subject's picture of himself, stripped of its proprioceptive elements, becomes confined to his visual field in the form of a more or less alien figure," like the original mirror reflection.[30]

Schilder emphasizes not only the tenuousness of the connection between the visual and sensational egos, but the looseness of the connection between bodily parts. "It is obvious that limbs and trunk can go their separate ways," he writes, "and that…psychological dismembering can take place" (114). In a remarkable passage which anticipates Lacan's theory of the *objet a*, Schilder also maintains that the body schema is continually losing certain elements, such as excrement, fingernails, and hair, which afterwards still remain in a psychological relation to the body (188). And in several other passages, he suggests that there is a way in which the bodily ego itself tends inexorably toward disintegration (121n, 191). However, in Schilder, this disintegration is beneficent rather than tragic; it is the precondition for change, what must transpire if the ego is to form anew. The author of *The Image and Appearance of the Human Body* thus gestures to the possibility of living the heterogeneity of the corporeal ego outside the logic of the psychic paradigm upon which Lacan places so much emphasis in "The Mirror Stage" and "Some Reflections on the Ego."

So far, I have not made sufficiently clear that this logic is one which Lacan identifies and anatomizes, not one in which he participates. At one point, he characterizes the coherence to which the classic subject aspires as "the armour of an alienating identity." He also associates that aspiration with an irreducible aggressivity toward any other who occupies the position of the ideal imago.[31] And in "Some Reflections on the Ego," he lays to rest the primary alibi of the subject who aspires to a coherent bodily ego—the notion that "wholeness" signifies psychic health. "The libidinal tension that shackles the subject to the constant pursuit of an illusory unity…is surely related to that agony of dereliction which is Man's particular and tragic destiny." He writes,

These reflections on the functions of the ego ought, above all else, to encourage us to reexamine certain notions that are sometimes accepted uncritically, such as the notion that it is psychologically advantageous to have a strong ego.

In actual fact, the classical neuroses always seem to be by-products of a strong ego. (16)

I will return in a moment to Wallon's account of the mirror stage, and use it as the occasion to interrogate more closely both the kind of identification through which the normative ego seeks to consolidate itself, and the very different identification through which the child initially relates to its specular reflection. Before doing so, however, I want to offer a few concluding remarks about the relation between the screen and what, for lack of a better phrase, I will call the "literal body." Although the first of these categories can in no way be said to reflect or follow logically from the second, it is also clear that it is on the basis of certain physical indices, such as the presence or absence of the penis, or the color of skin pigmentation, that the cultural gaze projects certain images onto certain bodies. What status are we to give these physical indices?

First, although at the level of the screen they provide the fantasmatic starting point for the elaboration not only of an entire visual *Gestalt*—or, to use an expression coined by Lacan in "Some Reflections on the Ego," an "imaginary anatomy" (13)—but of an essential identity, at the level of the real, they are neither the attributes of the body, nor the external signifiers of an indwelling self.

The second of these assertions will come as no surprise to even a casual reader of Lacan, who maintains the absolute discontinuity of the organic and the psychic. However, the first assertion follows just as inexorably from the texts which this chapter has assembled. The body does not exist even as a tenuous unity prior to its constitution through image, posture, and touch. Indeed, it cannot even be said to be "in pieces," since that implies that once assembled they would add up to a "whole." The physical indices through which "difference" is ostensibly identified are consequently no more than insignificant elements within an incoherent conglomeration, devoid of both form and value.

The Self-Same Body

Although in certain respects Wallon's account of the mirror stage would seem to offer a kind of meditation on Strachey's note about the bodily ego (and hence to be close to Freud's own thinking about that category), it articulates a different model of identification than that which is generally insisted upon within psychoanalysis. Freud's most extended treatment of identification, *Group Psychology and the Analysis of the Ego*, represents the process whereby one subject aligns him- or herself imaginarily with another as generally incorporative. Identification behaves, Freud writes, "like a derivative of the first, *oral* phase of the organization of the libido, in which the object that we long for and prize is assimilated by eating and is in that way annihilated as such."[32] In *Totem and Taboo,* Freud literalizes the cannibalistic metaphor through which he characterizes identification in *Group Psychology;* the patriarchal order is described as coming into existence through that double act whereby the horde of brothers murders and devours the primordial father, thereby in effect becoming him.[33] In "Mourning and Melancholia" and *The Ego and the Id,* two other texts that are centrally concerned with the formation of the ego, identification is again represented as the product of a process whereby the other is interiorized as the self—in the latter case, through the regulatory economy of the Oedipus complex; in the former, through the pathological logic of melancholia.[34]

My intention here is not to affirm the descriptive value of the exteriorizing identification described by Wallon at the expense of the very different identification theorized by Freud. On the contrary, I firmly believe an incorporative logic to be at the heart of normative adult subjectivity. Indeed, it provides the very basis for the formation of a "coherent" bodily ego. Rather, I want to place the identification elaborated by Wallon over and against that discussed by Freud, to suggest that its importance and radicality can best be grasped through its oppositional relation to the murderously assimilatory identification through which the self creates and fortifies itself. More specifically, I want to seize upon this excorporative identification as a mechanism for undoing the delusory unity and presence of the bodily ego.

Wallon's account of identity-at-a-distance is based primarily on early subjectivity. However, the German philosopher Max Scheler isolates two varieties of adult identification, one which follows an incorporative logic and another which reprises the Wallonian mirror stage. And far from pathologizing the Wallonian version, Scheler defines it as a profound form of sympathy. In the second edition of *The Nature of Sympathy* (1923), he characterizes that variety of identification which conforms to the classic psychoanalytic paradigm as "idiopathic," and, like Freud, he stresses its annihilatory relation to the other. Idiopathic identification, he says, effects "the total eclipse and absorption of another self by one's own, it being thus, as it were, completely dispossessed and deprived of all rights in its conscious existence and character."[35] Scheler refers to that variety of identification which pursues an excorporative trajectory as "heteropathic." Through heteropathic identification, the subject identifies at a distance from his or her proprioceptive self (19). The visual imago itself remains stubbornly exterior, like the original mirror reflection described by Wallon, at the expense of an imaginary bodily unity.

Scheler uses a story drawn from Schopenhauer as an allegory about heteropathy and idiopathy. This story obliges us to conceptualize both varieties of identification in corporeal terms—as bearing above all upon the bodily ego:

A white squirrel, having met the gaze of a snake, hanging on a tree and showing every sign of a mighty appetite for its prey, is so terrified by this that it gradually moves towards instead of away from the snake, and finally throws itself into the open jaws.... plainly the squirrel's instinct for self-preservation has succumbed to an ecstatic participation in the object of the snake's own appetitive nisus, namely "swallowing." The squirrel identifies in feeling with the snake, and thereupon spontaneously establishes corporeal identity with it, by disappearing down its throat. (21–22)

The white squirrel represents the heteropath, who identifies excorporatively, and in so doing surrenders his or her customary specular parameters for those of the other. The snake, on the other hand, metaphorizes idiopathic identification, which turns upon the ingestion of the other, and the resulting triumph of the subject's proprioceptive frame of reference.[36]

Scheler's allegory not only suggests that heteropathic identification can occur at the site of adult as well as infantile subjectivity, but it also helps us to understand better what it is that the idiopathic ego engorges. Having enlisted this tale primarily in the first of these capacities, I would now like to deploy it in the second. The story Scheler takes from Schopenhauer indicates that the ego consolidates itself by assimilating the corporeal coordinates of the other to its own—by devouring bodily otherness. The "coherent" ego subsequently maintains itself by repudiating whatever it cannot swallow—by refusing to live in and through alien corporealities. This is what I will henceforth refer to as the principle of the "self-same body."

I would like to suggest that it is this principle that lies behind many of the claims regarding the ego that Lacan makes in his first two seminars. When he observes that "the object is always more or less structured as the image of the body of the subject,"[37] for instance, or when he remarks that "the image of his body is the principle of every unity he perceives in objects,"[38] he attests less to the primacy of the isolated visual imago than to the function it serves when closely integrated with the proprioceptive ego. What is at issue here, in other words, is the insistence upon self-sameness or the *moi*—the refusal on the part of the normative subject to form an imaginary alignment with images which remain manifestly detached from his or her sensational body, and his or her stubborn clinging to those images which can be most easily incorporated. This normativity is only differentially available. As I suggested above, it can come into play only when the representations through which the gaze "photographs" the subject provide him or her with an idealized image of self. Only with such an image can the subject experience him- or herself to be at least momentarily and pleasurably at one.

The principle of the self-same body is consequently at the center of all of those varieties of "difference" which we have been concerned in recent years to understand and dismantle—most obviously gender and race, but also class and sexual preference. There is perhaps no more fundamental manifestation of these kinds of "difference" than the customary reluctance on the part of the sexually, racially, or economically privileged subject to identify outside of the bodily coordinates which confer that status upon him or her, to form imaginary alignments which would threaten the coherence and ideality of his or her corporeal ego. Typically, this subject either refuses "alien" identifications altogether, or forms them only on the basis of an idiopathic or assimilative model; he or she imaginarily occupies the position of the other, but only in the guise of the self or bodily ego. This kind of identification is familiar to all of us through that formula with which we extend sympathy to someone less fortunate than ourselves without in any way jeopardizing our *moi:* "I can imagine *myself* in his (or her) place."

To see the principle of the self-same body extravagantly at work, we need only turn to Freud's account of classic masculinity. The founding drama of sexual difference, as recounted in "Some Psychical Consequences of the Anatomical Distinction Between the Sexes," turns upon the inability of the exemplary little boy to "perceive" a body which does not replicate his own. Confronted with that spectacle, "he sees nothing or disavows what he has seen, he softens it down or looks about for expedients for bringing it into line with his expectations."[39] Even when he can no longer deny that this body is not in all respects identical to his own, the boy cannot think beyond the limits of his corporeality; the female body consequently figures not simply as slightly divergent from, but also as a castrated version of the male body—as the materialization of the punishment with which he is threatened. And "Some Psychical Consequences of the Anatomical Distinction Between the Sexes" indicates that the bodily ego may continue to assert itself with equal vehemence on the other side of the castration complex. Its author maintains that this event "permanently determines[s] the [conventional] boy's relations to women," leading to either "horror of the mutilated creature," or "triumphant contempt for her" (252).

Freud's essay on fetishism attests once again to the crisis which the image of the female body precipitates in the classically male subject, and to the lengths to which he is prepared to go in order to conform the body of the erotic object—an object which, as Lacan suggests, can only be desired through the frame of the self—to his own. The missing organ must somehow be attached to the female body, even if it has to be conjured forth through a shoe, or a shine on the nose.[40] As Irigaray writes in *Speculum of the Other Woman,* masculinity as it is conventionally defined, but seldom completely realized, attests to nothing so much as "the desire for the same, for the self-identical, the self (as) same, and again of the similar, the alter ego." Sexual difference is consequently "determined within the project, the projection, the sphere of representation, of the same."[41]

Since the preceding discussion of self-sameness may have seemed both too safely removed from my own subjectivity, and too narrowly limited to gender, I will suggest another way in which that principle might operate through a brief personal anecdote. Several times a week I must negotiate my way past the crowds of homeless people on Telegraph Avenue in Berkeley. Every time I do so, I am overcome with irrational panic. Initially, I rationalized this panic in strictly economic terms—as the imperative to give, but the impossibility of doing so to everyone who asks. I fantasized that my crisis would be solved if I could only find an intelligent formula for determining whom I should help. Yet I found myself unable to imagine what such a principle should be, and unable even to comprehend why I sometimes proffer a dollar or two, and at other times walk quickly past an outstretched hand.

Then, one day, I realized that I always studiously avoid looking at the homeless people, whom, with ruthless arbitrariness, I either help or don't help. And I began to understand that my panic on these occasions is not just economic, but specular. What I feel myself being asked to do, and what I resist with every fiber of my being, is to locate myself within bodies which would, quite simply, be ruinous of my middle-class self—within bodies that are calloused from sleeping on the pavement, chapped from their exposure to sun and rain, and grimy from weeks without access to a shower, and which can consequently make no claim to what, within our culture, passes for "ideality." More recently, it has occurred to me that I find it difficult but not impossible to identify with the structural position of homelessness, since I imagine that in such a situation I would still coincide with that corporeal fiction which I call "me." But the homeless bodies on Telegraph Avenue dispel this comforting fiction; they show me that, if homeless, I would precisely no longer be "myself." And rather than acceding to this politically imperative self-estrangement, I automatically avert my eyes.

I have recounted this story in part to encompass class as well as gender within the principle of the self-same body, and to implicate my own subjectivity in the latter's operations. Through it, I have also hoped to distance myself from any reading of this chapter which would propose the sexually, economically, or racially marked subject as somehow more inherently and progressively heteropathic than the white, male, heterosexual subject. First of all, I want to stress that the disenfranchised subject often identifies at a distance not with other disprized bodies, but with those that replicate the cultural ideal. Second, the aspiration to be "one" with such images can be very powerful indeed; the black subject who identifies with whiteness, like the female subject who identifies with masculinity, does not always remain willingly and joyfully at a distance from the idealizing mirror.

I have suggested that the jubilation about which Lacan writes in "The Mirror Stage" occurs when the sensational body is imaginarily conflated with an idealizing image, a conflation which requires the support of the cultural gaze.

Although this jubilation is always fleeting, since no one can in fact approximate the ideal, the struggle to attain it can be sustained over a lifetime. The aspiration to wholeness and unity not only has tragic personal consequences, but also calamitous social effects, since it represents one of the most important psychic manifestations of "difference." But so far, we have considered the bodily ego only from the point of view of those subjects who have cultural access to an idealizing imago. Let us now attempt to understand the corporeal quandary within which the subject finds him or herself when held to a deidealizing identification.

Fanon and the Black Male Bodily Ego

The account Fanon offers in *Black Skin, White Masks* of what it means to be black within a society which unquestioningly privileges whiteness attests once more to the necessity of including the categories of the gaze and the screen when attempting to understand the bodily ego. Fanon also obliges us to conceptualize something which is very far removed from both Lacan's and Wallon's accounts of the mirror stage—the psychic dilemma faced by the subject when obliged to identify with an image which provides neither idealization nor pleasure, and which is inimical to the formation of a "coherent" identity.

Fanon writes at length in *Black Skin, White Masks* about what might be called the "interpellation" into negritude of the dark-skinned male subject. His particular concern is with the psychic violence done to the typical male inhabitant of one of France's former colonies upon his entry into French society. Raised on a steady diet of Gallic culture, such an individual grew up during the colonial period perceiving himself more as "French" than as "black." However, upon leaving home and arriving in France, he was subjected to a violent corporeal redefinition, from which it was not easy to remain psychically aloof.

In Chapter 5, Fanon provides an anecdote which not only vividly dramatizes this corporeal reconfiguration, but also indicates precisely how a representation from which any subject would recoil can nevertheless turn into a "mirror," and induce a highly unpleasurable identification. Fanon describes going to a film in Paris, where he finds himself being addressed in a very disconcerting way. As he waits for the movie to begin, he feels himself being observed. To be more precise, he feels himself being seen through images which have not, as yet, materialized, but are already latent in the imaginations of those around him—images of a stereotypically menial blackness. "I cannot go to a film without seeing myself," Fanon remarks,

> I wait for me. In the interval, just before the film starts, I wait for me. The people in the theater are watching me, examining me, waiting for me. A Negro groom is going to appear. My heart makes my head swim.[42]

This passage serves as another important reminder that the subject does not accede to an image of self voluntarily, or in cultural isolation—that identification involves not only subject and image, but gaze. However, here, those categories are not clearly differentiated from each other; since the film has not yet begun, the representations within which Fanon feels obliged to recognize himself seem to derive directly from the personal prejudices of the audience. The power to confer meaning seems to be immanent within the collective white look.

In an earlier passage from *Black Skin, White Masks*, Fanon speaks again about the involuntary nature of his identification with negritude, and about the destructive effects of that identification upon what was previously his bodily ego. "Assailed at various points, [my preexisting] corporeal schema crumble[s]," he recounts, "I [subject] myself to an objective examination, I [discover] my blackness, my ethnic characteristics; and I [am] battered down by tom-toms, cannibalism, intellectual deficiency, fetishism [*sic*], racial defects, slave-ships, and above all: "Sho' good eatin'" (112). However, in this passage, Fanon also makes clear that if he is "photographed" in this guise, that is not because of the special power and productivity of the white look with respect to the black body, but rather because of the mobilization in the viewing situation he describes of the screen of "blackness"—the intervening agency of what he calls "a thousand details, anecdotes, stories" (111), or "legends, stories, history, and above all *historicity*" (112).

In the same passage, Fanon also clearly differentiates the white look from the gaze. He describes the peculiar way in which the gaze evaporates as he attempts to approach and specify it. Moving toward the other who has actually or metaphorically shouted, "Look, a Negro!"—the other who seems responsible for imposing upon Fanon an undesirable identification with negritude—this "evanescent other, hostile but not opaque, transparent, not there, disappear[s]" (112). Once again, the gaze turns out to be unlocalizable and "unapprehensible," at the same time everywhere and nowhere. If, from a distance, the white look is able to assume powers which it does not in fact possess, that is only because of the screen, which intervenes not just between the gaze and the subject, but also between the subject and the gaze. That mediating agency often aligns the gaze with both the male and the white look. To be more precise, it represents the white male look as the privileged "functionary" of the camera/gaze.[43]

As should be clear by now, the mirror which French society holds up to Fanon is radically deidealizing. Not surprisingly, then, the author of *Black Skin, White Masks* speaks of being "forever in combat with [his] own image" (194)—battling with it, as with a mortal enemy. The struggle here is not to *close* the distance between visual imago and the proprioceptive body, as in the classic account of identification, but to *maintain* it—to keep the screen of "blackness" at a safe remove from the sensational ego, lest it assume precisely that quality of self-sameness which is synonymous with a coherent ego.

Fanon speaks eloquently about the corporeal consequences of this forced identification with an abhorrent visual imago. Struggling to prevent that imago from being mapped onto his proprioceptive body, he refuses to confer "presence" upon it. Fanon's "corporeal schema crumble(s)," and he finds himself occupying not one point in space, but "two" or "three." "It was no longer a question of being aware of my body in the third person but in a triple person," he writes (112). Because of the extremely negative circumstances under which this decomposition occurs—because it is precipitated by an obligatory identification with an intolerable imago—it is experienced through the fantasy of the body in bits and pieces, as a violent mutilation. "I took myself far off from my own presence, far indeed, and made myself an object," he reminisces, "What else could it be for me but an amputation, an excision, a hemorrhage that spattered my whole body with black blood?"(112).

The black subject described by Fanon is not only in "combat" with the image through which he is "photographed" by the seemingly white gaze, but is also irresistibly drawn to the "mirror" of an ideal "whiteness." *Black Skin, White Masks* speaks about the black schoolboy in the Antilles who identifies with the "white man who carries truth to the savages," the Antillean movie spectator who identifies with Tarzan, and the Antillean children who write: "I like vacation because then I can run through the fields, breathe fresh air, and come home with *rosy* cheeks" (147, 152n, 162n). But at least within French culture of the 1950s, this ego-ideal can only entertain a highly disjunctive relation to the proprioceptive body, since, in order for the black subject to misrecognize himself within the image of a dazzling "whiteness," he must also be "seen" through it, and that is impossible. The ego-ideal consequently represents an unreachable bodily norm, what the self can never be.

Fanon's account of black male subjectivity is in many respects historically and culturally specific, and should not be recklessly universalized. At the same time, its theoretical value clearly exceeds its immediate context. Indeed, much of its discussion of what it means to be a black man in a predominently white society would still seem relevant today. *Black Skin, White Masks* helps us to understand, first of all, that our identifications must always be socially ratified. It also teaches us that only certain subjects have access to a flattering image of self, and that others have imposed upon them an image so deidealizing that no one would willingly identify with it. Under such circumstances, which are for the most part those in which black men still find themselves when confronted with dominant Western representation, the subject generally attempts to throw the "mirror" as far away as possible. *Black Skin, White Masks* makes clear that the resulting experience of bodily disintegration is not the beneficent decomposition Schilder describes but corresponds instead to the fantasy of the fragmented body. Finally, *Black Skin, White Masks* helps us to understand why a racially, sexually, or economically marginalized subject might identify hetero-pathically with normative corporeal parameters, rather than with those of a more despised corporeality. It lays bare the fascination of bodily ideality.

When I come to the topic of femininity, I will attempt to specify much more precisely the role played by idealization and its opposite in the formation of the corporeal ego. First, however, I want to comment briefly on what Fanon has to say about the relation between the black male subject and his white counter-part, since that relation would also still seem operative today. At one point, Fanon observes that "the Negro, because of his body, impedes the closing of the postural schema of the white man" (160). Elsewhere in the same chapter, he underscores what it is about the black male body which prevents the principle of self-same-ness from triumphing uninterruptedly at the site of the white male ego. The screen of negritude within Fanon's French culture (and our own) confers upon the black male subject a hyperbolic virility. To be more precise, it imputes to him a sexual organ whose proportions and capacities are in dramatic excess of his white counterpart's. "For the majority of white men," Fanon observes, "the Negro represents the sexual instinct (in its raw state). The Negro is the incarna-tion of a genital potency beyond all moralities and prohibitions…The Negro is taken as a terrifying penis" (177). Thus, as Mary Ann Doane points out in *Femmes Fatales,* black masculinity signifies not so much a "lack" as a "surplus" in relation to white masculinity.[44] What is the relationship between the phallus and this hyperbolic penis?

Jean-Joseph Goux has recently advanced the extremely interesting argument that far from equating the phallus with the penis, Greek philosophy aligned it instead with the *logos.* "It is by no means physical vigor but rather rational power…that Hermes's erect phallus signifies," he writes. "It is the emblem of guiding intelligence and…even of a political faculty that can manifest itself in spite of bodily infirmity."[45] Goux goes on a moment later to articulate the rela-tion between phallus and penis in even more starkly antithetical terms; in order to accede to the former, one must sacrifice or surrender the latter, since it is on the side of matter rather than spirit. Although this understanding of the pater-nal signifier is no longer available to us consciously, Goux maintains, it lives on within the contemporary unconscious, and is at the heart of Lacan's theory of the phallus.

Fanon proposes a similar account of the cultural logic behind the attribu-tion to the black man of an inflated virility. Since "every intellectual gain requires a loss in sexual potential," to confer a mythically large penis on the black man is not to associate him with the phallus, but to stress the distance which sepa-rates him from it (165). However, this is clearly only a very partial account of what it in fact means for the black man to be characterized in this way. If the black man is the recipient more of envy and contempt, that is not only because "the civilized white man retains an irrational longing for [the] unusual eras of sexual license, of orgiastic scenes, of unpunished rapes, of unrepressed incest" which he associates with black masculinity, but also because racial difference is always complexly imbricated with sexual difference (165).

The phallus can never be entirely abstracted from the penis for the simple reason that it is conferred upon men rather than women on the basis of a genital differentiation—a differentiation, moreover, which turns precisely upon a "more" and a "less." The clitoris, Freud maintains, is apprehended by the little boy, and later by the male unconscious, as a "small and inconspicuous organ."[46] The differentiation of the white man from the black man on the basis of the black man's hyperbolic penis consequently reverberates in disturbing ways within the domain of gender. It places the white man on the side of "less" rather than "more," and, so, threatens to erase the distinction between him and the white woman. This is the primary reason, I would argue, why the body of the black man disrupts the unity of the white male corporeal ego.

It is perhaps unnecessary to add that the female body poses a similar threat to the masculine psyche. Although it is on the basis of woman's anatomical "insufficiency" that the male subject lays claim to the phallus, the display of this ostensible lack often precipitates in him an intolerable anxiety concerning his own corporeal integrity. That anxiety is classically laid to rest through the fantasmatic reconstitution of the female body in the guise of the male. While this reconstitution clearly operates at the behest of the homologizing impulse I have emphasized in this chapter, it also works to erase the very antithesis through which the masculine ideal asserts itself. It should thus be evident by now that although the normative white male bodily ego is defined through its aspiration to coherence, the principle of the self-same body is, even there, never more than momentarily and delusorily victorious.

Freud and the Female Bodily Ego

It has been argued by certain French and American feminist theorists that the conventional female subject is "closer" to her body than is her male counterpart.[47] She is assumed not only to have a less metaphoric relation to her corporeality, but to be in danger of being psychically submerged by her literal body as well. However, as we have seen, the body does not exist prior to its cultural construction, and, so, can never be said to be directly "present" to the subject, whether male or female. Indeed, "presence" is itself only an imaginary effect of the integration of the visual imago and the sensational ego.

A variant of this formulation, against which I will argue at length in Chapter 2, is that the female subject is a less sophisticated reader of the images that define her—that she somehow tips over into the "mirror" of cultural representation, imagining that she really "is" what it depicts her as being.[48] However, several key

Freudian texts suggest that in fact the body represents much less of a "given" within female subjectivity than it does within its masculine counterpart, and that it is at least potentially less susceptible to a naive literalization. These texts take issue with the notions that the female subject has a direct relation to her real body, or that her imaginary captation is somehow more seamless than that of her masculine counterpart. They also indicate that her body may be obliged to accommodate a far more heterogeneous conglomeration of elements than the conventional male equivalent, and, so, may be capable of accommodating a greater diversity of corporeal identifications.

Before commenting on these texts, I want to indicate that I am once again sensitive to their historical and cultural specificity. All of the female patients available to Freud were white, and most were bourgeois. However, I believe that the explanatory power of the model I will be elaborating extends beyond the white, bourgeois, female subject. First of all, this model is far from monolithic; it accommodates a number of different narratives. Second, it focuses primarily on the Oedipus complex and the castration crisis, which—rather than being limited to a particular class or ethnic group—are the primary psychic structures through which gender and sexual preference are produced in Western culture, and through which the subject enters that culture. I would even go so far as to suggest that the actual family conditions which might distinguish one social group from another, and seemingly invalidate Freud's model—missing father, unusually potent or old mother, reversal of caretaking roles—can qualify, but not entirely militate against, the implementation of the scenarios that model describes. The Oedipus complex and the castration crisis do not necessarily occur punctually within the family, but are induced as an effect of the larger culture.[49]

Freud's essays "Femininity" and "Female Sexuality" point first of all to the ambiguity surrounding the question of what, for the female subject, constitutes her sensational or proprioceptive body, given that one erotogenic zone is expected within the normal course of things to yield to another. The clitoris, which generally provides the primary seat of erotic sensation during the phallic phase, when the mother is the love-object, "properly" gives way or is subordinated to the vagina during the positive Oedipus complex, when the mother is replaced by the father.[50] Freud stresses the radical upheaval which this proprioceptive transformation involves. When all goes according to cultural mandate, corporeal activity is transmuted into corporeal passivity. However, three paths fan out from the female castration crisis, and only one of those paths leads to normative femininity. Another leads to sexual anaesthesia, to the refusal to register gender at the site of the sensational body. A third leads to the so-called masculinity complex, a retreat to the negative Oedipus complex.[51]

In the last of these cases, in which the female subject fails to effect a complete transmutation from clitoris to vagina, the result may be either a defiantly clitoral proprioceptivity, or one with two culturally divergent erotic centers, one clitoral and one vaginal. Even at the level of the sensational ego, then, things are much more complicated and unpredictable in the case of the little girl than in that of the little boy.

The girl's relation to her visual imago conventionally undergoes a similar transformation at the moment of the castration crisis or mutation from the negative to the positive Oedipus complex. During the negative Oedipus complex, the girl misrecognizes herself primarily within the "mirror" of the mother, who, during that period, is not only the girl's love object, but also that which the girl aspires to be. Freud insists upon this convergence of identification and desire at the site of the mother in several key passages in "Femininity" and "Female Sexuality." He thereby suggests that during the negative Oedipus complex the girl typically identifies with a *lovable* image—with an image, that is, in which she is capable of investing libidinally.[52]

With the onset of the castration crisis, however, the typical girl's relation to her bodily image changes drastically. The castration crisis can perhaps best be understood as the moment at which the young female subject first apprehends herself no longer within the pleasurable frame of the original maternal imago, but within the radically deidealizing screen or cultural image-repertoire, which makes of her body the very image of "lack."[53] To be more precise, the castration crisis is synonymous with the moment at which the girl first feels herself *seen* in ways that are in radical excess of her negative Oedipal relation to the mother, and which are not those she would choose for herself. She is—as a consequence of this—held to an identification which she would otherwise refuse.

The normative female subject is simultaneously coerced into an identification with anatomical and discursive insufficiency, and exhorted over and over again to aspire to the ideal of the "exceptional woman," the woman whose extravagant physical beauty miraculously erases all marks of castration. She must thus embody both lack and its opposite: lack, so that the male subject's phallic attributes can be oppositionally articulated; plenitude, so that she can become adequate to his desire. This leads to a classic "double bind"; the female subject is under the imperative to be what she is at the same time prevented from approximating, structurally as well as ontologically.

Freud's claim that women typically love according to the narcissistic model makes no sense until it is read in relation to the narrative I have just related.[54] Only then, can there be seen some basis for differentiating the female subject in this respect from her male counterpart.[55] In effect, narcissistic object-choice provides yet another libidinal mechanism, analogous to sexual anaesthesia and the maculinity complex, through which the female subject can protest her forced identification with lack. The classic instance of that protest takes a form as culturally overdetermined as Fanon's identification with white masculinity. It is, of course, that unrequited love which many women direct toward the images of ideal femininity which they are exhorted to approximate, but prohibited from replicating. Significantly, this vain but nonetheless imperative quest after absolute beauty has nothing to do with self-love; it is predicated on the impossibility of loving the self. Only an imaginary union with the desired image would make possible a "jubilant" self-apprehension, but that image remains at an irreducible remove.

Narcissistic object-choice would also seem to represent the privileged libidinal economy of many women because it provides two other solutions to the impasse I outlined above, one "passive" and one "active." Narcissistic object-choice may involve self-love, love for what was once a part of the self, love for what one once was, and love for what one would like to be, but also love for the one who is able to love the subject in a way that compensates for the impossibility of self-love. Freud suggests in "On Narcissism" that the prototypical female subject may gravitate both to the fourth of these possibilities, which can be characterized as "active," and to the fifth, which can be characterized as "passive." He also suggests that some surprising gender displacements may take place when this subject loves another as what she would like to be.

When adopting the passive solution to the crisis of femininity, the subject positions herself as love object rather than as an actively loving subject, and attempts thereby to secure second-hand the libidinal sustenance which her bodily ego demands. In "On Narcissism," Freud writes about women who love themselves "with an intensity comparable to that of the man's love for them," and whose "need" lies not "in the direction of loving, but of being loved" (89). In such a case, the female subject might be said to seek access to self-love through another person's love for her.

But the female subject may also opt for what I characterized as the "active" solution to the crisis of femininity, and—rather than giving that position to the cold abstraction of exceptional femininity—put a man in the place of her ego-ideal. She can, in other words, project herself altogether outside the double-bind I described a moment ago by selecting as her ego-ideal someone of the opposite sex. Freud says of such a woman that she typically chooses to love someone who represents "the narcissistic ideal of the man whom [she] had wished to become."[56]

Such a solution to the dilemma of femininity represents a further challenge to the principle of the self-same body, which is already under siege from many directions. Not only are the ego and the ego-ideal organized around two very different bodily images, but the ego-ideal cannot be even partially mapped onto the proprioceptive body of the subject who orients herself in an imaginary and erotic relation to it. Here, as with the exemplary femininity she is exhorted and forbidden to embody, the female subject is "farther" away from the "mirror" within which she would like to recognize herself than is her male counterpart.

Once again, this distance is rarely turned to political advantage. It is more frequently the occasion for subordination and dependency. However, it instanciates an identificatory flexibility which is not to be found where the principle of the self-same body triumphs. When the subject does not have easy cultural access to an idealizing image of self, he or she can become very adroit at identifying heteropathically with alternative images. Freud's essay "A Child Is Being Beaten" provides a striking example of this principle by suggesting that the female subject can cross gender lines not only in romantic love but also at the level of her unconscious fantasmatic.

In stage three of the feminine version of the group beating fantasy recounted by Freud in that text, the female subject imagines herself being beaten by the father, not *in propria persona* but rather in the guise of a group of boys. And as in Fanon, the identification in question assumes an exteriorizing rather than an interiorizing form. The female subject feels herself, but does not see herself, looking on as this event takes place; proprioceptively she stands on the margins, but visually she is fully excorporated, assimilated to the image of the male body.[57] The masculine version of the beating fantasy has no comparable stage; in all three of the modulations which are specific to that fantasy, the male subject clings to his usual terms of bodily reference. It is only the figure performing the punishment whose identity remains in a state of flux (196–99).

Thus, like "On Narcissism," "A Child Is Being Beaten" provides the psychoanalytic rationale for a claim which has been reiterated several times within feminist film theory—that the conventional female spectator enjoys greater identificatory freedom than does her male counterpart. After writing "Visual Pleasure and Narrative Cinema," Laura Mulvey was often asked why that essay theorizes only the male viewing position.[58] Years later, in an "Afterward" to "Visual Pleasure," Mulvey suggested that she had in fact been theorizing a subject-position which is conventionally available to the female as well as the male viewer, since the former easily slips out of her own and into "transvestite" clothes.[59] Teresa de Lauretis elaborates another version of this argument in *Alice Doesn't: Feminism, Semiotics, Cinema*. She maintains that the female spectator is classically split between identification with "the image on the screen, perceived as spatially static, fixed, in frame," and feminine, and identification with the camera, "apprehended as temporal, active or in movement," and masculine.[60]

Finally, although the female spectator's cross-gender peregrinations often work only to confirm libidinally the values traditionally attributed to the male body at the site of the cultural screen, such is not the case in "A Child Is Being Beaten." There, the male body with which the girl identifies is erotically centered on the anus rather than the penis, and is defined as the recipient rather than the agent of erotic punishment. The female version of the beating fantasy thus makes heteropathic identification simultaneous with a reworking of gender, and at least hints at the possibility implicit in that psychic transaction for a disruption or reconfiguration of other forms of "difference."

Of course, the principle of the self-same body is far from being completely unfamiliar to the feminine psyche. Although the female subject is sexually defined as "lacking," she often has access in other respects to a more flattering corporeal imago. A middle-class white woman, for instance, is culturally encouraged to see herself as the bodily ideal in relation to which both the black woman and the homeless man are widely perceived as inferior or insufficient. To the degree to which she in fact does so, she effects a pleasurable captation with her "own" specular imago.

Nor is every female subject content to relegate to the man she loves the representation of her corporeal longings. There are also women who attempt to claim the image of masculinity for themselves rather than identifying with it through the intervening agency of another body—women who seek to embody the man who represents their narcissistic ideal. Sometimes this visual performance of masculinity is conducted for "camp" or deconstructive purposes, or at least with an apprehension of the performance as a masquerade. In such cases, the screen is recognized as such, and manipulated in creative and subversive ways. The image of masculinity is then more "worn" than assumed.

In other cases, the female subject has recourse to the masculine image because it conforms to her own sense of who she is. Since identification requires a cultural ratification, she also attempts to be seen through the representational parameters of that image. However, the gaze for the most part resists this solicitation,[61] and—on the basis of certain bodily traits, which are themselves devoid of meaning or formal coherence but through which every culture "fantasizes" gender—either projects onto the subject the unwanted screen of femininity or pathologizes the assumed signifiers of masculinity.[62] In the former instance, we are face to face with another version of that unhappy and one-sided love affair I spoke about earlier—only this time, one focusing upon masculinity rather than an exemplary and exceptional femininity. In the latter, the imaginary accession to masculinity is often "photographed" as a travesty or perversion of the "real thing," and so fails to lead to the desired identification with ideality.[63] In neither of these cases does the female bodily ego achieve even an imaginary coherence, a state of affairs which could be, but generally is not, efficacious.

Prolegomena to a Fuller Discussion of Idealization
I want to stress once again that my intent in the last two sections of this chapter has not been to privilege the sexually or racially marked subject, but rather to dramatize what it means for a culture to valorize a particular bodily configuration at the level of the screen. This valorization precipitates a dangerous *mécon-*

naissance on the part of certain subjects, which prevents them from identifying outside extremely restrictive bodily limits. It encourages others to live the irreducibly disjunctive relation between the sensational ego and the specular imago in a pathological way, i.e., as personal insufficiency and failure. As a result, all kinds of potentially transformative opportunities are lost.

I am not arguing against idealization—without which human existence would be unendurable, and which is the precondition for every loving access to the other, whether identificatory or erotic—but against the smooth meshing of that psychic operation with culturally defined norms. The colonization of idealization by the screen not only restricts ideality to certain subjects, while rendering others unworthy of love, but also naturalizes the former as essentially ideal. We need to learn how to idealize oppositionally and provisionally.

It is equally imperative that we learn to idealize outside the corporeal parameters of the self. To do so would be to escape from the vicious circle which leads inexorably from the aspiration to perfection to the experience of corporeal fragmentation, and which makes the subject irreducibly aggressive toward anyone who seems capable of approximating what he or she cannot. To do so would also mean to situate oneself at a necessary distance from *das Ding* or the impossible nonobject of desire, and thereby consolidate oneself as a subject of lack. Finally, to do so would be to make possible our identification at a distance with bodies which we would otherwise phobically avoid, to facilitate our leap out of "difference" and into bodily otherness.

Since idealization is clearly an operation whose roots extend deep into the unconscious, it cannot be simply decreed through conscious edict. We consequently require textual assistance in carrying out the project I have just described. We need visual texts which activate in us the capacity to idealize bodies which diverge as widely as possible both from ourselves and from the cultural norm. Those representations should also be ones which do not at the same time work to naturalize the end result of that psychic activity in a way that might be ultimately productive simply of new, reified ideals. The bodily representations which I am imagining here are ones that would not so much incarnate ideality as wear it, like a removable cloak.

2

From the Ideal-Ego to the Active Gift of Love

There is nothing more intoxicating than self-love. On those rare occasions when we imaginarily coincide with the ideal imago which we usually worship languishingly from afar, we experience an absolutely thrilling euphoria—what Lacan, in his essay on the mirror stage, does not hesitate to call "jubilation."[1] Indeed, I would go so far as to suggest that the pleasures afforded by even the most intense object-love pale by comparison with those provided by this narcissistic transport.

However, at such rapturous moments, the subject is "filled up" in a dangerous way. Not only is the *moi* bloated with importance, but it functions in this distended form to conceal from the subject what founds him or her: lack, or *manque-à-être*. Although imaginary, this surfeit is inimical to the operations of desire, and, therefore, to human existence in all its manifold dimensions. As long as it continues, there is in effect no other, and no world. And if capable of infinite prolongation, it would spell certain death.

Moreover, the ideal image is impossible to approach except in moments of mania or delusion. For the most part, the subject who yearns to approximate it experiences not repletion, but insufficiency, not wholeness, but discordance and disarray. He or she vaguely apprehends the irreducible heterogeneity of the bodily ego, the distance of his or her proprioceptive coordinates from the specular ideal, but only via the extremely dystopic fantasy of the body in bits and pieces. This fantasy elicits feelings of extreme aggression toward any other who is imagined to be intact or complete, a rivalry to the death over the right to occupy the frame of the idealizing image. And it is only such an other who really figures psychically for the subject who is my present concern.

Finally, the subject who aspires to incarnate or embody the ideal most typically derives his or her definition of that ideal from normative representation. He or she thereby surrenders all negotiating distance with respect to ideality, and all agency within the larger field of vision. He or she is not only compliant with the dominant values of the screen, but also deprived of any capacity to put its images to new uses, or to work transformatively upon them. This subject can only passionately but passively reaffirm the specular status quo.

Some further clarification of the last paragraph would seem necessary. By "idealization," I mean the increase in an object's value which occurs when it is elevated to the level of *das Ding,* or the impossible nonobject of desire.[2] Idealization is a strictly human activity. Representational practice generally works to establish which objects are worthy of being idealized. It does so, as I will explain in greater detail later, by embedding them in a symbolic matrix which extends and deepens their semantic range, and so solicits libidinal investment. Certain objects are so widely represented as being worthy of idealization that they assume the status of normative ideals. Nevertheless, no matter how often it is reiterated, an ideal remains a bloodless abstraction until it is has been psychically affirmed. We alone are thus finally responsible for the production of ideals.

When the subject idealizes what is most culturally valorized, the idealized object becomes almost automatically fetishized, in the Marxian rather than the Freudian sense of the word.[3] Affirmed both representationally and psychically, it begins to seem intrinsically more valuable than other objects, substantially superior. Although the subject has constituted that object as an ideal, he or she often falls prostrate before it, in thrall to its fascinating luster.

It might seem to follow logically from this discussion that the human subject should somehow learn to live without ideality. However, such is not the conclusion toward which the present chapter will move. Idealization has a crucial role to play in the psychic existence of even that individual who most fully and relentlessly confronts the void upon which all subjectivity pivots. This is only in part the case because human existence would be intolerable without ideality. By putting objects in the place of the unattainable nonobject of desire, one also maintains one's distance from that nonobject, thereby becoming, in the strongest sense of the word, the subject of lack. Even more crucially, idealization is something we cannot do without because under the right circumstances it facilitates not so much rivalrous as *loving* identifications—because it alone makes possible a genuine *relation* to the other. Finally, and equally importantly, it can open up identifications which would otherwise be foreclosed by the imperatives of normative representation and the ego. However, ideality can only serve these vital functions when it is bestowed at the greatest possible distance from the self, and when that bestowal is *active* rather than *passive*.

As the preceding paragraphs make clear, this chapter is devoted to the subject of idealization. Most of it will be given over to a theoretical elaboration and textual dramatization of the perils involved in self-idealization. However, in the final two sections, I will address the psychic and social functions served by idealization when it is directed not toward the self, but toward the other. I will then attempt to specify the conditions under which idealization might work to position the subject actively within the field of vision, and to effect a radical redistribution of value at the site of the screen.

Although the writings of Lacan are central to this chapter, the argument here and in the next chapter may seem very alien to the reader of his late seminars. What I am attempting to imagine or construct is an alternative to Lacan's itinerary—a route along which he takes a first few hesitant steps in *Seminar I*, and again in *Seminars VII* and *XI*. Following up on the implications of several remarks in the earlier text on the topic of the "active gift of love," I will move not toward the conclusion that there can be no real relation between man and woman,[4] but toward an elaboration of the terms under which precisely such a relation might be possible. The Lacan who figures here thus speaks with a very different voice from the one made famous through *Seminar XX*.

The Ideal-Ego

In *Seminar I*, Lacan first effects a deconstruction of the human/animal opposition, then reintroduces the difference between those two terms at an unexpected juncture. He attempts to dispel the illusion that animals inhabit a purely natural domain by suggesting that the imaginary register is as central to their existence as it is to that of the human subject. However, he then contrasts the animal realm to that of the human on the basis of the divergent relationship each sustains with the image.

Visual representation is as necessary to the maturation of an animal as it is to that of a human being, he suggests; both conventionally effect an erotic approach to the other only via the image. However, whereas the representation which "lures" an animal into sexuality facilitates its relation to other members of the same species, in the case of the human subject, it is more generative "of fragmentation, of rupture, of breaking up, of lack of adaptation, of inadequation."[5] The image precipitates not only desire for another human body, but also something which is prior to and often at odds with both the sexual conjunction of one individual with another, and their peaceful cohabitation: the *moi*.

Lacan suggests that in the case of the animal, the image functions to define it as a member of a species rather than as an individual. Its productivity is exhausted in encouraging the animal to effect only those sexual conjunctions through which it will reproduce the biological paradigm of which it is a representative. Lacan maintains that the animal is "so much a captive of the type" that it is "already dead in relation to the eternal life" of that species.[6] Somehow both the animal's typicality and the smooth operation of its sexuality are intimately connected to the fact that the image functions for it more as a window than a mirror—it opens onto the other, rather than the self.

Things are very different with the human subject. Classically, his or her central preoccupation throughout life is to overcome that inadequacy to him- or herself which is the result first of the prematurity of birth, and later of a whole series of divisions and losses, most particularly those induced through the entry into language. The image consequently functions less as a window than a reflecting surface. When confronted with an idealizing representation, he or she generally searches first for the self rather than for the other. However, since "it is [always] in the other that [the subject] will…rediscover his [or her] ideal ego" (I, 282), not even the most jubilant captation can be prolonged forever; sooner or later, the subject apprehends his or her distance from the actual or metaphoric mirror.

At the moment that he or she perceives the "otherness" of the idealizing image, the subject classically responds to it as an enemy and a rival, one whose separate existence is inimical to his or her own. He or she strives desperately to close the gap between it and the sensational body, so as to assert the unity of the self. The result is the negation of either that entity, or the other. To the degree that the subject succeeds in affirming him- or herself as image, the world is in effect annihilated. To the degree that he or she fails to do so, he or she experiences that corporeal disintegration which Lacan associates with the fantasy of the fragmented body. This is the "either you or me" logic which informs the subject's relation to the other:[7]

> [the object] appears in the guise of an object from which man is irremediably separated, [it]…shows him the very figure of his dehiscence within the world…. Inversely, when he grasps his unity, on the contrary it is the world which for him becomes decomposed, loses its meaning, and takes on an alienated and discordant aspect. (II, 166)

Seminar I thus stresses both the murderous and suicidal logic of this narcissistic relation to the image. It makes clear that what I have called the "principle of the self-same body" entails more than the repudiation of bodily otherness, or its assimilation to the subject's own corporeal coordinates. It also involves an aspiration to be "one" with the ideal image, and a relationship of fatal rivalry with anyone who seemingly occupies the position of that image.

At the same time, *Seminar I* makes clear that it is only through the mirror that each of us is able to love an other. "What we call libidinal investment is what makes an object become desirable, that is to say how it becomes confused with this more or less structured image which, in diverse ways, we carry with us," observes Lacan. "It's one's own ego that one loves in love, one's own ego made real on the imaginary level" (141–42). It is consequently not through its radical alterity that we effect a libidinal approach to an object, but rather through its evocation of an image which we would like to call our own.

However, "love" does not necessarily imply entering into a generous relation to another. Love can represent the demand that this other prostrate him- or herself before our image, and submit in every way to our demands. As Lacan observes, such a love "is expressed in a sort of bodily agglutinating of freedom. We want to become for the other an object that has the same limiting value for him as does, in relation to his freedom, his own body.... We require that a freedom accept its own renunciation so as to be, from that moment on, limited to everything capricious, imperfect, in truth inferior, the paths along which it is swept by its captation by that object which we ourselves are" (I, 217). A generously loving relation to the other implies something very different, something which can best be described as my recognition of that other as an other.

Since, as Lacan insists, such a relation is still narcissistic in nature, it implies at the same time the specification of that person as what I would like to be. The necessary simultaneity of these two actions means that if I am to relate to the loved other outside the vicious logic of the "you or me,"[8] I must accept that the image within which I would like to see myself reflected does not show me myself, but someone else. To state the matter slightly differently, I must confer ideality upon the face and lineaments of another.

This formulation may seem to grant an exhorbitant privilege to the body within the economy of love. However, Lacan not only stresses over and over again in his writings and seminars that the body is the frame within which the subject apprehends both self and other,[9] but he even insists in *Seminar VII* on the absolute centrality of that term to the operation of idealization, an operation without which there is no love, and no pleasurable identification. "Even in Kant's time," he observes, "it is the form of the human body that is presented to us as the limit of the possibilities of the beautiful, as ideal *Erscheinen*. It once was, though it no longer is, a divine form. It is the cloak of all possible fantasms of human desire. The flowers of desire are contained in this vase whose contours we attempt to define."[10] Paul Schilder also stresses the centrality of the human body to our notion of beauty, which might be said to represent one of the most important end results of idealization. "We regard beauty as being primarily connected with the beauty of the human body," he writes; "The problem of beauty is therefore closely linked with the problem of the body-image."[11] But why is idealization so intimately connected with the human body?

Seminar VII suggests that if the body is "the cloak of all possible fantasms of human desire," that is for fundamentally narcissistic reasons. As the key to a psychoanalytic understanding of idealization, it proposes the subject's relation to its corporeal imago in the mirror stage. *Seminar VII* thereby intimates that idealization is an activity which the subject performs first and foremost in relation to the corporeal image within which he or she most aspires to see him or herself. All other images which are subsequently idealized are somehow related to it. Indeed, to idealize an image is to posit it as a desired mirror. The mirror image derives its preeminent value from its capacity to substitute for what has been lost to the subject through his or her entry into language. Through identification with it, the subject imputes a fictive reality to him- or herself, and thereby elevates the *moi* to the status of *das Ding.*

In a passage immediately following the one quoted above, Lacan invokes both the mirror stage and the subject's *mangue-à-être,* and insists upon the necessity of conceptualizing them in relation to each other. In so doing, he gives the lie to the notion that the mirror stage could be said in any simple way to "precede" the inauguration of lack. He suggests that the mirror stage plays more of a compensatory role than a preparatory one with respect to lack:

> ...the body, and especially its image, as I have previously articulated it in the function of narcissism, [is] that which from a certain point of view represents the relationship of man to his second death, the signifier of his desire, his visible desire. (298)

But *Seminar VII* represents the mirror image as more than a conventional pivot for desire. It is also a "mirage" preventing the subject from apprehending his or her fundamental nothingness or "being-for-death," a lure encouraging him or her to pursue endlessly that imaginary plenitude whose unavoidable sequel is the fantasy of bodily fragmentation. The subject's attempt to approximate the ideal imago can be read as proof positive of lack. However, it is also through this imago that he or she protects him- or herself against knowledge of that lack. Lacan suggests that the idealizing reflection provided by the real or metaphoric mirror

> ...both indicates the site of desire insofar as it is desire of nothing, the relationship of man to his lack of being, and prevents that site from being seen. (298)

It is often assumed that a strictly symbolic differentiation provides the only path leading out of the dead-end described in this passage from Lacan, and that such a differentiation is antipathetic both to the image and to ideality. However,

Seminar VII makes clear that far from discouraging idealization, the symbolic order relies upon it. The symbolic order does not so much impede ideality as exploit and colonize it. As I will demonstrate later in this chapter, Lacan also makes abundantly evident both in *Seminar VII* and elsewhere that there is no subjectivity without the image, and that idealization represents a vital psychic function. The crucial project is not to move from the imaginary to the symbolic, since there is no "getting out" of the one to the other. The all-important undertaking with respect to the domain of images is to idealize at a distance from the self. To state the matter in terms closer to the present discussion, the goal is to confer ideality upon an image which cannot be even delusorily mapped onto one's sensational body.

For Lacan, this project implies replacing the ideal-ego with the ego-ideal. However, the ego-ideal generally demands the subject's psychic subordination, and his or her allegience to dominant cultural values, both of which are at odds with the *active* idealization toward which I gestured in the previous chapter. I will consequently advance a rather different formulation than the one to which Lacan is primarily committed. First, I will attempt to specify in more insistently political terms what it means to idealize. I will also attempt to determine how we might do so not only outside the parameters of the self, but also outside those of normative representation. Finally, I will attempt to elaborate an identificatory model which does not replicate the negative power dynamic instanciated by the relation of the ego to the ego-ideal.

But before exploring how idealization might work to facilitate rather than to render impossible a genuine relation to the other, I would like to offer an extended reading of a film which addresses with great urgency many of the issues raised so far in this book: Ulrike Ottinger's *Bildnis einer Trinkerin* (*Ticket of No Return*). This text dramatizes the difficulties the white female subject is likely to encounter when she takes seriously the cultural imperative imposed upon her to embody an exemplary femininity, and, so, to *become* the image. It consequently provides a visual and narrative specification of the dangers of self-idealization. It also showcases both the fantasy of bodily decomposition which haunts such a project, and the deadly rivalry which it encourages in the subject vis-à-vis the ideal image, whether human or representational. Through an analysis of *Bildnis einer Trinkerin,* I hope to make evident how important it is that ideality be dispensed at the greatest possible distance from the self.

The Ideal-Ego and the Fantasy of the Body in Bits and Pieces: 1

At first glance, *Bildnis einer Trinkerin* (1979) seems to provide an extended illustration of two of the most accepted tenets of feminist film theory. Like the theories of Laura Mulvey and Mary Ann Doane, it seems to suggest that there is a certain collapse between woman and the image,[12] and to propose as an alternative to this specular implosion the masquerade of femininity.[13] Its female protagonist is pathologically obsessed with her own mirror reflection; that reflection engrosses all of her desire, and completely defines her relations to all of the other characters in the film. A long fantasy sequence in the second half of *Bildnis,* however, shows her assuming in succession a whole range of professional roles, and in the process manipulating the contours of her bodily imago. Here, she seems to have achieved some distance from the mirror, to be detached from the identities which it figures forth. Because of the parodic aspect of the fantasy sequence, this detachment might well be taken for irony, and the images it inflects as a politically enabling masquerade of femininity.

I want to advance a very different reading of *Bildnis einer Trinkerin,* to show that, from the very beginning, "Madame" (Tabea Blumenschein) stands at an irreducible distance from the mirror, and that her pathological relation to her own reflection is the logical extension not of too complete a specular "captation," but of her inability to accept her exteriority to the idealizing image. I also want to use Ottinger's film to challenge the larger assumption—which sometimes informs the equation of woman and spectacle—that the female subject stands outside lack, along with the particular reading of psychoanalysis from which that assumption proceeds.[14]

Bildnis provides a wide-ranging commentary on what Lacan calls the "imaginary," on the psychic register that is specific to identification and narcissism, and which the author of *Seminar II* places in the closest possible relation with the specular.[15] *Bildnis* tells the story of a woman who abandons her past, and with it her name, in order to dedicate herself uninterruptedly to the adoration and exhibition of herself-as-image. More precisely, it recounts the narrative of a woman who decides to take seriously the impossible mandate which is culturally imposed upon the white female subject: that she conform to the visual specifications of an ideal femininity. *Bildnis* brilliantly dramatizes the fantasy of bodily disintegration which haunts this project, and the consequent self-hatred into which self-love constantly threatens to devolve. However, it refuses to characterize the imaginary as a "feminine" domain, as a presymbolic space from which woman never fully emerges, or to which she easily regresses from the symbolic order.

Rather, like Lacan's early seminars, which will figure prominently in the following pages, *Bildnis* shows the imaginary to be fundamentally *reparative,* and, hence, unthinkable prior to the subject's symbolic structuration. It suggests, that is, that the images of an ideal unity within which the subject attempts to locate herself are not only always inflected by meaning, but are also conjurations against the void which is introduced by language. And if the imaginary cannot be thought apart from the symbolic, neither can the symbolic be "entered" without imaginary mediation; it is only through the coordinates of that necessary fiction, the self, as *Bildnis* shows, that the subject is able to apprehend the other.

The theoretical gendering of the imaginary as "feminine" consequently represents a misrecognition of the part that register plays within all subjectivity. Finally, Ottinger's fourth feature film takes very seriously both the dangers and impasses to which the logic of the imaginary can lead, and its undeniable seductions, pleasures, and powers—seductions, pleasures, and powers which are at the heart of its own spectatorial appeal.

In "Film and the Masquerade," Mary Ann Doane claims that for the female spectator, who is here representative of the normative female subject, "there is a certain overpresence of the image—she *is* the image." She argues that because of the "closeness" of this relationship, "the female spectator's desire can be described only in terms of a kind of narcissism—the female look demands a becoming. It thus appears to negate the very distance or gap specified by Metz and Burch as the essential precondition for voyeurism" (22). Although Doane is careful to specify this "overpresence of the image" as a theoretical construction, her own insistence upon the importance of masquerade as a mechanism for opening up an interval between the female spectator and the spectacle confers upon that construction a certain psychic reality, at least within the present symbolic order.[16]

The white protagonist of *Bildnis* is not introduced in terms of her biographical specificity—we are in fact never given a single concrete detail about her past—but rather in terms of what might be called her "mission." A disembodied female voice-over characterizes her as someone destined to embody the feminine ideal. It invokes this ideal by enumerating a number of the names with which it has been associated throughout the history of Western representation:

> She, a belle of antique grace and raphaelic harmony, a woman, created like no other to be Medea, Madonna, Beatrice, Iphigenia, Aspasia, decided one sunny winter day to leave La Rotunda. She bought a one-way ticket to Berlin-Tegel.

However, this proliferation of names attests to the impossibility of locating the feminine ideal within any individual woman, even within the realm of literature or art; it can only be conjured forth through a range of mythical figures. The images which accompany the voice-over commentary attest further to the abstract nature of this ideal. Ottinger's "belle of antique grace and raphaelic harmony" is not depicted through the specificity of feature or limb, but through the spectacle of swirling red fabric, and the sound of high-heeled shoes tapping with exaggerated precision on a green marble floor.

When we are finally given a close-up of Madame's face, it is shot through a glass door, as if to stress its distance from actuality. But even this guarded attempt to corporealize the ideal is doomed to failure. Almost immediately, the exquisitely composed image of Madame's face and raised hand is "liquified" or destabilized by the cleaning woman, who squeezes water out of cloth onto the other side of the door's transparent surface [figure 1].

figure 1

This series of shots demands to be read in relation to the project outlined in the opening monologue. There, we are told that Madame is leaving La Rotunda for Berlin because Berlin seems to her a place where she will be able to devote herself uninterruptedly to a very singular goal:

> She wanted to forget her past, rather leave it like a ragged house. With heart and soul she wanted to concentrate on one affair. Her affair. To finally follow her destiny was her sole wish. Berlin, foreign to her, appeared to be the right place to live her passion undisturbed. Her passion was to drink, live to drink—a drunken life, life of a drunkard. Upon landing at Berlin-Tegel, her decision had become irrevocable. Inspired by a Berlin folder that was presented to her by a friendly stewardess, she decided to set up a drinking schedule…. She decided to do a sort of boozer's sightseeing, briefly, to use sightseeing for her very private needs…. Her plans for a narcissistic worship of loneliness have deepened and intensified to the point where they have entered a stage worthy to be lived, not to risk being lost in realms of phantasy. Now had come the time to let everything come true.

As this commentary makes clear, the object of the passion to which Madame commits herself for the duration of *Bildnis* is only ostensibly alcohol. The consumption of wine and brandy is really a metaphor for another kind of incorporation, one much more difficult to effect. It is a metaphor, that is, for Madame's attempt to assimilate or become the specular ideal in relation to which she, like all female subjects, is (negatively) defined. However, whereas for Doane the dilemma of femininity is the excessive proximity of the mirror, for Madame the problem is rather its irreducible distance.

Alcoholism functions as an appropriate metaphor for the project described by the voice-over for two reasons. First of all, the consumption of alcohol leaves behind no permanent "deposit" or residue. It results only in a very transitory

The Threshold of the Visible World

and delusory euphoria, which then gives way to a sense of emptiness and loss, and must consequently be endlessly repeated if its effects are to be sustained. Alcohol also lends itself to Ottinger's purposes because it is a fluid substance. Implicit in the Narcissus myth, as in Ottinger's retelling of it, is an insistence on the impossibility of the lover's incorporative desire for the idealized self, and liquidity assumes a privileged role in the articulation of this impossibility. Because the image which engrosses him is reflected in a pool, he cannot embrace it without shattering it.

Lacan provides an important definition of the fragmented body in *Seminar I*. He suggests that it is "an image essentially dismemberable from its body" (148), that it provides the fantasy through which the subject acknowledges his or her distance from the idealizing representation within which he or she would like to find his or her "self." It could thus be said that any attempt to enter the impossible frame of that representation leads inexorably, as in the Narcissus legend, to the subject's "fall" into an image which is the very opposite of the one which is desired: his or her headlong "plunge," that is, into an image of bodily decomposition.

As we will see, the shot in which water streaks down the window separating Madame's face from the camera is only the first of many occasions on which her attempt to approximate the status of an exemplary spectacle ultimately leads to an experience of a radical corporeal disintegration. Over and over again, the protagonist of *Bildnis* ventures into the streets of Berlin in the guise of the image which she wishes to become, only to have that image quickly lose its shape and coherence as she commences her evening of drinking. However, the film never permits the spectator to imagine that he or she stands safely outside the insane project to which Madame devotes herself. It prolongs the moment of *méconnaissance* long enough to remind us of the jubilation it affords—long enough, that is, to evoke in us once again our own inextinguishable desire to approximate the ideal.

The airport scene provides a witty dramatization of the no-exit logic of the narcissism to which Madame commits herself upon her arrival in Berlin. She is thwarted in her first attempt to leave Tegel by the window washer who stands on the other side of the door. Her second attempt initially meets with no greater success; the electric door in front of which she stands fails to open, and Madame searches in vain for a knob to turn. The claustral binarism which leads relentlessly from the desire for unity to the fantasy of the fragmented body is of course a trademark of the imaginary register. However, *Bildnis* emphasizes more than once during this scene that although the imaginary promotes closure, it is not itself isolated from the symbolic. Not only does the female voice-over evoke the ideal femininity which Madame seeks to embody with names that are redolent with cultural significance, but she arrives in Berlin at the same time as three "professional" women in extravagantly styled houndstooth suits.

As their names suggest—Common Sense (Monika von Cube), Social Question (Magdalena Montezuma), and Exact Statistics (Orpha Termin)—these figures provide parodic representatives of the symbolic order. Although one of their primary functions in the film is to demonstrate the inadequacy of a whole range of social discourses to account for the peculiar pleasures and dangers to which Madame surrenders herself, their presence in virtually every important public scene also speaks to all of the ways in which the symbolic intrudes into the imaginary register. The obsessive conversational return of each of the houndstooth women to the comforting certitudes of her professional discourse also suggests the extension of the imaginary into the symbolic.

The scene following Madame's arrival at Tegel begins with a spectacular shot of her leaving her hotel, which once again stresses the close imbrication of imaginary and symbolic. Dressed in an exquisite black dress and matching hat, with a golden spiral hanging from each ear, she is emphatically situated within the *mise-en-scène* of her desire, on the side of a hyperbolically idealized image [figure 2]. That image is also classically articulated, organized according to the strictest perspectival principles. At the moment when Madame first comes into sharp focus, she is framed by an ornate interior doorway, and she stays within this frame until she is lost from sight. Even her movement through this doorway fails to disrupt the fixity of the composition, since it is in turn framed by a second doorway. And the interior entrance seems to lead to yet another doorway, which represents a kind of vanishing point. This shot functions as a powerful reminder that, even at its most imaginarily alluring, the field of vision is never free of symbolic definition.

figure 2

The casino where Madame begins her "sightseeing" tour of Berlin provides the site for one of the film's most explicit repudiations of the heterosexual imperative at the heart of classic cinema. In the elevator leading to the gambling room, a uniformed man attempts without success to interest her, first by exhibiting his card tricks, then by showing her the photos of naked women on the reverse side of the cards. Although here, as in many other scenes in the film, the protagonist of *Bildnis* functions emphatically as an erotic spectacle, it is not for the benefit of the male look.[17] Her indifference to the uniformed man strips that look of its usual phallic pretensions, not the least of which is its claim to confer meaning on the female body.

A later shot in the same scene again situates Madame beyond the reach of the male scopic drive, and outside the libidinal economy which it conventionally implies. This shot begins with a close-up of her black-gloved hand placing an elegant glass of white wine on the casino table. The contents of this glass, which now occupies the center of the frame, are brilliantly illuminated, gold against a black background. Significantly, however, this light does not radiate outward, but is entirely contained by the contours of the glass, as if—like the protagonist of *Bildnis*—it shines only for itself. A man's fingers reach from right frame toward Madame's hand, which lies beside her drink. She immediately frees herself from his hold, and slowly lifts the glass to her lips [figure 3]. The glass casts a luminescent reflection on her face and neck, a reflection which is framed and echoed by her long spiral earrings. Lacan suggests in *Seminar II* that the shadow of the ego always falls upon the object (166). Here, that relation is reversed, attesting to both the initial exteriority of the images through which the ego constitutes itself, and the infinite reversibility of its relation to the object.

figure 3

The camera shares Madame's indifference to the man's appropriative hand; like her, it never even turns to glance at the man. However, although the feminist spectator might be tempted to offer a lesbian reading of this indifference—a reading which many other scenes in the film support—the shot under discussion points unequivocally in a different direction. Here, Madame is clearly locked in a narcissistic self-embrace. Alcohol is ostensibly an external substance, pointing at least tentatively to the possibility of a libidinal investment in the exterior world. However, the shimmering reflection of the glass on Madame's face and neck makes clear that her relation to its contents is less under the sign of "having" than "being."[18]

When she appears in the ornate double doorway of her hotel prior to leaving for the casino, Madame seems at least momentarily to approximate the image around which her desire revolves. The ensuing cab ride, however, already attests to a certain unravelling of this coherence. Initially, she is located firmly in the back seat of the car, but eventually she projects herself imaginarily into the driver's seat, in the guise of a young white man with a moustache and black leather jacket [figure 4]. Significantly, this masculine masquerade fails to alter the terms of her self-address. What this scene dramatizes is less the production of an ironic distance from the mirror than the conjuration of yet another ideal image of self, this time male rather than female. As is so frequently the case in *Bildnis,* either the image cannot be assumed, or it quickly loses its seductive luster. The fantasmatic cab driven by Madame in her capacity as male driver knocks over the cart of Lutze, a homeless white woman, and spills its contents all over the street. This accident provides another demonstration of the inability of the self to contain the images out of which it is ostensibly composed. But here, at least, the specter of disintegration is successfully exteriorized.

figure 4

As she leaves the casino, Madame once again encounters Lutze, who helps her into a cab and washes one of its windows with spit and a rag. Like that important series of shots organized around window washing in the airport scene, Lutze's actions serve to liquify or destabilize the image on the other side of the glass. Her face also functions as a kind of alternative mirror. As Lutze wipes the window with her rag, Madame stares intently at her features, even turning to look back when the cab pulls away. This scene clearly positions the wealthy woman in a narcissistic relation to her homeless counterpart. However, this relation differs markedly from that described by Lacan in "The Mirror Stage." Lutze does not provide Madame with an idealized self-image, but with the opposite; she literalizes the fantasy of the body in bits and pieces, which constantly threatens to undermine that image.

Back in her hotel room at the end of her first day in Berlin, Madame resorts once more to alcohol as a device for closing the gap between herself and ideality. Her room has been transformed into a narcissistic shrine: two identical photographs of its occupant in masculine clothing hang on the wall above the bed, each lit by three lights in the shape of votive candles. Madame again positions herself in relation not only to feminine perfection, but also to what might be called "the man she would like to have been."[19] *Bildnis einer Trinkerin* thus equips its protagonist with both a female and a male ego-ideal. And, unlike the woman about whom Freud writes,[20] Madame reserves for herself the right to approximate each in turn.

The wine Madame consumes facilitates a series of extraordinary fantasies. Because these fantasies are "actualized" at the level of the image, but not the narrative, they dramatize the resistance that the spectacle of woman can offer to the forward movement of the story. Each takes the spectator into what Mulvey calls "a no man's land outside its own time and space," and gives "the quality of a cut-out or icon, rather than verisimilitude, to the screen"(20). Of course, given its larger preoccupation with female specularity, and, most particularly, with those idealized images of femininity which can be neither temporally nor spatially localized, this quality inheres as well in many of the film's other images; this fantasy sequence merely represents its apotheosis.

In the first shot of the sequence, a dwarf (Paul Glauer) stands to the right of an elaborate granite fountain, bowing and gesturing to Madame to approach. She enters from the other side, sits down on the ledge of the fountain, and drinks from its contents [figure 5]. The hyperreal acuity of the sounds made by her approaching footsteps and the placement of her glass on the ledge evoke the clink of ice cubes in a glass. This acoustic version of the alcohol metaphor surfaces again in the next fantasy, where it is given a visual analogue. Here, Madame and the dwarf slowly climb a glass-enclosed stairway [figure 6]. This structure has the shape and the opaque consistency of the glasses conventionally used for iced tea or mint juleps. The third fantasy shows the dwarf, in extreme long-shot, carrying a drink on a tray toward a pagoda, in which Madame sits. She raises the glass to her lips.

figure 5   *figure 6*

In the final, and most aesthetically compelling fantasy, Madame and the dwarf ceremonially cross a brook on the round steps provided for that purpose, again producing a sound evocative of ice against glass. Here, as in the other fantasies, her clothing, the music, and the general *mise-en-scène* connote "the Orient." The dwarf plucks an orange flower from the water and hands it, as if it were a glass, to Madame. She raises it to her lips, her head thrown back voluptuously [figure 7]. Three more shots repeat this gesture, emphasizing the contrast between the intense orange of the flower, the rich black and blue of Madame's dress, and the exaggerated pallor of her complexion [figures 8, 9, 10].

figure 7

figure 8

figure 9

figure 10

Each of the first three fantasies consists of only one isolated shot, as if to insist at a formal as well as conceptual level on its status as "cut-out" or "icon." The final fantasy, on the other hand, consists of four shots. Interestingly, however, this recourse to montage does not serve to advance the narrative; each subsequent shot merely works to reiterate the action shown in the preceding one. The final fantasy does nevertheless dramatize an "advance," but one which is spatial rather than temporal. Whereas the camera remains at a discreet remove from its human subjects in the first three fantasies, in the last one it abandons this principle. In each of its four shots, the distance between Madame and the camera diminishes, until her face is finally shown in an eroticizing close-up which isolates the activity of drinking from all else. I say "the distance between Madame and the camera," but what is really at issue here is the distance between the protagonist of *Bildnis* and her ideal imago. In the first three fantasies, that imago remains unapproachable, but in the final four shots, Madame moves closer and closer to the desired mirror, until she almost achieves in relation to it that proximity which Doane characterizes as the feminine norm.

Significantly, in the shot immediately preceding the fantasy sequence, Madame is shown lying with her back to the images that hang on the wall above the bed. Consequently, she is not overtly positioned as an external spectator in relation to the ideal she seeks to approximate, which presumably facilitates the imaginary approach to it dramatized by the flower-drinking shots. However, not only are all of the fantasy images marked by a high degree of "unreality," located in a "no man's time and space"—a place, that is, where no one can actually "be"—but each is emphatically displayed for an implied viewer, who can only be Madame. The final shot of her lifting the flower to her mouth gives way to two scenes in which the axis of vision is much more fully foregrounded, in ways which work to place her once again at an irreducible distance from ideality. Here, Madame is subordinated to the gaze, in her capacity both as spectacle and as look.

The Ideal-Ego and the Fantasy of the Body in Bits and Pieces: 2

The first of the two scenes to foreground the axis of vision does so by deploying the gaze to problematize Madame's quest to approximate the feminine ideal. In it, she sits at a table in a coffee shop drinking brandy after brandy, the empty glasses ranged in front of her. Here, the ingestion of alcohol offers none of the narcissistic gratification it provides in the fantasy sequence; instead, it is manifestly desperate and obsessional. Madame faces a window, toward which she repeatedly grimaces and gesticulates [figure 11]. At first, she appears to be addressing someone on the other side of the window, but as the scene progresses, it becomes increasingly apparent that the window is important less for its transparent properties than its

figure 11

reflective ones. Madame's gestures and grimaces are not directed to the world outside the restaurant, but to the body in bits and pieces, or—to state the case somewhat differently—to the principle of decomposition which now threatens to gain the upper hand. Significantly, that principle is once again represented by Lutze, who is now placed in an even more intimate psychic relation to Madame than in the cab scene. In the only shot which purports to show what Madame sees when she looks at the window, Lutze pushes her cart toward the restaurant from the rear of the frame, until she stands directly behind the reflection cast on the glass by Madame [figure 12]. This shot not only indicates that the window functions as a mirror in the coffee house scene, but it also incontrovertibly establishes Lutze as the image which that mirror shows.

figure 12   figure 13

Significantly, Lutze passes through the window which maintains her exteriority in the cab scene, and into the space where the other woman sits. Madame summons her inside the restaurant, in an explicit acknowledgement of the psychic affinities which link her to the "bag lady." The two women drink several double brandies, but the alcohol again fails to provide Madame with the desired *méconnaissance*. Finally, in a reversal of the Narcissus legend, she attempts to shatter rather than embrace the mirror. She tosses the contents of a glass of brandy onto the window, much as one might throw something into a pool of water to disrupt the image formed there. As she does so, two other patrons of the coffee shop quickly pull out their cameras. They point them not at Madame or Lutze, who replicates the action of her friend, but at the streaming surface of the window [figure 13]. They thus photograph Madame not as "herself," but in the guise of the image she attempts to efface.

The photographers' action serves as another potent reminder that self-recognition is never a purely imaginary transaction. That transaction involves not only subject and image, represented in the restaurant scene by Madame and the window/Lutze, but also the gaze, which is metaphorized—as it is in Lacan's eleventh seminar[21]—by the camera. The gaze, which can perhaps best be defined as the inscription of Otherness within the field of vision, radically exceeds the human looks through which it often manifests itself. It impresses itself upon us phenomenologically through that sense which we all have at moments of acute self-apprehension of being seen from a position outside ourselves, a position which *Bildnis* inscribes through the flash of the camera. That experience of specularization constitutes a necessary feature of identification; we can only effect a satisfactory captation when we not only see ourselves, but *feel ourselves being seen* in the shape of a particular image.

I say "particular image" because the gaze does not photograph us directly, but through the cultural representations which intervene between it and us— representations which Lacan calls the "screen."[22] Although we often treat these representations as simple mirrors, they do not so much reflect us as cast their reflection upon us. They are carriers of—among other things—sexual, racial, and class difference. For these reasons, the subject does not always occupy the field of vision happily. No image can be comfortably assumed by the subject unless it is affirmed by the gaze, but the gaze does not necessarily photograph the subject in ways that are conducive to pleasure. As is so clearly the case in this scene, the gaze often imposes upon the subject an unwanted identity.

Even before the actual cameras are pointed at the window within which Madame sees herself as a body in bits and pieces, the screen is firmly in place. It manifests itself through a conversation taking place elsewhere in the restaurant. At a certain point in this scene, Common Sense, Social Question, and Exact Statistics enter, and order "Houndstooth" desserts. As they eat their sweets, they engage in a conversation about alcohol abuse. At the precise moment that Madame and Lutze are ejected from the coffee house, one of them provides a verbal gloss on the screen through which those figures have been "photographed": "Disgusting! Women getting drunk in public!"

This commentary serves an extremely important function. It suggests that the image of the fragmented body is no more "authentic" than those within which Madame more jubilantly apprehends herself. In other words, it disposes of any temptation on the part of the spectator to see the restaurant window as the mirror in which Madame discovers her "true" self. Like the spectacle of ideal femininity, that of corporeal disintegration is culturally produced, and projected onto certain bodies by the social gaze. Not surprisingly, then, when Madame apprehends the distance which separates her from that femininity, she visualizes herself in the guise of Lutze. As I stressed in Chapter 1, in our culture, homeless bodies signify the very unravelling of the bodily ego.

The next morning, an unseen hand pushes under Madame's hotel room door a copy of a newspaper with the headline "Wealthy Foreign Lady Raised the Roof at Coffee-House 'Mohring.'" When Madame picks up the paper, she discovers that it also features one of the unflattering pictures taken of her the day before. She carries the picture to the mirror, ostensibly to compare it with her reflected image. But the dissatisfied expression on her face shows that she is unable to separate the two representations. After several more unsuccessful attempts to isolate the mirror image from the newspaper photograph, she throws the contents of a glass of wine against her recalcitrant reflection, in a repetition of the previous day's action and looks at it once more [figure 14]. Again, *Bildnis* stresses that there can be no direct access to the "self," and that even the subject's relation to the literal mirror involves all kinds of cultural coercions.

figure 14

The film cuts immediately from this shot to a scene which, although clearly fantasmatic, is nevertheless curiously embedded in the larger narrative, and which again draws attention to the gaze. This scene begins with the oblique image of a sexually ambiguous figure whistling and gesturing, as if signalling the opening of a circus performance. This is followed by an overhead shot which shows a large auditorium, with a conspicuously empty orchestra space. Five women, all dressed in black, file ceremoniously down the aisle and sit in the front row. A second whistle is heard. Madame enters and is escorted to her seat by the androgynous figure. The camera cuts to a medium shot of the black-clothed women, who turn around *en masse* to stare at Madame [figure 15]. Their faces have been dramatically made up, as if for a dumb show. The character presiding over this strange "event," who can now be seen to be an elderly woman, brings Madame a glass and a bottle of champagne. Madame

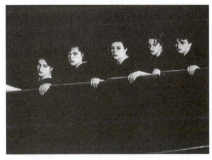

figure 15

takes a sip of the champagne, and gestures her enthusiasm to her server. Again, the camera cuts away to the five women in the front row, who continue to stare fixedly at the drinking woman. There is a final shot of Madame; she takes another sip from the glass, puts on her dark glasses, and adopts a theatrically spectatorial position [figure 16].

figure 16

figure 17

This scene, which might be said to make a spectacle out of spectatorship, demands to be read in relation to the one which follows it. This next scene begins with a close-up of the blue video monitor in Madame's room. It shows the dwarf carrying a large cooked turkey on a platter into the same room. He stands motionless for several moments, as if displaying the turkey, and then carries it over to the bedside table and bows. The camera then pans away from the monitor to the right, revealing the "actual" night table and turkey. Madame enters the frame, picks up the carving knife that accompanies the bird, and stabs with it violently around one of the two images of herself hanging on the wall [figure 17]. Again, that image is illuminated by a bracket of candle-shaped electric lights, as if it were a shrine. Madame is dressed in the same pink satin nightgown that she wears when tossing the wine against the mirror, suggesting that this scene is the continuation of that one.

Whereas in earlier scenes Madame lay with her back to the images on the wall, she is now manifestly a viewer of them. This unwanted exteriority pro-motes aggressivity; located at a stubborn distance from the figure standing in front of it, the idealizing representation becomes a threatening rival which must be destroyed. This scene thus dramatizes the "despair" side of what Mulvey characterizes as the "long love affair/despair between image and self-image"(18).

In the auditorium fantasy, the desire for the elimination of the hated rival finds dramatic fulfilment. Again, Madame is positioned as spectator rather than spectacle, but now the stage remains conspicuously empty. This void permits her once again to make a narcissistic claim on ideality, this time from the position of spectatorship. She attempts, in other words, to retreat from specularity to vision—to position herself as gaze, and thereby to achieve the narcissistic gratification which is denied her in her capacity as image. But this is an impossible aspiration. The subject always looks from a position within the field of vision. Even when adopting a spectatorial position, in other words, he or she is subordinate to the gaze, which remains outside. The impossibility of Madame's project is signified in this scene not only by the hyperbolic specularization of her look, but also by the fixed stare of the five black-clothed women.

I have interpreted the auditorium scene as though it followed the scene in Madame's room, but that is not the order decreed by *Bildnis*. When these two scenes are considered in their actual sequence, the second assumes the status of the spectacle which is called for by the first. The shot that begins with the video monitor and ends with Madame stabbing around her portrait comes as the "reverse" counterpart to the one of her sitting in the auditorium in an attitude of exaggerated scopic anticipation. In the transition from the one to the other, her look is even more emphatically disassociated from the gaze. She is transferred from the seemingly transcendental viewing position of a theater spectator to one in front of the ideal imago, a position manifestly defined by exclusion and insufficiency.

The Ideal-Ego and the Fantasy of the Body in Bits and Pieces: 3

Yet another fantasy sequence occurs immediately after Madame and Lutze visit the lesbian bar. In this sequence, Madame aspires to occupy not only the position of the gaze, but also that of the spectacle "photographed" by the gaze. This sequence is initiated by an extreme long shot of Madame sitting in a sky-blue dress on a decorative park bench, symmetrically positioned in front of a bridge over the Spree, and framed by trees. Again, the compositional impulse is classical. The dwarf enters from the left, places a picture of himself on the ground beside the bench, and exits to the left. A close-up of Madame's left eye follows, accompanied by the click of a camera [figure 18]. This image gives way to six more shots of her sitting in the same place. The camera moves progressively closer to its human subject [figure 19], cutting back between each shot to the close-up of her

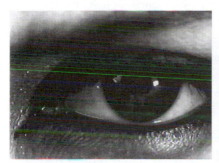

figure 18

figure 19

eye. The last of the eye images introduces a series of six "professional" fantasies. At the end of this series, the frame sequence is repeated in reverse, beginning with a close-up of Madame's eye, and concluding with an extreme long shot of her sitting on the park bench while the dwarf removes his photograph. In the latter, the dwarf enters from the left, and carries away his portrait.

The close-ups of Madame's eye that are interspersed between the images of her on the park bench are extremely brief, more like "flashes" than composed images. Like the sound which accompanies them, they suggest the opening and closing of a still camera shutter. Because of the metaphoric value afforded the camera in the restaurant scene, these shots make very evident Madame's renewed aspiration to occupy the position of the gaze. However, whereas the auditorium scene dramatizes her attempt to abolish the spectacle she cannot inhabit, the situation here is more complicated. The eye/park bench series does not dramatize Madame's ambition to become a transcendental gaze, outside spectacle, but rather her attempt to occupy the point from which she is "photographed." She seeks to safeguard the ideality of herself as spectacle by functioning simultaneously as the gaze, thereby imposing a purely imaginary logic on the field of vision.

Once again, *Bildnis* attests in all kinds of ways not only to the alterity of the gaze, but also to the unavoidable imbrication of imaginary and symbolic. To begin with, in each of the professional fantasies, Madame "performs" not for herself, but for the houndstooth women, who, as I have already suggested, offer a parodic personification of the symbolic order. Moreover, although Madame never produces "embodied" speech in any of these fantasies, each depends in some central way upon a verbal text, whether it be the soliloquy from *Hamlet*, the outraged monologue a business owner directs toward his recalcitrant secretary, an advertising brochure for coffins, the words of a popular song, or the exclamations of onlookers during a tightrope performance. Sometimes these texts are spoken by a voice-over, and at other times they are spoken by a voice internal to the fiction, but we are never given images uninflected by language. The professional fantasies are also characterized by a certain degree of narrative elaboration, which, like the centrality of language and the spectatorial role played by the houndstooth ladies, testifies to the omnipresence of the symbolic.

The eye/bench sequence introduces yet another term that cannot be assimilated to a hermetic narcissism: the photograph which the dwarf places on the ground beside Madame. That photograph does not show the fantasizing subject, but an image seemingly extraneous to her specularization. Nevertheless, its introduction works somehow to precipitate the ensuing sounds and images, suggesting that for Madame—as for the subject described by Lacan—the self is an "other." The images that constitute the *moi* come from outside, and cannot be "owned."

The figure of the dwarf is an element in excess both of a hermetic narcissism, and a claustral imaginary. Miriam Hansen characterizes that figure as the representative of Madame's "death wish," and the "master of ceremonies" within the domain of her fantasies.[23] He performs some version of each of these functions in the eye/bench sequence. His appearance in the park both opens and closes that sequence, and the first fantasy begins when he pulls back the curtain from the stage on which Madame will subsequently "deliver" Hamlet's most famous soliloquy. That gesture suggests that the scenes that follow are being ordered or "managed" from another "scene," and that Madame's desires are the desires of the Other. The soliloquy from *Hamlet*, moreover, immediately introduces a topic which will resurface repeatedly in the professional fantasies, only to be subordinated each time to a concern with "appearances." The first words Madame "speaks" after appearing on the stage are "To be or not to be—that is the question." The subsumption of death to a narcissistic problematic indicates perhaps more strikingly than anything else that the fantasy sequence represents an imaginary displacement of a symbolic problematic.

In his second seminar, Lacan remarks that the fully constituted subject is a dead subject, he or she "engage[s] in the register of life" only from a place "outside life" (90). The Rome discourse also attributes an annihilatory force to the symbolic order; the signifier murders what it designates.[24] And in *Seminar XI*, Lacan proposes that the subject accedes to language only at the cost of "being." He allegorizes the entry into the symbolic as an old-fashioned highway robbery, in which the alternatives are not money or life, but meaning or life. The subject, of course, always chooses meaning, and hence speaks from the domain of death.[25]

However, Lacan writes in the *Écrits* that "fear of death" is subordinate to "narcissistic fear of damage to one's own body" (28). He thereby underscores the reluctance of the subject to arrive at a conscious acceptance of his or her "being-for-death"—his or her unwillingness, that is, to confront the nothingness or *manque-à-être* out of which desire issues. The ego represents the primary vehicle of this denial, that through which the subject procures for him or herself an illusory plenitude.

As is so often the case within the psychic domain, we are not dealing here with a simple denial, but with a simultaneous avowal and disavowal. The only ego capable of filling the lack at the heart of subjectivity is the one which affords a "jubilant" self-recognition, and this exemplary unity—which always assumes in the first instance a corporeal form—is impossible to sustain. It inexorably gives way to its antithesis, corporeal decomposition. The body in bits and pieces might thus be said to provide the imaginary construct through which the subject indirectly apprehends both his or her distance from the mirror, and his or her *manque-à-être.*

The eye/bench fantasy sequence enacts precisely the displacement I have just described. The *Hamlet* soliloquy offers yet another version of the old-fashioned highway robbery, only here the options are more starkly stated; the alternatives are, quite simply, life and death. But even as this grim choice is articulated, it undergoes an imaginary transmogrification. While listening to the famous monologue, Social Question, Common Sense, and Exact Statistics comment not on the relative merits of the two possibilities it presents, but on Madame's unsuitability for the role she plays. "The lead is totally drunk!" one of them exclaims. Another complains that Hamlet is a "breeches" rather than a female part. Again, attention is deflected away from death to the specular domain, or, to state the case slightly differently, from *manque-à-être* to the *moi.*

The subsequent fantasies subordinate death even more fully to a "fear of narcissistic damage to the body." Madame literally falls out of her assigned role in two of these fantasies, dramatically opening up that gap between the subject and its ideal imago which Lacan associates with the fantasy of the fragmented body. In one scene, she loses her balance while attempting to walk a tightrope and plummets to the ground; in another, she rolls unconscious off the hood of a stunt car after it drives through a wall of flames. *Bildnis* shows this last fall three times, with virtually identical shots, as if to emphasize the loss of corporeal control. In the remaining fantasies, Madame's fall out of the idealizing frame is more metaphorically rendered. In the scenes in which she represents an advertising consultant, a secretary, a singer, and a coffin salesman, she remains manifestly exterior to the roles she plays. This exteriority is perhaps most strikingly communicated through the sound track; the voices which speak "for" Madam are not synchronized or "married" to her body, but manifestly derive from elsewhere.[26]

Parts of the fantasy sequence might seem to provide precisely that masquerade which Doane presents as an alternative to classic femininity. However, Madame's dislocation from the parts she plays in that sequence is only obscurely and intermittently parodic. For the most part, it does not represent an ironic deformation of the social *vraisemblance,* or the production of a psychically and politically enabling distance from the images which would otherwise engulf her, but a manifestation of the abyss separating the female subject from an exemplary specularity. In other words, it is a signifier of the impasse at the heart of traditional femininity: the impossibility of approximating the images in relation to which one is constantly and inflexibly judged. In this fantasy sequence, as in those which precede it, *Bildnis* suggests that if the specular domain figures more centrally in conventional female subjectivity than it does in its masculine counterpart, that is not because woman *is* the image, but because—more than man—she is *supposed* to be.

The scene which follows immediately after the eye/bench fantasy sequence provides a further caution against a too easy assimilation of that sequence to a masquerade paradigm. In it, an already drunk and slightly dishevelled Madame boards a fish-shaped boat, orders a bottle of wine, and initiates a glass-breaking competition with a group of other passengers. She is abruptly ejected from the boat, and stumbles with her wine bottle along the edge of the Spree to a cheap café, where she finds Lutze and her cart. The two women then wander from bar to bar in an alcoholic haze, a spectacle which constitutes the very opposite of mastery.

The Ideal-Ego and the Fantasy of the Body in Pieces: 4

The next two shot sequences, which represent the events of a single day, but which do not cohere "scenically," offer several more images of an idealized femininity. Significantly, however, *Bildnis* does not provide the female spectator with easy identificatory access to these images. The first sequence positions Madame in the same frame as Lutze, stressing once again the intimate relation between the ideal imago and the fragmented body. Those two figures walk away from the camera, which occupies a fixed, low-angle position, toward the Column of Victory. At a certain moment, they simultaneously—and seemingly involuntarily—drop their purses. In keeping with the metaphoric value consistently attributed to its owner, Lutze's bag spills its contents on the ground. Madame's, on the other hand, remains closed, an apparently sealed unity. Lutze returns for her possessions, but Madame continues walking after dropping hers [figure 20].

A photographer picks up the abandoned purse and follows Madame for a time, as if to return it to her. Eventually, he abandons his pursuit, empties the contents of the bag on the curb, and photographs them one after another. These photographs, which are presented as six brief close-ups, reveal in succession a bottle of medicine, a tube of lipstick, a small pink heart, an address book, a watch, and a pocket knife. As the inclusion of the heart would suggest, these objects represent less another inscription of the fragmented body than a half-humorous catalogue of the elements of Madame's "interiority." If the contents of her psyche can be so easily exteriorized, it is clearly because they derive in the first instance from outside. Once again, then, *Bildnis* works to deconstruct the notion of the "self."

figure 20

The six objects found in Madame's handbag testify as much to her symbolic structuration as they do to her imaginary captation. The address book connects her not only to the order of language, but to that of the name and—by implication—kinship. The watch signifies the social and economic regulation of time, and belies any easy relegation of Madame to a presymbolic space. The tube of lipstick offers an obvious synechdoche for woman-as-spectacle or, to be more precise, for all of the feminine props and appurtenances through which the female subject attempts to approximate the ideal image. The pocket knife surfaces again in a closely adjacent scene, where it evokes the aggressivity implicit within the subject's relation to that image. Together with the medicine bottle, the knife represents the culturally induced "malady" at the heart of classic femininity.

In this series of shots, as in the restaurant scene and the final fantasy sequence, the camera clearly represents the gaze. Significantly, it is once again situated at an emphatic remove from Madame's look; it "takes" her from behind, from a position which is inaccessible to her vision. However, although the gaze constitutes both a literal and a metaphoric third term in relation to Madame and Lutze, and so stands outside the insistently dyadic logic through which the imaginary articulates the interactions of self and other, ego and reflection, it is once again shown to play a determinative "backstage" role. And as in the coffee shop scene, it does not "photograph" its object directly, but through a series of intervening images.

Madame makes one final attempt to embody the image of her desire later in the same day. She leaves the bar where she has been drinking with Lutze and walks out into the dark, past a series of shop windows, and down to the pavement below. A spotlight illuminates her as she progresses, and her high heels produce the by-now familiar sound of ice against glass. At the end of this shot, Madame lifts her arms dramatically toward the sky. For a brief moment, she lays claim not only to a generalized ideality, but also to a very specific image from the history of Western representation—the image of Rita Hayworth in a black sheath dress and gloves, singing "Put the blame on Mame."

This citation from Charles Vidor's *Gilda* (1946) serves a complex function. Although the scene in question inscribes such an idealized feminine eroticism that Hayworth was to feel inadequate to the task of representing it in day-to-day life for ever after, it is constantly on the verge of giving way to the body in bits and pieces. Disintegration haunts Gilda's performance from the very beginning of this scene, and ultimately it triumphs as she begins removing her clothing, and is dragged from the dance floor in a state of masochistic intoxication. The spotlit image of Madame raising her arms to the darkened sky is also placed in the closest possible intimacy with the fragmented body, although here that relation is conveyed formally rather than narratively. This shot is cross-cut with the scene in which Willi and Lutze stagger drunkenly amid the debris surrounding the railroad tracks, and finally embrace incoherently in a ruined glass railway station.

Lest the spectator fail to note the significance of this montage, *Bildnis* cuts from the final shot of Willi and Lutze in the railway station to a medium close-up of Madame's hand reaching into the left of the frame with a knife [figure 21]. The knife casts a theatrical shadow against the wall. Almost immediately, this shot yields to a series of rapid-fire images. First, a shadow of the hand and knife appears against the wall from the left frame, followed by a smaller version of this shadow in the lower right frame. Then, in a jump cut, Madame walks into the frame from the right, her outstretched hand still holding the knife, and crosses over to the corner of the room. She stabs the wall around the edges of her shadow with the weapon. This shot gives way first to the shadow image of a hand-held knife striking the wall from the left frame, and then to one of an ambiguous body shadow.

figure 21

In shot seven of this sequence, the shadow of a second person appears on the left, also with knife in hand. Shot eight reveals the person to be Lutze. Her right arm, which holds the sharpened implement, is dramatically extended, and she is framed by a large shadow. Madame stands next to her, facing away from the camera, one arm protectively lifted. She struggles with Lutze, who says, "It's me, Madame! I'm your only friend, Madame! Stop that rubbish, Madame!" She "combs" her own hair and that of her friend with the knife. Madame faces Lutze acquiescently, and the two embrace.

In this shot sequence, as in that which follows, Madame wears a dress composed primarily of silver foil. She has attempted to close the gap between herself and her ideal imago by literally "putting on" the mirror. However, the dress does not entirely close in the back, and in the final moments of the film this gap will become more and more pronounced. The exaggerated shadows cast on the white wall throughout this sequence also render visible that dislocation of body and image which is for Lacan the very definition of corporeal fragmentation. As before, the exteriority of the idealizing representation provokes violence; in asserting its independence from the desiring subject, the beloved imago becomes a hated rival and must be destroyed. Significantly, the sound of the knife striking the wall is connected acoustically to all the many variations of the sound of ice cubes clinking in a glass; indeed, the ice cubes clinking can be heard in the knife stabs, and vice versa.

The final sequence of *Bildnis* is organized around a text by Peter Rosei. This text, titled "Drinkers," circulates among a series of narratively inconsequential characters, each of whom reads a passage aloud. Ottinger herself initiates this textual relay, in the guise of a derelict alcoholic. Sitting on a bench with a bottle of alcohol, she reads,

> "Wondrous plan: to heighten a pleasure so much that it torments one to death. Lately I talked it over with Lipsky. He meant: 'Our manias are nothing but Eryns in the theater of cruelty.' I said: 'So we hate ourselves.' 'Yes,' Lipsky said, 'It's not that bad.'"

This passage makes explicit the metaphoric connection between alcohol and narcissism. It also suggests once again that a libidinal economy organized entirely around the attempt to approximate an ideal imago could more justly be characterized as "self-hatred" than "self-love," since the demands it makes on the subject are impossible to sustain for more than a delusory moment. However, since the "intoxication" of that moment is so extreme that all other pleasures pale by comparison, there is nothing more addictive.

The final section read from the Rosei text also emphasizes the thrill that comes from being lifted even briefly into the rarefied atmosphere of ideality. It compares that experience to planetary travel; "drinkers are travellers," reads a businessman into whose open suitcase Madam has dropped the book, "they're...moved without moving. You pick them up, you give a lift. Can you see the galaxy?" The Rosei text stresses not just the pleasures, but also the life-threatening dangers of this sublation. To identify with ideality is to refuse lack, and with it desire; consequently, it is to turn away from life itself. For this reason, the Rosei passage concludes, "self-sufficiency could only be ruin[ous]."

The penultimate shot of *Bildnis* shows Madame lying unconscious on a flight of stairs leading to a train station. Lutze finds her there and attempts to lift her to a standing position. As she does so, a crowd of people rush down the stairs, obscuring the two women from our view. Lutze screams in terror, indicating that Madame has been trampled to death by the crowd. This shot must be read in relation to the one with which the film concludes. In it, Madame walks down a hallway constructed entirely of mirrors in her silver-foil dress [figure 22]. As she proceeds, she crushes her own reflection underfoot. This shot, which has no narrative locus, repeats the one which precedes it at a metacritical level. It thus makes clear that Madame's death is less literal than symbolic—the event outside the train station is to be understood not as her physical demise, but as a signifier for her full and final surrender to the morbidity of that psychic trajectory which leads from self-idealization to self-disgust. Madame's destruction of the many mirrors which reflect her image back to her in the final shot of the film is only the most dramatic instance of that aggressivity toward the ideal image which follows inexorably from the aspiration to ideality, here brilliantly indexed through the silver-foil dress.

figure 22

Bildnis einer Trinkerin dramatizes vividly the closed logic of the psychic loop which leads from the aspiration to ideality to the fantasy of the body in pieces, and back again. However, it has nothing to say about how we might break out of this closed logic, and into a relational field which includes the other. It also affords us no alternative model for conceptualizing how idealization might work. We are left with the sense that its operations always annihilate the other and the self alternately, that having once exalted an object, the subject will first attempt to murder it so as to take its place, and then fall in turn into radical self-disarray.

The Ego-ideal

It would be a grave mistake to assume that the psychic condition dramatized by *Bildnis* represents an isolated malady, or even one specific to femininity. The imaginary register is as central to human subjectivity as is language. Lacan maintains that the world can be seen only on the other side of the mirror stage, and that long after that "event" the bodily ego continues to provide each of us with "the very framework of [our] categories, of [our] apprehension of the world" (I, 282).

I indicated earlier in this chapter that for Lacan love always necessitates an imaginary facilitation (I, 122), but it is now necessary to make an even more global claim on his behalf: there can be no relation to the other except through the frame of the ego. As Lacan remarks in *Seminar I,* "the object relation must always submit to the narcissistic framework and be inscribed in it" (174).[27] Finally, the relation between the subject and language—the relation, that is, through which lack is installed—will always "pass via the intermediary of these imaginary substrates, the ego and the other, which constitute the imaginary foundation of the object" (II, 323).

As we have seen, this means that the subject often attempts to avoid confronting his or her *manque-à-être* by attempting to diminish the distance between the sensational body and ideal images. However, it also implies that even for the subject who knows him or herself to be both "nothing" and "nowhere," there can be no sustainable existence without those idealizing (and hence narcissistically inflected) representations through which we attempt to give feature and substance to our ultimately unspecifiable desire. This is so not only because life would be barren and the relational inconceivable without ideality, but because—as I will explain later in this chapter—the articulation of desire is precisely what maintains the subject at a distance from *das Ding,* and inscribes him or her as lacking.

But although Lacan suggests that without such representations the subject would not be a "man" but a "moon," he characterizes as a "madman" someone "who adheres to the imaginary, purely and simply" (II, 243). For such a person, the other has only a fleeting existence, since it is no sooner apprehended than it is either repudiated or assimilated as "self." The world of objects, in other words, has no temporal consistency, hence no real existence (II, 169). For Lacan, the subject gains access to objects which persist over time only through the mediation of the ego-ideal.

At times, Lacan associates the ego-ideal almost exclusively with language. In *Seminar I,* he defines it as both the "legal exchange which can only be embodied in the verbal exchange between human beings" (141), and as "the other as speaking, the other in so far as he has a symbolic relation to me" (142). He associates it, that is, both with that linguistic signifier which creates the "time" or temporal stability of the object, and with the recognition of the other as a subject. Although "recognition" here resonates in all kinds of ways with Kojève's reading of Hegel,[28] it ostensibly represents a step beyond that imaginary impasse which Lacan associates with the master/slave dialectic: it supposedly implies the mutual affirmation of the other as an other on the part of two subjects—their joint acknowledgment of their equality before the Law (177).

However, Lacan also suggests in *Seminar I* that the ego-ideal needs to be conceptualized in relation to the ideal-ego, which it in certain respects resembles, and from which it in other respects differs (142). He goes on immediately in the same passage to talk about the domain of visual representation as that within which both this difference and this similarity are registered. The passage in question serves as a useful reminder that, like the ideal-ego, the ego-ideal is in the first instance an *idealized image of the body.* It consists among other things of a corporeal representation or set of representations constituting at the very least a subcultural, and more often a broadly cultural, standard.

Finally, Lacan maintains that the ego-ideal is a "guide" to an ethical relation to the other. This claim is not so easy to reconcile with the notion of the ego-ideal as an idealized image of the body, but obviously warrants the closest possible attention in the present discussion. In order to arrive at a clearer sense as to how the ego-ideal can for Lacan be simultaneously an idealized image of the body and an ethical guide to the other, we need a more precise definition of the connection between idealization and identification. We also need to ascertain in precisely what sense the subject identifies with the ideal image which constitutes the ego-ideal.

Identification can clearly occur without idealization. The first of those psychic operations often assumes not only imaginary, but also symbolic or structural forms; the subject can identify not only with an image, but also with a position or "place." In addition, identification can come powerfully into play—as Chapter 6 will suggest—precisely around the distance separating two subjects from ideality. However, idealization cannot be thought apart from identification. Indeed, drawing upon Freud's "On Narcissism" and *Group Psychology and the Analysis of the Ego,* I would like to suggest that they are two sides of the same operation. We cannot idealize an object without at the same time identifying with it.

Identification always follows close on the heels of idealization because idealization refers back to the subject's bodily ego. As I suggested earlier in this chapter, all ideal images are linked to the first and most important of those images, the specular imago. Through idealization, the subject also posits an object as capable of filling the void at the heart of his or her psyche, which puts him or her in a definitionally identificatory relation to it. Freud makes the same point in slightly different terms. In "On Narcissism," he writes, "What man projects before him as his ideal is the substitute for the lost narcissism of his childhood" (94). And in *Group Psychology and the Analysis of the Ego,* he maintains that when we idealize an image or an object, "a considerable amount of narcissistic libido overflows on to [it].... We love it on account of the perfections which we have striven to reach for our own ego, and which we should now like to procure in this roundabout way as a means of satisfying our narcissism" (112–13).

But identification can take two forms in relation to the idealized object: it can acknowledge that object's separateness, or it can seek to abolish it. As we have seen, during the rare moments that it can be sustained, the second of these forms of identification results in jubilation. The subject establishes such an intimate imaginary relation with the ideal image or other as to believe him- or herself to be ideal. The first of these forms of identification is specific to the condition of love, in the most profound and generous sense of that word. It implies forming an imaginary alignment with bodily coordinates which cannot be assimilated to one's own.

Freud also makes clear in *Group Psychology* that whereas the aspiration to become the ideal is idiopathic or incorporative in nature, love—which for him entails the externalization of the ego-ideal—is fundamentally heteropathic or excorporative.[29] He describes the successful alignment of the subject's sensational ego with an idealized image or object as involving an "introjection," and as leading to a state of enrichment (113). In love, on the other hand, the subject "surrender[s] itself to the object," resulting in the "impoverish[ment]" of the ego.[30]

I would like to suggest that the diminution of the ego, which for Freud is coincident with love, should not be understood as referring in the first instance to the subordination of the lover to the beloved. When read through Lacan, this passage can be seen to designate in some more fundamental sense the productive dissipation of the "mirage" concealing lack which the love relation facilitates. In other words, the "shrinking" of the ego can be grasped less as a necessary "surrender to the object" than as the clearing of the narcissistic mist which generally prevents the subject from accepting that he or she desires out of an irreducible void. The apprehension of this enabling void as an inadequacy vis-à-vis the other results only when the latter is conversely exalted as substantially ideal, when he or she is assumed to possess the wholeness and unity of which the subject is deprived. The "impoverishment of the ego" assumes a negative value, in other words, when the object is *passively* idealized. I will suggest later that the object can instead be actively idealized.

The subject's relation to the ego-ideal also turns upon an excorporative identification. Like the love object, the ego-ideal represents an unassimilable ideal. Indeed, the ego-ideal implies—and is even created through—the idealization of a bodily image which is to varying degrees different from what the subject sees when he or she looks in the mirror. At the same time, it is the mirror within which he or she would like to see him or herself. It might thus be said to provide identity-at-a-distance, much like the exteroceptive *moi* in the Wallonian mirror stage. It is for this reason, I would argue, that Lacan privileges the ego-ideal. In Lacan's account, the ego-ideal provides an ethical guide to the other because it shows that that relation depends on the location of ideality outside the confines of the self.

The fact that I have spent so much time clarifying the argument through which Lacan represents the ego-ideal as an ethical guide to the other should not be taken as implying that I agree with it. Crucial as the category of the ego-ideal is to the theorization of an excorporative or heteropathic identification, it fails in other respects to model the terms of an exemplary relation to the other.

First of all, that psychic entity does not always work to promote the absolute disjunction of sensational body and visual imago for which I argued in Chapter 1. Although the establishment of the ego-ideal opens up a psychically salutary gap between the subject and the image, it does not necessarily imply either an acceptance of corporeal heterogeneity, or identification outside the narrow limits of what is culturally valorized. As Freud suggests in "On Narcissism," there is usually a close convergence between the ego-ideal and the values of the larger culture within which it is formed (101). Certain corporeal indices are consequently likely to be privileged at the level of the psyche, regardless of a given subject's gender, race, and class. It may consequently result in certain cases (such as that of a white man, whose ego-ideal is likely to be both white and masculine) in the idealization of corporeal parameters which are only slightly divergent from those of the bodily ego. In others (such as that of the black male subject described by Fanon, whose ego-ideal is white and masculine), it may lead to the idealization of corporeal parameters which, although sharply divergent from those of the bodily ego, are in keeping with normative representation.

The ego-ideal also represents a problematical model through which to conceptualize identity-at-a-distance because the subject's relationship to it represents only an inverted version of that affective tie which Lacan calls "imaginary love." Within the latter, as I have already indicated, the subject seeks to captate the other, to be to him or her the image to which he or she is in thrall. In the relation between the subject and the ego-ideal, this situation is reversed. The subject remains at a distance both from the ego-ideal and those others who at times actualize it for him or her not only because the latter are marked by alterity, but because the subject also feels him- or herself so enamored of—though so inadequate to—the norm they represent.

Lacan comments on this unfortunate power dynamic in *Seminar VII.* "The [ego-ideal] makes room for itself alone," he observes, "within the subject it gives form to something which is preferred and to which it will henceforth submit…[it] places the subject in a state of dependence relative to an idealized, forced image of itself" (98). He makes the same point about the love object in a passage from *Seminar I* in which he comments on the externalization of the ego-ideal in love. "The loved object, when invested in love, is, through its captative effect on the subject, strictly equivalent to the ego-ideal," he remarks. "It is for this reason that, in suggestion, in hypnosis, we encounter the state of dependency, such an important economic function, in which there is a genuine perversion of reality through the fascination with the loved object and its overestimation" (126).[31]

Lacan makes clear that the ideality which the subject confers upon the ego-ideal or its representative is not freely given—it is more the recognition which the slave accords the master than that through which one subject recognizes another as separate from him- or herself. Lacan also suggests that the subject imputes an absolute reality to that ideality, that he or she believes the construct in question to be *essentially* perfect. In both cases, then, the subject once again idealizes passively. Since what is thereby idealized is generally a normative set of bodily and other values, this naturalization is doubly problematic.

The Gift of Love

In *Seminar I*, Lacan alludes briefly to another model of heteropathic identification, one which lends itself much more fully to the ethical-political project of this book. In that text, he counterposes to imaginary love a very different relation to the other, which he designates "the active gift of love." In the passage in question, Lacan maintains that such a love is always directed "towards the being of the loved subject, towards his particularity" (276). He thereby suggests that it is predicated on the perception of the other as a subject, rather than an object, and as separate from, rather than an extension of, the self. But Lacan does not indicate what precisely the loving subject might be said to "give" to this other. He also neglects to clarify the role played within this libidinal economy by the image.

The active gift of love is never adequately theorized by Lacan. However, some of his later *Seminars* specify at least some of the parameters within which such a theorization should take place. I therefore propose to begin my elaboration of that affective relation by looking at the relevant passages from *Seminar VII* and *Seminar XI*. Later, I will indicate the points at which my own notion of the active gift of love altogether exceeds the Lacanian paradigm.

Although *Seminar VII* does not mention the *active* gift of love, it does refer to the gift of love (150). Significantly, it links the gift of love not only to idealization, but to sublimation as well. Indeed, Lacan suggests that where there is sublimation there is also idealization. He illustrates what he means by the gift of love with an extended discussion of courtly love (139–54); in that discussion, he associates courtly love with an "idealizing exaltation" (151). A page earlier, he also suggests that courtly love—and, by implication, the active gift of love—is an instance of sublimation (150).

Before engaging with *Seminar VII* in a more detailed way, it is crucial that we understand that Lacan presents sublimation there in very different terms from those made familiar by Freud. In his essay on narcissism, Freud argues that idealization needs to be differentiated from sublimation, with which it is often confused. Idealization is something that happens to the *object* of a drive; sublimation is something that happens to the *aim* of a drive (94). Idealization, that is, involves the exaltation of an object, while sublimation involves the deflection of the drive away from a sexual to a more culturally esteemed aim.

However, whereas Freud rigorously distinguishes sublimation from idealization, Lacan suggests that sublimation produces one form of idealization. Indeed, he goes so far as to suggest that to sublimate is to confer ideality upon an object, in contradistinction to the self—or, to state the case more precisely, in contradistinction to that image or object which one attempts to assimilate to the self. Sublimation in Lacan also has nothing to do with desexualization; it can coexist with absolute carnality (161).[32]

In *Seminar VII,* Lacan suggests that sublimation inheres in the displacement away from *das Ding* to *die Sache* (112), in the shift away from the impossible nonobject of desire which is produced with the entry into language and the "fading" of the real to a nameable and specifiable object. Otherwise stated, he proposes that it involves the elevation of a thing to the status of the Thing. He thus equates it with that process whereby something is posited as the object capable of making good the subject's lack, with the activity whereby the desire for something which has neither face nor name is given imaginary lineaments. When one treats an object in this way, one of course idealizes it. To sublimate is thus to confer ideality on that someone or something through which the subject articulates his or her ineffable desire.

It is vital to my own theorization of the active gift of love that sublimation be understood not only as the conferral of ideality upon an object, but also as idealization, and so identification, *at a distance from the self.* When the subject sublimates, he or she agrees to posit the other rather than the self as the cause of desire—to see perfection in the features of another. A number of passages from *Seminar VII* and *Seminar XI* suggest as much, albeit indirectly.

In the passage in which Lacan encourages us to equate the gift of love with sublimation, he once again indicates that the former, like the latter, is somehow bound up with that "primary symbolization" through which the subject names his or her fundamentally unnameable desire (150), and thereby confers ideality upon it. However, this time he goes further. By putting an object in the place of *das Ding,* sublimation or the gift of love consolidates that operation which Lacan elsewhere characterizes as primal repression or the entry into language. Crucially, what is at issue here is more than the plugging of the hole through which the real might otherwise flood back into the psyche with representations of what has been lost through primal repression. Sublimation or the gift of love also delegates that representative function to signifiers capable of directing the subject away from his or her "self" to the other. It transfers ideality from the first to the second of those terms, a displacement which is crucial to the assumption of lack, and—by implication—of desire.

Seminar VII twice stresses that sublimation is an operation turning upon the object rather than the ego. At one point, Lacan quotes Freud approvingly as saying that sublimation concerns *object* rather than *ego* libido (95). Since, as even the casual reader of Freud knows, libido is neither inherently narcissistic nor altruistic, but capable of being invested either in the object or the ego, what this really means is that sublimation works to the "credit" or enrichment of the object rather than the ego. A few pages later, Lacan suggests that sublimation is also somehow a way out of the no-exit logic so richly dramatized by *Bildnis einer Trinkerin* (98). It is a mechanism for getting beyond what he calls the "mirage relation" to the object, in which the latter "introduces itself only insofar as it is perpetually interchangeable with the love that the subject has for its own image" (98), and into a more productive interaction with that object.

In the "Drives and Lures" section of *Seminar VII,* Lacan indicates again that to elevate an object to the status of the Thing is to constitute it as an *objet a* (99). In the same passage, he proposes that the psychic operation whereby the subject installs *die Sache* in the place of *das Ding* can be designated through the algorithm for fantasy, $\$ \lozenge a$, an algorithm which he elsewhere decodes as the desire of the lacking subject ($\$$) of or for ($\lozenge$) the object which stands in for *das Ding* or "being" (a).[33]

Although *Seminar XI* is not concerned with sublimation per se, it addresses at great length the relation of the subject to the *objet a* in the transaction implied by $\$ \lozenge a$, and the terms in which it does so are absolutely crucial to an understanding of the gift of love. In that text, Lacan proposes a slightly different schematization for what *Seminar VII* calls "sublimation," one better calculated to show that the sublimating subject never really takes possession of the *objet a,* but respects its separateness. The schematization, which designates the itinerary of the drive, is a loop. Inside that loop is situated the *objet a:*

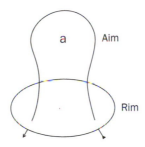

This diagram shows the progression of the drive from its source in the rimlike opening of an erotogenic zone toward and around the *objet a,* and back once again to that opening. It consists of an outward and a backward movement, designated in the $\$\Diamond$ a algorithm by $\langle$ and $\rangle$, respectively (209). Although it might seem that the drive here traces a hermetic trajectory, returning punctually to the point from which it begins, the subject attains through that trajectory what Lacan calls "heterogeneity" or the "dimension of the capital Other" (194). Through the loop diagrammed above, the subject travels away from him- or herself toward what resides outside.

It is also important to understand that the subject returns from this journey with "empty hands." His or her hands are empty not only because the return journey is made without the *objet a,* but because the outward journey is synonymous with a certain bequest, which has been made at the expense of the self, with the conferral of ideality on the *objet a.* And since that object by definition represents what the subject lacks, the return journey might also be said to inscribe the subject as "barred" ($\$$) or insufficient unto him- or herself. As Lacan puts it at one point, "the subject sees himself caused as a lack by *a*" (270), or, several pages earlier, "Through the function of the *objet a,* the subject separates himself off, ceases to be linked to the vacillation of being" (258).[34]

At this point, it would seem crucial to reiterate once again that although sublimation or the gift of love concerns the object rather than the ego, it does not involve merely the substitution of love for identification. The gift of love is loving in the most profound sense of the word, not because it abolishes identification, but because it involves idealization, and hence identification, at a distance from the self—because it strives to keep the cherished "image" outside.

Lacan associates the gift of love with heteropathic identification in *Seminar VII.* In a key passage from that text, he acknowledges that courtly love—his primary example of the gift of love—is "fundamentally narcissistic in character" (151). He thereby indicates that, due to the attractions which have been conferred upon the object, even here, the subject cannot help but place him- or herself in an identificatory relation to it. However, he maintains that this "mirror function" is anamorphic or off-center—it does not work according to the usual incorporative logic. Two paragraphs later, he goes on to clarify why: courtly love defined the lady as *unapproachable;* it radically isolated the idealizing lover from the object of his idealization.[35]

Even more explicitly and axiomatically, *Four Fundamental Concepts of Psycho-Analysis* associates the loop around the *objet a* with an identification "of a strangely different kind" from that which obtains within the conventional narcissistic relation (257). At one point in that text, Lacan specifies this identification in terms which contrast strikingly with those conventionally deployed not only in the essay on the mirror stage, but in Freud's *Totem and Taboo.* Whereas identification normally operates cannibalistically to annihilate the otherness of the other, sublimation or the active gift of love works to inhibit any such incorporation by maintaining the object at an uncrossable distance. The *objet a* is "presented precisely, in the field of the mirage of the narcissistic function of desire, as the object that cannot be swallowed, as it were" (270). The only possible identificatory relation is excorporative.

Making the Gift of Love Active

Now that we have established that the gift of love involves idealization and, therefore, identification at a distance from the self, let us attempt to determine precisely what it might mean for the latter to be "active." I suggested above that passive idealization involves misrecognizing the ideality which one has conferred upon the other as the other's essence. The gift of love must consequently be "active" in the first sense of that word when it somehow inhibits this substantialization, when it prevents the congealing of ideality into an intrinsic quality of the beloved. This gloss on "active" is also available in Lacan.

Seminar VII proposes that sublimation is in its most exemplary forms not only part of that process through which "emptiness" is produced in the subject, but is itself an organization which *implies* emptiness:

> In every form of sublimation, emptiness is determinative.... All art is characterized by a certain mode of organization around this emptiness.... Religion in all its forms consists of avoiding this emptiness.... Yet although the whole ceremonial phase of the body of religious practices...enters into this framework...the emptiness remains in the center, and that is precisely why sublimation is involved.

In an extremely unfortunate recourse to anatomy, Lacan proposes that in the case of courtly love the inscription of emptiness might be said to have resided at the site of the female genitals (168–69). However, elsewhere in *Seminar VII,* he suggests a much more interesting account of how a particular act of sublimation might work not only to produce, but also to point to emptiness. In that passage, Lacan maintains that the object which is elevated to the status of the Thing should both stand in for the Thing and indicate its own purely substitutive character—it should render the Thing "both present and *absent* [my emphasis]" (141). He thereby encourages us to think of the luster which the subject confers upon an other through the active gift of love as something which does not seamlessly adhere to the other, but—unlike that which illuminates the ideal-ego or the ego-ideal—retains a borrowed and provisional quality.

Lacan dramatizes the gap between the loved other and the ideality which the subject imparts to him or her through his primary example of sublimation, courtly love. He indicates first of all that the cult of courtly love installed the lady in a position which was startlingly divergent from that to which she was socially confined. He thereby inadvertently gestures toward the possibility of idealizing outside the normative parameters of the screen, a point to which I will return. Lacan also suggests that although it transformed relations between the sexes, courtly love made no attempt to effect a close match between the images through which it exalted the lady and the physical attributes of the real women who benefited from this exaltation:

> [the lady] is presented with depersonalized characteristics. As a result, writers have noted that all the poets seem to be addressing the same person.
> The fact that on occasion her body is described as *g'ra delgat e gen*—that means that plumpness was part of the sex appeal of the period, *e gen* signifying graceful—should not deceive you, since she is always described in that way. (149)

Once again, the ideality conferred upon the other through this most exemplary of all sublimations is described as fitting the other more like a draped toga than a luminous skin.[36]

Thus, whereas the subject classically prostrates him- or herself before the ego-ideal or its human substitute, and responds to the latter as something intrinsically exalted, to give someone the active gift of love implies assuming a *productive* relation to him or her. It means not only to "crystallize" the other, as Stendhal would say[37]—to encrust that other with the diamonds of ideality— but to do so knowingly, and without forgetting for a moment that he or she is also a subject marked by lack. The active gift of love consequently implies both idealizing beyond the parameters of the "self," and doing so with a full understanding of one's own creative participation with respect to the end result. It means to *confer* ideality, not to *find* it. Lacan further stresses that such a relationship involves generosity, but not subordination, when he remarks in *Seminar I* that although the actively loving subject can "accept to such a great extent" the "weaknesses," "detours," and "errors" of the other, "there is a point at which [his or her generosity] comes to a halt, a point which is only located in relation to being—when the loved being goes too far in his betrayal of himself and persists in self-deception, love can no longer follow" (276).

The adjectives "active" and "passive" can be construed in a completely other sense as well, one more germane to the field of vision elaborated in Chapter 1 than to Lacan's dispersed remarks upon the gift of love. The loving subject can subordinate him- or herself not only to that other to whom he or she gives the gift of love, but to the restrictive mandates of the cultural screen. This second dependency is perhaps even more problematic than the first. "Active," on the other hand, might be said to qualify most profoundly that process of idealization which, rather than blindly and involuntarily conforming to what the cultural screen mandates as "ideal," lights up with a glittering radiance bodies long accustomed to a forced alignment with debased images. This active process of idealization conjures into existence something genuinely "new," as did the courtly lover when he idealized his lady.

I want to pause here briefly to indicate that it is very difficult for the gift of love to be given actively in the first of the ways I have just specified when it is not also given actively in the second. Every culture attempts to map out in advance which objects can be raised to the status of the Thing, to "colonize the field of *das Ding* with imaginary schemes," as Lacan puts it in *Seminar VII*. It is consequently in "forms that are historically and socially specific" that the *objet a* usually presents itself to the subject (99). However, an ideal remains lifeless until it has also been libidinally validated. The libidinal process through which such a validation occurs is of course idealization.

It is because the psychic operation is necessary to ratify the cultural one that there can be such energetic contestation around the values at the heart of a given society. This is what permits those values to be questioned, even derealized, and others affirmed in their place. However, when an object is validated at the level of the psyche as well as the screen, it exercises an almost irresistible reality-effect; all too easily, it assumes the status of something intrinsically or essentially ideal, before which the idealizing subject must subordinate him- or herself. The result is very different when we libidinally valorize an object which does not enjoy an equivalent cultural legitimation. Here, the resulting ideality is not prone to a similar naturalization, and is thus more easily sustained in the mode of a bequest.

As should be clear by now, the active gift of love represents more than an alternative model of romantic passion to that described by Freud, in which the loved other comes to take the place of the ego-ideal. It is first and foremost an account of how identification, that psychic operation without which there would be no subject, no world, and no possible relation to the other, might work outside the libidinal economy which Lacan associates with the master/slave relationship. In other words, it is an account of how identification might function in a way that results in neither the triumph of self-sameness, nor craven submission to an exteriorized but essentialized ideal. As it has been elaborated here, the active gift of love also provides the basis for conceptualizing how we might idealize outside the narrow mandates of the screen; how we might put ourselves in a positive identificatory relation to bodies which we have been taught to abhor and repudiate.

But how, precisely, does one give the active gift of love? Here, Lacan is often less than helpful—in fact, I would go so far as to suggest that he can be positively misleading. At times, he speaks about that psychic transaction as though it could be voluntarily effected, as if idealization could be somehow consciously and volitionally "steered." At other times, he seems to propose that this particular variety of sublimation, which involves the foregrounding of the image as a signifier, could be effected entirely unconsciously. Both of these assumptions seem to me incorrect.

First of all, idealization is not something which any of us can simply decree. It is an activity which extends deep into the unconscious, and cannot be consciously mandated. Second, the gift of love cannot be actively given at the level of the unconscious, since no unconscious act of idealization is capable of inscribing itself in the guise of an investiture, or *Belehnung;* the unconscious always substantializes, treating representations as things, and appendages as essences. The "active" moment in the gift of love can only occur at a conscious level, because it implies epistemological access to what would otherwise remain occluded in the mists of the imaginary—the coming of the subject to the knowledge that if something dazzles him or her, that is because he or she has rendered it dazzling. And as Freud observes in *The Ego and the Id,* "All our knowledge is invariably bound up with consciousness."[38]

Within the domain of individual human subjectivity, the adjective "active" can consequently only be understood to qualify the gift of love according to the logic of a deferred action, or *Nachträglichkeit.* We cannot confer that gift actively, but we can come to be in an active relation to it after the fact; at a conscious level, in other words, we can affirm our productivity with respect to what we unconsciously idealize, and thereby desubstantialize the latter in our waking, if not in our sleeping life. This is a finite notion of agency, but one whose reverberations could be made to resound within the entire field of a given subject's interpersonal relations.

While I in no way want to understate the importance of this ethical project, it should be clear that it satisfies the meaning of "active" in only one of the senses enumerated above. How can the gift of love come to be active in the second, and ultimately more radical sense? How, that is, can we learn to idealize not only consciously but unconsciously outside the narrow confines of what is culturally decreed to be "ideal"? How can we be brought at the most profound level of our psyches to confer an imaginary luster on bodies that are culturally profoundly devalued?

I stress the normative nature of unconscious idealization because it is unfortunately the case that the subject more often than not libidinally affirms what is culturally valorized. As I emphasized earlier, the objects which are repeatedly represented by a particular society as "the ideal" can exercise an almost irresistible attraction. Thus, the project I am calling for necessarily exceeds the limits of the purely ethical; it necessitates a political intervention into the domain where our culture "colonizes" *das Ding.* But what is that field?

Lacan suggests that it is through textual production, specifically in its visual or "imaginary forms," that the subject is encouraged to idealize certain corporeal parameters over others. As he puts it in *Seminar VII,* it is through the fantasies produced by "artists, artisans, designers of dresses and hats, and the creators of imaginary forms in general" that certain bodies come to seem worthier of our libidinal affirmation than others (99). Although in 1995 we would be likelier to name cinema, television, and photography as the primary contributors to our cultural screen, most of us would not dispute the overarching logic of this formulation. The conclusion which we are encouraged to draw is stunning in its simplicity: if it is through textual production, especially in its visual or imaginary forms, that the subject is encouraged to idealize certain bodily parameters, it can only be through the creation and circulation of alternative images and words that he or she can be given access to new identificatory coordinates.

Consequently, I would like to suggest that the gift of love can only be active in all of the ways I have specified as a result of a ceaseless textual intervention. The textual intervention I have in mind is one which would "light up" dark corners of the cultural screen, and thereby make it possible for us to identify both consciously and unconsciously with bodies which we would otherwise reject with horror and contempt. It would also inhibit our attempt to assimilate those coordinates to our own in order to "become" the ideal image. Finally, it would bring us to a conscious knowledge of both the purely provisional nature of the illuminated image, and our own capacity to turn the light on or off.

3

Political Ecstasy

Brecht and Cinema

Although Anglo-American film theory has in recent years relaxed its vigilance against popular narrative cinema, since the 1970s there has been no systematic attempt to elaborate a model of political cinema. Consequently, the privileged paradigm for such a cinema continues to be one which derives from Brecht, and stands in opposition to Hollywood. Surprisingly, this model achieved preeminence in *Screen,* the journal that was also most vocal in articulating and promoting a psychoanalytic film theory. During the 1970s, *Screen* published such by-now classic texts of psychoanalytic film theory as Laura Mulvey's "Visual Pleasure and Narrative Cinema," Christian Metz's "The Imaginary Signifier," Jacqueline Rose's "Paranoia and the Film System," and Stephen Heath's "Anata Mo."[1] But at the same time, *Screen* published two issues devoted exclusively to Brecht.[2] And one of the most important essays in those two issues—Heath's "Lessons from Brecht"—elaborates the notion of "separation," or the fourth wall, through Freud's theory of fetishism.[3] So intimately did psychoanalysis cohabit with a Brechtian model of political cinema during the period of *Screen's* intellectual dominance that Sylvia Harvey later found film theory's recovery of Brecht to have been "effected from within the parameters of an interest in audience subjectivity largely specified in psychoanalytic terms."[4]

In characterizing this theoretical alignment as surprising, I do not mean to imply that we must choose between Brecht and psychoanalysis. Rather, I want to point to the fact that in his best-known theoretical writings, Brecht seeks to exorcise identification, precisely that relation which psychoanalysis posits as an irreducible condition of subjectivity, and which, consequently, has been one of the primary concerns of recent film theory. This Brecht dreams of a theater uncontaminated by the imaginary, a theater that would "appeal to the reason,"[5] and engage the spectator more at the level of the conscious than the unconscious.[6] To this end, he decrees the isolation not only of the actor from the role, each scene from every other (37), and the music from the spectacle,[7] but, above all, the spectator from the fictional character. "So long as the arts are supposed to be 'fused' together," Brecht writes,

> the various elements will all be equally degraded, and each will act as a mere "feed" to the rest. The process of fusion extends to the spectator, who gets thrown into the melting pot too and becomes a passive (suffering) part of the total work of art. Witchcraft of this sort must of course be fought against.[8]

Brecht proposes to combat this "process of fusion" with the knife—or, as he at one point puts it, the "scissors"[9]—of symbolic differentiation. The only variety of spectatorial identification that he is willing to tolerate is one with the actor as "observer" of the role he or she plays.

The theoretical texts which are most explicitly concerned with the articulation of a model of political cinema also militate against the notion of an easy character identification, although the authors of these texts do not all call for the complete suspension of that psychic operation. In a landmark essay from 1972, Peter Wollen maintains that the Brechtian counter-cinema illustrated by Godard's *Vent d'est* is exemplary not only for its anti-illusionism and refusal of closure, but also for its inhibition of identification.[10] Heath makes a similar argument on behalf of Oshima's *Death by Hanging* in *Questions of Cinema*. He critiques classic cinema primarily on the grounds that it converts screen "space" into a narrative "place," and in so doing encourages the intimate psychic alignment of spectator and character. *Death by Hanging*, on the other hand, provides an important model for an alternative film practice because it frustrates identification through its constant troubling of the categories of "identity" and "motive."[11] And in "Towards a Feminist Film Practice: Some Theses" Claire Johnston critiques Hollywood cinema for promoting an "imaginary sense of identity," and calls for a feminist cinema which would "achieve a different constitution of the subject in relation to ideology."[12]

Why this adversarial relation to identification, particularly in its "secondary" or diegetic forms? It follows, first of all, from the assumption that it is primarily through identification that the conventional narrative film simultaneously works on the spectator, and renders him or her oblivious to that work. Implicit in the call for an alternative cinema is the notion that the viewer could some-how be led out of the "cave" of the imaginary into the clear light of day—released from the captation to which he or she is unknowingly in thrall, and endowed with a politically enabling knowledge about cinema and its structuring effects. Such a cinema would itself be a model for this pellucid state of consciousness; uncompromised by the imaginary, it would at all times render its own activities legible.

It was also assumed during the seventies—and we are far from being liberated of this assumption today—that the pleasure of identifying with a fictional character always turns on the spectator's rediscovery of his or her preordained place within gender, class, and race. Secondary identification, in other words, is frequently equated with interpellation into the dominant fiction.[13] In *The Subject of Semiotics,* I helped to promote such an equation by theorizing cinematic identification so insistently in terms of the subject's insertion into a normative position.[14] Anne Friedberg offers a more extreme version of the same argument in a recent essay, in which she claims that

> identification can only be made through recognition, and all recognition is itself an implicit confirmation of the ideology of the *status quo.* The institutional sanction of stars as ego ideals establishes normative figures, authenticates gender norms.[15]

It logically follows from such a formulation that only a cinema which thwarts identification can be truly transformative.

In the previous chapter, I attempted to dispense in advance with the first of these assumptions by demonstrating both the centrality of the imaginary register to every aspect of human existence, and the impossibility of exiting from it into the rarefied atmosphere of pure rationality. In this chapter, I will consequently be less concerned to demonstrate the irreducibility of identification than to argue for its potential importance as an agency of psychic and social change. I will endeavor to show that we have been too hasty in assuming that operation to be inherently and automatically at the service of the dominant fiction, and, hence, antithetical to the operations of an exemplary political cinema. Indeed, I will be insisting that what has been frequently assumed to be one of film's primary limitations with respect to an oppositional project—its identificatory "lure"—may be, on the contrary, one of its greatest political assets, since it represents the potential vehicle for a spectatorial self-estrangement.

Implicit in what I have just said is my belief that the alienation of the viewer from the filmic screen cannot by itself constitute the primary goal of a political cinema. Equally important is the alienation of the spectator from his or her sensational ego, and that requires a reconsideration of the place within such a cinema of identification. The self is the site not of an emancipatory reason but of a murderous narcissism. That narcissism cannot be combated with a textual practice which attempts to abolish identification, since such a practice would fail to challenge the principle of corporeal sameness upon which the normative ego is predicated.

But the spectator can only come into a politically productive relation to bodily otherness when he or she is encouraged to identify according to an exteriorizing, rather than an interiorizing, logic—when the screen succeeds in soliciting the love he or she normally preserves for the ideal-ego, but no longer reflects back to him or her an image which can be assimilated to the self. Crucial to the encouragement and maintenance of a heteropathic identification is the designation of the scene of representation as radically discontinuous with the world of the spectator. The Brechtian model clearly accepts the close relationship between these two operations since it attempts to circumvent the first by avoiding the second.

Brecht objects to character identification because it carries the spectator away from him- or herself.[16] He thus conceptualizes that transaction according to an excorporative rather than an incorporative model. With epic theater, Brecht seeks to inhibit such a "carrying away." Brilliantly grasping that this imaginary transport somehow depends upon the presence of the fourth wall, he calls for its elimination.[17] Brecht seeks thereby to make it possible for the spectator to think critically, an activity which is for him antipathetic to identification. However, in so doing, he suspends, just when it is most needed, the principle that governs every other aspect of his aesthetic model—the *V-Effekt.*

Brecht's famous *Verfremdungsffekt* is conventionally translated in film theory as "distanciation" rather than "alienation-effect." This translation puts a spatial metaphor at the heart of the Brechtian textual model; it suggests that a quintessentially Brechtian theater or cinema would be one where the representational scene is in all respects more "removed" from the spectator than is customary. In fact, Brecht's aesthetic turns upon distance in many respects. It promotes in the spectator a critical detachment from or irony toward the spectacle and its ideological values. It also isolates textual elements from one another so that each can comment on the others, rather than seeming to be part of an ostensibly harmonious whole.

However, there is one crucial way in which Brecht's aesthetic might be said to bring the theatrical or cinematic event "closer": it seeks to place that event on a continuum with the auditorium. As Walter Benjamin observes in "What is Epic Theatre?" Brechtian theater—and, by extension, Brechtian cinema—is concerned above all else with "the filling-in of the orchestra pit," the equalization of spectator and spectacle. Hence,

the abyss which separates the actors from the audience like the dead from the living, the abyss whose silence heightens the sublime in drama, whose resonance heightens the intoxication of opera, this abyss which, of all the elements of the stage, most indelibly bears the traces of its sacral origins, has lost its function. The stage is still elevated, but it no longer rises from an immeasurable depth; it has become a public platform. Upon this platform the theatre now has to install itself.[18]

It might seem as though this paradoxical closeness at the heart of Brechtian distanciation is only the hallucinatory product of an infelicitous translation. At first glance, *Verfremdungseffekt* does not seem to imply a spatial metaphor. It literally means "to alienate," or more precisely, "to render the familiar strange."[19] However, the same paradox manifests itself with respect to this concept as with respect to "distanciation," since there is one theatrical element where the *Verfremdungseffekt* precisely does not come into play: the theatrical space. Brecht wanted the spectator of epic theater to be on such intimate terms with the stage that he or she would not hesitate to smoke a cigar during the performance, as if watching events unfolding in his or her own living room.[20]

This invitation to the spectator to make him or herself at home in the theater again foregrounds the paradoxical closeness at the heart of Brechtian distanciation. That closeness can, moveover, now be seen even more clearly to imply an action which is precisely the opposite of what *Verfremdungseffekt* is generally assumed to mean: rather than making the familiar strange, the Brechtian aesthetic involves making the strange familiar.

It would seem that there is something here which is spared the self-estrangement to which every other element of the theatrical event is subjected. It is, of course, the spectatorial ego. By making the stage continuous with the auditorium, Brecht safeguards that ego against alien images, and, so, leaves unchallenged the terms of its bodily parameters. He thereby installs the principle of the self-same body at the heart of epic theater.

Although, on occasion, theater has managed to make one continuous space of the stage and the auditorium, the gap separating those two domains is less easily bridged in the case of cinema. In fact, as I will argue in much greater detail later in this chapter, no film has ever managed to completely abolish the fourth wall. As is well known, Brecht's "fundamental reproach" against the cinematic text is that it is not possible for the spectator to intervene in that text during its screening in the same way that he or she could during the performance of a play.[21] This is in part because in cinema there is a "failure to meet of the voyeur and the exhibitionist," as Metz puts it in *The Imaginary Signifier;* the cinematic actor and spectator are never made physically present to each other.[22]

Though Brecht would argue that the irreducible distance dividing the auditorium from the screen severely limits cinema's political usefulness, I want to show that, in fact, the opposite is the case. I will attempt to demonstrate that implicit in the gap separating the spectator from the spectacle is the possibility of bringing about an even more radical distanciation than the one about which Brecht wrote—the possibility of alienating the spectator from his or her corporeal coordinates. Consequently, I will argue not only for the radical potential of cinematic identification, but also for the hyperbolization rather than the abolition of the fourth wall.

Cinematic Identification

Recent film theory has, for the most part, accounted for cinematic identification in terms of the dominant psychoanalytic paradigm. It consequently figures there primarily as the imaginary internalization of an external image. Ann Friedberg, for instance, maintains that film depends upon "introjective identification," while providing only "the illusion of projective identification."[23] Mary Ann Doane, another theorist who has written specifically about identification, does not even acknowledge any version of that psychic operation other than the incorporative variety. She accounts for secondary identification in "Misrecognition and Identity" according to the Freudian model,[24] and in *The Desire to Desire* she establishes an intimate connection between consumption and cinematic identification.[25] Although drawing more on Lacan than on Freud, Christian Metz's very influential discussion of identification in *The Imaginary Signifier* also conceptualizes cinematic spectatorship as an assimilation; when discussing secondary identification, he invokes the by-now standard account of the mirror stage, and when commenting on primary identification, he suggests that the viewer does not so much identify with the camera as with "himself as spectator," in a triumphant affirmation of self-sameness (42–57).

However, several early film theorists conceptualize the experience of going to the movies more as a transport or abduction of the spectator. Indeed, they find cinematic identification to be fundamentally excorporative or heteropathic, rather than incorporative or idiopathic. Since the texts in question offer crucial support for my own argument, I would like to comment on them briefly.

In *Theory of the Film*, Béla Balázs characterizes secondary identification as a process whereby the spectator is lifted out of his or her seat, and projected into the interior of the cinematic spectacle. He illustrates this psychic transport through an account of what it means to be a spectator watching a filmed adaptation of Shakespeare's *Romeo and Juliet*:

In the cinema the camera carries the spectator into the film picture itself.... Although we sit in our seats...we do not see Romeo and Juliet from there. We look up to Juliet's balcony with Romeo's eyes and look down on Romeo with Juliet's. Our eye and with it our consciousness is identified with the characters in the film, we look at the world out of their eyes and have no angle of vision of our own. We walk amid crowds, ride, fly or fall with the hero and if one character looks into the other's eyes, he looks into our eyes from the screen, for, our eyes are in the camera and become identical with the gaze of the characters. They see with our eyes.[26]

In the final sentence of this passage, Balázs invokes the conventional model of identification, one predicated on spectatorial incorporation. However, most of the passage is given over to the elaboration of a very different kind of identification—one which alters the terms of bodily reference. The spectator no longer looks with his or her own eyes, but with those of the other. This deliteralization of the spectator's body is rendered particularly striking by the fact that in this case identification occurs across gender lines; the viewer invoked by Balázs occupies, in rapid succession, both Romeo's body and Juliet's body. The subsequent conversion of this exteriorizing identification into an interiorizing one is signaled by the triumph of the spectator's "own" corporeal frame of reference. The fictional characters now look through the spectator's eyes, rather than the spectator looking through theirs.

Significantly, Balázs illustrates cinema's propensity for carrying away the spectator through the example of a filmed version of a play, as if to underscore what would be different about it from a theatrical version. In addition, he immediately goes on to assert that "nothing like this [exteriorizing] 'identification' has ever occurred as the effect of any other system of art." He thereby suggests that there is something about film which is unusually conducive to heteropathic identification.

In the little drama described by Balázs, the spectator ultimately recovers his or her customary terms of bodily reference. However, in a closely related passage from *Theory of the Film,* Balázs elaborates the story of a Chinese painter as an allegory about cinema's propensity for taking the spectator "elsewhere." Here, there is no moment of ostensible self-recovery. The spectator disappears forever into the cinematic spectacle:

There was once a painter who one day painted a landscape. It was a beautiful valley with wonderful trees and with a winding path leading away toward the mountains. The artist was so delighted with his picture that he felt an irresistible urge to walk along the path winding away towards the distant mountains. He entered the picture and followed the path towards the mountains and was never seen again by any man. (50)

This passage suggests that filmic identification may have the potential to effect a more lasting spectatorial abduction than the one described in relation to Romeo and Juliet—it may be capable of estranging the viewer forever from his or her habitual bodily parameters.[27]

In an essay titled "L'Acte perceptif et le cinéma" (1953), which Metz draws on extensively in *The Imaginary Signifier*, Henri Wallon also stresses the excorporative logic of cinematic identification. Indeed, he accounts for filmic spectatorship in terms remarkably similar to those which, elsewhere, he uses to describe the child's early relation to its specular image.[28] There is, however, one salutary difference: the emphasis in this essay falls much less upon the early formation of the ego than upon the disintegration of the imaginarily coherent self.

In "L'Acte perceptif et le cinéma," Wallon distinguishes once again between the proprioceptive ego and the scene of representation, seeing them now not merely as being exterior to each other, but in open competition. He speaks of them as two mutually exclusive or "incompatible" series, one of which must necessarily be sacrificed to the other.[29] But whereas, in *Les Origines du caractère chez l'enfant*, "proprioceptivity" designates only the "sensational body," here it implies the spectator's corporeal ego in its entirety—his or her self.[30] To the degree that the spectator succeeds in maintaining his or her integrity during the screening of a film, he or she remains quite simply detached from that text's sounds and images. No identification occurs. But if the film prevails over the bodily ego—if it successfully captates the spectator—the latter's self is obliterated as such. A heterogeneous and stubbornly exterior image displaces the one previously mapped imaginarily onto the subject's sensational coordinates. At such moments, Wallon writes, "I forget myself, nothing but the visual series any longer exists; this visual series engrosses me, and…abolishes in me the feeling of being a separate person [*le sentiment de ma propre personne*]" (294). The principle of the self-same body gives way, in other words, to an identity-at-a-distance. Wallon thus suggests that, at least during the screening of a film, cinematic identification is fundamentally heteropathic.

Siegfried Kracauer also makes use of the allegory about the Chinese painting to characterize cinema's engrossment of the spectator.[31] However, it is Eisenstein who meditates at greatest length upon cinema as a vehicle for taking the viewer "elsewhere." Since he also addresses the potential political uses of this transport, his discussion of the "ecstatic" bases of filmic identification warrants a closer look.

The Leap into Opposition

During the second half of the 1930s, Eisenstein articulated a model of political cinema which is the very opposite of that which has been extrapolated from Brecht's theoretical writings. In "Film Form: New Problems," an essay from 1935, Eisenstein takes a position that seems very much at odds with his earlier film practice: he defends the recent emergence of the individual protagonist in Soviet cinema.[32] Indeed, he claims that this phenomenon is part of "a phase of yet more distinct Bolshevization, a phase of yet more pointed ideological and essential militant sharpness" (124). It is not until he begins to talk about the imaginary relation of the actor to his or her fictional role that it is possible to understand how this new concern with subjectivity could serve a revolutionary function.

In that passage, Eisenstein speaks about the transubstantiation whereby the method actor "becomes" the part he or she plays. As an exemplary commentary on that process, he quotes several extraordinary lines from the memoirs of contemporary actors: "'I am already not me,'" "'I am already so and so,'" and "'See, I'm beginning to be him'" (137). These lines attest to a self-annihilatory identification not unlike that about which Wallon and Scheler write. Once again, rather than the ego being constituted at the expense of the other, it is the other who emerges at the expense of the self. The "I" becomes a "he" or "she," an objectification reminiscent of the subject's initial relation to the mirror image. Over the course of "Film Form" and "The Structure of the Film," the essay which follows it in the same volume, this story about method acting becomes emblematic of another exteriorizing transubstantiation—that involving the cinematic spectator.

In "The Structure of the Film," Eisenstein suggests that when cinematic identification is properly "guided" it can induce the spectator not only to "depart" from him- or herself, but also to effect a "transition to something else."[33] It can even precipitate a "dialectical leap" into opposition[34]—catapult the spectator out of one social order, and into one whose organizing principles are the opposite of the first:

> …a leaping imagist movement from quality to quality is *not a mere formula of growth,* but is more, *a formula of development*—a development that involves us in its canon, not only as *a single "vegetative" unit, subordinate to the evolutionary laws of nature,* but makes us, instead, *a collective and social unit, consciously participating in its development.* For we know that this very leap…is present in those revolutions to which social development and the movement of society are directed.[35]

It is crucial that we understand the full extremity of the Eisensteinian argument. For him, political cinema cannot be understood apart from identification, since it is the privileged mechanism whereby the spectator can be not only integrated into a new social collectivity, but also induced to occupy a subject-position which is antithetical to his or her psychic formation (i.e., to his or her self). Eisenstein speaks of breaking down "the resistance even of that spectator whose class allegiance is in sharp opposition to the direction taken by the subject and the theme of the work, i.e. those spectators for whom neither theme nor subject is 'organic.'"[36] He proposes to effect this integration not through rational persuasion, but through heteropathic identification. In the passage I just quoted

Eisenstein from the spectator's optimal relation to the development of a new social order is characterized as a conscious participation. However, his emphasis elsewhere in the same text on the "ecstatic" bases of that participation suggests that it would have to involve the unconscious as well.

Twice in *Film Form*, Eisenstein comes close to suggesting that the rapture he writes about turns in some central way upon the body. In "The Filmic Fourth Dimension," in the middle of a discussion of "creative ecstasy" in *Old and New*, he speaks about the "'psycho-physiological' vibrations" induced in the spectator by that film's montage structure.[37] And in "Methods of Montage," he associates the "sensation of physical displacement" with overtonal montage, again in relation to ecstasy in *Old and New*.[38] However, the only body which figures within "Film Form" and "The Structure of the Film" is that new social body which Eisenstein hopes to constitute by transporting the spectator out of him- or herself. The first of those essays speaks at length about the unity which the exemplary political film both prefigures and helps to bring about, and its metaphors are all drawn from the realm of nature; through this film, Eisenstein writes, "each spectator feels himself organically related, fused, [and] united…just as he senses himself united and fused with organic nature around him" (161).

Fredric Jameson maintains that the body can have no political value when put to non-metaphoric uses—that it has legitimacy only as a trope for the "knitting" together of the members of a society into a "genuine organism," and not as a term in its own right. In *The Political Unconscious*, he objects to any "reprivatiz[ation]" of the body "in the henceforth purely individual terms of the isolated body and the merely personal ecstasy."[39] However, what should by now be clear is that there can be no "isolated body." The body figures psychically only as the "projection" of culturally induced sensations, and culturally orchestrated representations. The conditions under which those two sets of elements are— or are not—brought together within certain subjectivities are also an effect of larger discourses and institutions. The body can consequently never be strictly "private," although it often presents itself in this guise. Just as every fantasy is always a group fantasy, so every body is always a "group body." Moreover, since the body provides the primary terrain across which the principle of self-sameness maps itself, it has a crucial part to play in the maintenance of a culture's existing categories of identity. It is, consequently, directly social. Although a political cinema for our time would still be one which induces the bourgeois spectator not only to vote, but also to identify in opposition to his or her class allegiance, this can no longer be the limit of its project.

The cinema I am imagining would, first, challenge the very principle of an integral self, both because that principle is tantamount to an inexorable insistence upon sameness, and because of its hostile or colonizing relation to the realm of the other. Confronted with difference, the ostensibly coherent bodily ego will either reject it as an unacceptable "mirror," or reconstitute it in digestible terms. The cinema I am elaborating here would dismantle the illusory unity of the body schema, and situate the visual imago insistently outside, where it can be renegotiated.

Second, such a cinema would position the subject in an identificatory relation with precisely those others at whose expense his or her *moi* previously maintained itself. This, I would argue, is how we should today construe Eisenstein's notion of a "leap" into opposition. This cinema would project the male subject into the bodily parameters of femininity, the white subject into those of blackness, the middle-class subject into those of homelessness, and the heterosexual subject into those of homosexuality. It would also eroticize this identity-at-a-distance, and, so, make it the source of new and intoxicating pleasures. Only a cinema providing such pleasures would be able to prevent the self-estranging "mirror" from later being either rejected, or "swallowed up" by the reconstituted *moi*. Although film has not traditionally performed either of these functions very well, they would together seem to constitute one important mandate for a political cinema of the 1990s.

Cinema and the Aura

But what is it about cinema which makes it such a privileged potential vehicle for what might be called "political ecstasy"? I would like to suggest that film's propensity for abducting the spectator out of him- or herself can best be theorized through Walter Benjamin's concept of the "aura." Although that concept would seem absolutely antipathetic to our usual ways of thinking about political cinema, in fact, it has important oppositional uses.

These oppositional uses can only be apprehended by reading "The Work of Art in the Age of Mechanical Reproduction" and "A Short History of Photography" in relation to a text which has been for the most part neglected by film theory: Benjamin's "On Some Motifs in Baudelaire."[40] When the first two texts are juxtaposed with the Baudelaire essay, it becomes evident that the notion of the aura does not irrevocably imply certain traditional aesthetic values to which mechanical reproduction is inimical. Rather, more profoundly, it designates a subjective relation enabling what Lacan calls "a whole affective assumption of one's neighbour."[41] An aesthetic text might consequently be said to be "auratic" not when it defies mechanical reproduction, but when it promotes that subjective relation. It does so when it engages in two simultaneous and equally necessary activities: when it maximizes the so-called fourth wall, and when it irradiates the scene of representation with ideality.

Benjamin begins "The Work of Art in the Age of Mechanical Reproduction" by equating the aura with the "authenticity," "authority," and "unique existence at the place where it happens to be" of the traditional work of art.[42] He seems to imply that the aura is something inherent in an aesthetic object, something which is lost with mechanical reproduction. A few pages later, however, Benjamin associates the aura with the "cult" value enjoyed by the work of art before the advent of photography (223–24), suggesting that it would be more correct to characterize the aura in terms of a social "attitude" toward the work of art, than a property inherent in it. Benjamin also deconstructs the notion of "authenticity" by suggesting that it can be better understood as the ideological construct of a particular age than as a specific attribute of a text.

And when, elsewhere in the text, he finally arrives at the definition of the aura which he will most insist upon in "A Short History of Photography" and "Some Motifs in Baudelaire," and which assumes paramount importance in subsequent pages of "The Work of Art in the Age of Mechanical Reproduction," that value assumes emphatically subjective proportions. Benjamin also generalizes it beyond a strictly aesthetic frame of reference by drawing his primary examples from nature rather than art. "The concept of aura which was proposed…with reference to historical objects may usefully be illustrated with reference to the aura of natural ones," he writes. "We define the aura of the latter as the unique phenomenon of a distance, however close it may be. If, while resting on a summer afternoon, you follow with your eyes a mountain range on the horizon or a branch which casts its shadow over you, you experience the aura of those mountains, of that branch" (222–23).

A footnote to "The Work of Art in the Age of Mechanical Reproduction" provides a partial clarification of this notion of "distance." Benjamin links it to the "unapproachability" of the cult image (243, n5), thereby indicating that it is not so much physical as psychic. In several much-discussed passages from "Some Motifs in Baudelaire," he provides a somewhat fuller elaboration of the "distance" with which the aura is synonymous, specifying it not only in subjective, but also in explicitly *psycho-visual* terms. In a footnote to that text, he associates it with a particular way of looking at an object,[43] and, in the text itself, he characterizes that way of looking as an "investiture" or *Belehnung* of the object (188). The object derives its aura of "unapproachability" from what one German critic calls the "productive attention of the spectator."[44]

Benjamin describes this investiture or enrichment in two ways. First, he suggests that, through it, the object is given the capacity to look back. In the passage in which he proposes this understanding of *Belehnung*, he describes it as essentially intersubjective, and indicates that it comes into play in the aesthetic domain only through a metaphoric extrapolation. He suggests, that is, that *Belehnung* involves primarily the relation between an individual and the other, and only secondarily between the viewer and the work of art:

> Experience of the aura…rests on the transposition of a response common in

human relationships to the relationship between the inanimate or natural object and man. The person we look at, or who feels he is being looked at, looks at us in turn. To perceive the aura of an object we look at means to invest it with the ability to look at us in return. (188)

To invest the other with the ability to return our look is seemingly to accept the other as an other, or—to state the case rather more precisely—to concede that he or she is also a subject.

Since Benjamin provides his second definition of *Belehnung* or investiture in the very next passage, it, too, would seem to have a fundamentally intersubjective reference. Here, the aura implies less the imputation to the other of the capacity to return our look than his or her exaltation. Benjamin suggests that this exaltation happens through the articulation or naming of desire. He characterizes the production of an inexhaustible and ultimately unconsumable beauty—a beauty which one can, as it were, "loop" around but never incorporate—as the end result of such an exaltation.[45] Benjamin says of this beauty, quoting Valéry, that "no mode of behavior that it suggests we adopt could exhaust it or dispose of it." It "reflects back at us that of which our eyes will never have their fill," because "what it contains that fulfils the original desire [is] the very same stuff on which the desire continuously feeds" (186–87). This particular investiture might thus be said to entail the radical *idealization* of the other, his or her elevation to the status not only of the beloved, but of the very *cause* of desire.

How are we to understand these two forms of investiture through which "distance" is created—the attribution to the other of the capacity to return our look, and the elevation of him or her to the status of a "ceremonial image"? It is probably evident by now that there are a number of intimate connections between Benjamin's notion of *Belehnung*, and Lacan's concept of the gift of love. The exaltation of the other described in "On Some Motifs in Baudelaire" closely coincides with that process of sublimation whereby a person or thing is raised to the status of the Thing, and is thereby cloaked in ideality. In both cases, that impossible nonobject of desire is given imaginary lineaments, and is thereby put at that distance which consolidates lack and renders desire fundamentally unfulfillable. The object which stands in for *das Ding* assumes in turn the value that properly belongs to *das Ding*; the object comes to signify that absolute beauty of which one can never have one's fill.

But, for both Benjamin and Lacan, idealization alone is insufficient to establish a viable relation to the other. It is also crucial that the subject maintain his or her distance from the scene of illumination—he or she must not assimilate the "ceremonial image" through an incorporatory identification. The attribution to the other of the capacity to return our look is crucial here, since it implies our acknowledgment of him or her as an independent equal. As Birgit Recki puts it in her analysis of the Benjaminian aura, through looking back, the other "shows the spectator that [he or she] is on the same level"—not a "dead thing," in the way that the mirror might be said to be, but a being equivalent to him or herself (24). The identification which always accompanies idealization thus here necessarily follows an excorporative trajectory.

The look also has a crucial part to play in Lacan's account of this subject-to-subject recognition. In an important passage from *Four Fundamental Concepts,* Lacan first distinguishes "the dimension of the capital Other" from that idiopathic operation whereby one loves oneself through the other. He then proposes that that which "responds in the Other" when it is apprehended as such—that which, in other words, might be said to be synonymous with the other in his or her capacity as subject—is the look.[46]

It is not only Lacan who helps to clarify the process described by Benjamin, but Benjamin who specifies something which Lacan leaves only half-explained: the mechanism through which this sublimating idealization takes place. The subject gives the other the gift of love by situating him or her in an intimate relation to those libidinally saturated and specifically visual memories which Benjamin qualifies as "involuntary" or "unconscious." The experience of the aura, he observes, "corresponds to the data of the *mémoire involontaire.*" Benjamin goes on to add, parenthetically, that

> These data…are unique: they are lost to the memory that seeks to retain them. Thus they lend support to a concept of the aura that comprises the "unique manifestation of a distance." This designation has the advantage of clarifying the ceremonial character of the phenomenon. The essentially distant is the inapproachable: inapproachability is in fact the primary quality of the ceremonial image. (184)

Lacan also suggests, in the context of another discussion, that the nameless cause of desire is both semanticized and kept at a fixed distance by embedding the object which takes its place in a network of libidinally resonant memories. This network or "quantity" of memories eventually gives way to a qualitative "complexity" through the displacement from one of these privileged signifiers to another.[47] It is through this signifying "complexification" that something is constituted as a representative of the Thing, and so as an object of desire. A person or thing thus comes to radiate ideality not through any inherent value, but through its emplacement within a dense and libidinally saturated metaphoric field.

This investiture is somehow synonymous with illumination in both Benjamin and Lacan. It produces what might be described as a "lit-up" image. When Benjamin writes about the *Erscheinung* of the aura, it is clear that he means us to understand that signifier not only as "appearance," "apparition," or "vision," but as "*Schein*," which in German carries the additional meanings "glow" and "light." Similarly, when Lacan describes the process whereby ideality is produced through the displacement from one representative of desire to another, he observes: "In a kind of expansion of the lighted zone of the neuronic organism…it lights up according to the laws of associative facilitation, or constellations of *Vorstellungen* which regulate the association of ideas."[48] As we will see later, this ideality is so closely linked with illumination that it can even be conferred upon an object in a film or photograph by the way in which it is lit.[49]

Just as "distance" finally turns out to imply more of a subjective relation than something immanent in the traditional art work, so does the contrary value of "nearness." In the passage in "The Work of Art in the Age of Mechanical Reproduction" in which Benjamin first introduces the notion that the aura is in decline, he suggests that the traditional work of art is indissolubly anchored to "the place where it happens to be." The mechanically reproduced image, on the other hand, "enables the original to meet the beholder halfway, be it in the form of a photograph or a phonograph record," and so to come "closer" (220–21). He thereby specifies "nearness" in spatial terms. However, two pages later, Benjamin elaborates "nearness" in ways which are analogous to those he ultimately uses to specify "distance." He indicates that "nearness," like "distance," has less to do with mechanical reproduction than with a particular relation between the subject and the object—or, to state the case more precisely, with a certain "positioning" of the subject vis-à-vis the object:

> [The decay of the aura] rests on two circumstances, both of which are related to the increasing significance of the masses in contemporary life. Namely, the desire of contemporary masses to bring things "closer" spatially and humanly, which is just as ardent as their bent toward overcoming the uniqueness of every reality by accepting its reproduction. Every day the urge grows stronger to get hold of an object at very close range by way of its likeness, its reproduction…. To pry an object from its shell, to destroy its aura, is the mark of a perception whose "sense of the universal equality of things" has increased to such a degree that it extracts it even from a unique object by means of reproduction. (223)

As this passage makes clear, "nearness" for Benjamin finally implies not only the triumph of the subject's frame of reference over that of the external image, whether it derive from an artistic representation or another human being, but also his or her assimilation of the image. It means to apprehend that image in and through myself, to make it not merely "mine" but "me." Benjamin's language makes evident the violence that this appropriation does to the real or metaphoric other: through it, I remove the latter from the only context in which he or she can sustain life, or *be* (the "shell"). I also effect his or her veritable destruction. Whereas the bequest and maintainance of the aura finally implies heteropathic identification, the contrary value of "nearness" suggests an idiopathic or interiorizing version of that psychic transaction.

Now that we have established the primarily subjective valence of the concepts of "distance" and "closeness," the moment has come to find some space in this model for the aesthetic—and, specifically, the cinematic—text. Let us explore the conditions under which a work of art might prompt its spectator to confer the gift of love upon corporeal coordinates which cannot be assimilated to his or her proprioceptive body, and so to identify at a distance from the latter.

As I indicated earlier, for theorists like Balázs and Eisenstein, cinema lends itself more than any other aesthetic form to such a project. These theorists do not, however, specify why this should be the case. Benjamin, on the other hand, seems to see cinematic identification as fundamentally idiopathic. Indeed, while he, too, invokes the allegory of the Chinese painter, he does so as a parable of what cinema is not, rather than of what it is.[50] Benjamin further complicates our effort to understand why film should facilitate heteropathic identification by characterizing it as the primary representative of mechanical reproduction, and so as fundamentally antiauratic.

However, Benjamin also provides at least the bare outlines of an aesthetic theory of the aura, and this theory does more to clarify why cinema should be ideally suited to perform the identificatory function designated by early film theory than to consolidate his own claim for it as an antiauratic representational form. Not only is the opposition of mechanical reproduction and traditional art not nearly as pivotal as might at first appear to Benjamin's model of the auratic text, but cinema almost ineluctably emerges as the model's primary exemplum. And the auratic features of cinema turn out to be precisely what encourage the spectator to idealize—and, so, to identify—at a distance from the self.

Significantly, although Benjamin begins his discussion of the aura in "The Work of Art in the Age of Mechanical Reproduction" by establishing a schematic antithesis between traditional art and the mechanically reproduced image, his account of the aesthetic conditions through which the aura is created ultimately turns upon the same signifier he uses to define *Belehnung:* "distance." And, once again, that signifier derives its meaning from its opposition to "closeness."

"Closeness," whose privileged instance is that variety of photography pioneered by Atget, involves, first of all, the falling away of the artistic or representational frame of an image, and a radical heightening of its "evidentiary" or referential axis. Benjamin writes that Atget photographed the streets of Paris "like scenes of crimes," and that, from this point forward, the referential photograph has been assumed to provide "standard evidence for historical occurrences" (226). Thus, rather than opening onto another world, as a Renaissance painting does, such a representation seems to provide a fuller access to our own.

To bring an image "closer" is also to "liquidate" its specificity (221), to standardize it, to strip it of its particularity. Although Benjamin gives as his example of this "liquidation" the substitution through mechanical reproduction of "a plurality of copies for a unique existence" (221), this textual strategy can perhaps best be understood as the homogenization of heterogeneity—the triumph of normative representation and the self over diversity. Finally, "closeness" signifies possession, that "belong-to-me" quality which is such a notable feature of certain contemporary images. It implies not only the substitution of the subject's own frame of reference for that specific to the object (221), but the possibility of "getting hold" of it at "very short range," i.e., of appropriating it (223).

"Distance," by contrast, would seem to necessitate a foregrounding of the frame separating an image from the world of objects, and the marking of it as a representation. It would seem to require, in other words, the hyperbolization of the fourth wall. "Distance" would also seem to entail the preservation or reconstitution of the context specific to an image. Finally, "distance" would seem to be part of the viewing experience of an aesthetic text when that text focuses on what falls outside the purview of both the "mirror" and the dominant coordinates of the cultural screen—on what is "strange" or "unfamiliar." The function of all of these discursive strategies is to mark the otherness or alterity of the image with respect not only to normative representation, but also to the viewer, and to thwart the drive toward possession. Through them, the viewer apprehends the image very precisely in the guise of the "not me."

However, when attempting to specify the aesthetic conditions through which the aura is imparted to something, it is crucial to remember that Benjamin does not merely associate the aura with distance. He says, more precisely, that it involves the perception of remoteness with respect to what is near. In so doing, he emphasizes the necessity for an identificatory relation between the viewer and the auratic object, a relation which can only be enabled through idealization, or the elevation of that object to the status of a "ceremonial image." As in the psychic domain, that elevation would seem, above all, to require the object's insertion into a representational network sufficiently complex to "light" it up in new ways, and so to solicit the spectator's imaginary relation to what would otherwise remain merely alien. However, as I emphasized in the last chapter, this idealizing activity generally occurs on an unconscious level. Under what terms can the work of art intervene in this process?

"On Some Motifs in Baudelaire" provides us with an interesting answer to this question. The issue of unconscious memory is at the heart of that text, and throughout, Benjamin emphasizes its opposition to consciousness. However, "On Some Motifs in Baudelaire" also moves from a strictly psychoanalytic account of unconscious memory to a discussion of its place in art, and, so, implicitly poses the possibility of somehow gaining access, if not to that domain itself, then to the mechanisms through which it operates. His primary example of the latter is Proust's *A la recherche du temps perdu,* which provides for Benjamin what might be called the textual "analogue" to unconscious memory.[51]

In Section XI of "On Some Motifs in Baudelaire," Benjamin attributes the idealizing aspect of the aura to "the associations which, at home in the *mémoire involontaire,* tend to cluster around the object of perception" (186). In so doing, he not only identifies, once again, the formation of metaphoric and metonymic networks as a vehicle of exaltation, but intimates that the faculty for forming such networks can be transferred from unconscious memory to artisitc production. Benjamin writes that this faculty is not a fixed resident of unconscious memory, but only most "at home" there, suggesting the possibility of occasional visits elsewhere. At another point in that essay, Benjamin confirms this assumption by putting forward Baudelaire's *correspondance* another aesthetic equivalent of unconscious memory.

Significantly, given the centrality of *A la recherche du temps perdu* to his larger argument, Benjamin makes this last point via a passage from Proust. This passage suggests that, like the *mémoire involontaire,* the *correspondance* always conveys the object in the guise of an associative network which irradiates and libidinally extends it, and is capable of weaving that cloak of metaphors and metonymies through which one drapes ideality around the shoulders of an other. "'There is no one else [but Baudelaire] who pursues the interconnected *correspondances* with such leisurely care, fastidiously and yet nonchalantly—in a woman's smell, for instance, in the fragrance of her hair or her breasts—*correspondances* which then yield him lines like 'the azure of the vast, vaulted sea' or 'a harbour full of flames and masts'" (183).

But the Proust passage also attests to the crucial difference between unconscious memory, on the one hand, and *Fleurs du mal* and *A la recherche du temps perdu,* on the other. Baudelaire, like Proust, does not so much *unconsciously remember* as *create in the mode of unconscious recollection.* Indeed, I will go further, and suggest that Baudelaire and Proust, like all authors who know how to "light up" the objects about which they write, do so by synthetically producing in the reader the effects of unconscious memories. "[Baudelaire's *correspondances*] are not occasioned by chance," writes Proust, "and this, to my mind, is what gives them their crucial importance'" (183).

In characterizing this process as "synthetic," I have deliberately left open the question of whether an artist produces such an effect consciously or unconsciously. I have done so because I agree with Benjamin that, in the creative process, the conscious and unconscious faculties "lose their mutual exclusiveness" (160), and become amenable to mutual influence. Drawing upon his or her own unconscious resources, but working in a form at least partly available to consciousness, a poet, novelist, or filmmaker can create a metaphoric or metonymic network of images capable of precipitating in the reader or viewer an analogous apprehension of ideality to that normally produced via the workings of unconscious memory. Once received, these "implanted" recollections will also communicate in complex ways with those which are more indigenous to the reader's or viewer's psyche, both at the level of the preconscious and at that of the unconscious. And, once again, there is likely to be a rich interaction between those two domains.

The central difficulty posed to my argument by "The Work of Art" is its notion that cinema is inherently destructive of, rather than constitutive of, the aura. That essay proceeds from the assumption that film is irremediably wed to photography, and so to the representational logic Benjamin associates with "closeness." However, I would like to emphasize not only that the properties Benjamin attributes to Atget's photographs are not typical of all photographs, but also that both "closeness" and "distance" do not mean the same thing in the case of cinema as they do in photography.

A crucial difference distinguishes the photographic from the cinematic image, and that difference turns very precisely on a spatial metaphor. Each is somehow "distant" from the spectator in certain respects, and "close" in others. However, that distance and that closeness are not equivalent in both cases. The photograph involves temporal remoteness, but spatial proximity. It brings its referent before us, but only in the guise of what once was. Roland Barthes suggests that its "reality" is consequently less of a "being there" than of a "having-been-there."[52] The cinematic image might be said to reverse this formulation—to imply temporal immediacy and spatial remoteness. As Barthes goes on to say in the same essay, in film "the having-been-there gives way before a being there of the thing" (45).

Both because filmic sounds and images inhabit time, and because—due to their extraordinary sensory vividness—they are often able to pass themselves off as perceptions rather than representations, they invade the present in a way that the photograph does not. At the moment an image passes through the gate of the projector and materializes on the screen, or a sound fills the room of the auditorium, it manifests itself to us in the guise of an absolute "now." However, the perceptual order onto which cinema seemingly opens is not that of our daily life. The filmic spectacle and the auditorium are sharply differentiated from each other not only by the curtain which frames the images, and by an articulation of space which is unblushingly evocative of the proscenium stage, but also by the illumination of the screen, and the darkness of the auditorium. I stress this last point in particular because the beam of light through which filmic images are conveyed to us is more than a practical necessity; it also imparts to those images a pulsatile and dazzling quality which photographs conventionally lack, a quality which is perhaps irreducibly "auratic."

Moreover, whereas photography is distinguished in its everyday use by, above all else, its evidentiary or indexical relation to what we take to be the "real," cinematic pleasure is intimately tied to the alterity of the filmic image—or, to be more precise, to its capacity to posit a world apart from and discontinuous with the one we inhabit, but capable of preempting the latter within the domain of the present. As Bazin observes in "Theater and Cinema—Part 2," "the world of the screen and our world cannot be juxtaposed." Rather, "the screen of necessity substitutes for [our world] since the very concept of universe is spatially exclusive. For a time, the film is the Universe, the world, or if you like, Nature."[53]

Because of the real and metaphoric radiance of the cinematic image, and the irreducibility of the gap dividing it from the space of the auditorium, filmic identification is almost definitionally excorporative. Heteropathy takes priority over idiopathy for the simple reason that the literal and metaphoric illumination of the screen and the separation decried by Brecht are generally apprehended by the spectator as the intoxicating possibility of going "elsewhere" and being "other"—as an invitation to "be" someone else for two hours, to leave one's self behind. The ideality of the image and the schism of screen and auditorium thus together open up a space for viewing pleasures which are at least potentially inimical to the coherent ego and the principle of the self-same body.

However, while the experience of cinematic viewing is perhaps inevitably heteropathic, it is clear that the radical project I have just described is seldom realized as such. Either the bodily parameters within which the spectator is encouraged to situate him- or herself do not significantly challenge those upon which his or her *moi* is based, or they are those which are customarily valorized at the level of the screen. Consequently, after the curtains are closed and the auditorium lights come on they are incorporated either at the level of the ego, or at that of the normatively disjunctive ego-ideal.[54] Albeit initially conforming to an exteriorizing trajectory, the identifications promoted by narrative cinema are, in other words, customarily subject to the rule of what Althusser would call the "always-already." Consequently, they do not often effect a dramatic estrangement of the viewer both from his or her proprioceptive parameters, and from dominant representation.

Nevertheless, it seems to me that a political cinema for today must be one which, rather than lamenting the identification at the center of the cinematic experience, seizes upon it as a vehicle for taking the spectator somewhere he or she has never been before, and which discourages the return journey. Central to this project, as I have repeatedly stressed, is the idealization of bodily coordinates within which the viewer is not accustomed to finding him- or herself, and which have been routinely devalued at the site of the cultural screen. Equally important is the elaboration of strategies for inhibiting the ultimate assimilation of the unfamiliar to the familiar, for maintaining the alterity of the new corporeal parameters to which the spectating subject accedes.

The most important of the textual strategies through which bodily ideality is maintained in its otherness are those through which the cinematic aura is not only foregrounded, but exaggerated, and not those through which—as Brecht would argue—it is neutralized and dispelled. A cinema devoted to the maintenance of alterity would thus involve, above all else, the emphatic marking and maintenance of the representational frame; an insistence upon particularity over and against standardization and stereotype; and the frustration at the level of image, sound, narrative, and characterological system of the "belong-to-me" quality which Benjamin associates with "closeness," and which—despite the irreducibility of the cinematic fourth wall—is such a prominent feature of many Hollywood films.

However, these textual strategies would not by themselves pose a sufficiently radical challenge to the principle of corporeal self-sameness. The ideality which a genuinely alternative cinema would encourage the viewer to confer upon bodies long unaccustomed to such radiance must be actively bestowed. It must, in other words, be marked as a garment rather than as the body itself. And it is here that the political cinema I have been dreaming about would draw on both Benjamin's theory of the aura, and the seemingly very different notion of *Verfremdung*. Such a cinema would put all of the many representational devices elaborated by Brecht for "alienating" one component of a play from all of the others to a new purpose: it would use them to make manifest the gap separating the gift of ideality from its recipient. It would prevent us from imputing to the recipient an essential or intrinsic ideality by bringing us to a knowledge of our own productivity with respect to that ideality.

As I indicated in the previous chapter, such knowledge is a strictly conscious affair, having little or nothing to do with the unconscious processes through which the subject idealizes or negates an object. Consequently, it can come into play only according to the logic of *Nachträglichkeit*, or deferred action. We can only retroactively make our gift of love an active one by arriving at a conscious perception of our unconscious idealizing activities.

As Freud's account of the female beating fantasy would indicate, it would seem possible for unconscious identification to follow an exteriorizing or heteropathic logic. In the unconscious version of that fantasy, the girl stands manifestly outside the image with which she identifies, an image whose corporeal parameters are unassimilable to her own.[55] Both the formation of the ego-ideal, and the state of being in love as Freud describes it—a state which involves the exteriorization of the ego-ideal—also involve an identification at a distance which is predominantly (although not exclusively) unconscious.[56] However, the unconscious has no capacity to apprehend an object as an signifier or stand-in for what exceeds it; it treats words as things, and dream images as if they actually were what they symbolically replace.[57] Consequently, it cannot grasp that the cloak of ideality in which an object is sheathed might be "borrowed." It is only through a conscious coming-to-knowlege that the unconscious substantialization of ideality can be undone, and the idealizing spectator moved from a position of prostration to one of active generosity. I say "spectator" rather than text because idealization is a strictly human activity. A text may encourage that activity, but it cannot effect it.

Although consciousness may have often appeared to play a small role in the political cinema to which this chapter is devoted, I hope it can now be seen that this role is nevertheless absolutely indispensable. The same is true of the Brechtian paradigm. Distanciation offers little assistance in shifting unconscious desire, or reordering the terms of the bodily ego. However, it figures necessarily and centrally at that point at which the gift of love shifts from a passive to an active modality. Because distanciation aims precisely and above all else at the inculcation of conscious knowledge in the spectator, it is the preeminent epistemological tool within the aesthetic domain.

Let us now attempt to specify this cinema of rapture more precisely through the film which has more than any other permitted me to dream it: Isaac Julien's *Looking for Langston*.

The Ceremonial Image

Looking for Langston is ostensibly "about" the Harlem Renaissance writer Langston Hughes. However, we are never allowed to take possession of that figure. Rather than providing us with the cinematic equivalent of a "pocket" Hughes, Julien's film weaves around the name "Langston": a complex web of poetry, music, and photographic and cinematic images, which is itself imbricated with a wide range of discursive concerns, ranging from the Harlem Renaissance to contemporary gay sexuality. It thereby refuses to pry Langston from his "shell," to extract him from his context so as to facilitate his easy assimilation to the spectator's own subjective parameters. Indeed, it goes even further. Julien's film creates a veritable aura out of the network of associations within which it embeds Langston.

Looking for Langston further militates against a spectatorial "raid" or appropriation through an insistent marking of the fourth wall, that is, through the repeated specification of itself as a world apart from the auditorium. When, at the end of the film, a group of policemen and thugs attempts to penetrate the nightclub in which the wake party is taking place, they come to enforce the norm of heterosexuality, to eliminate that which threatens their own "self-sameness." However, when they enter the party room, they find no one there; the revellers have disappeared without a trace. Julien thus makes clear that one can only enter the world of *Looking for Langston* through a radical self-estrangement, by leaving everything familiar behind. Any other approach is doomed to failure.

Looking for Langston overtly signals its difference from the conventional cinematic "homage" in two ways. First, it characterizes itself as "a Meditation upon Langston Hughes (1902–1962) and the Harlem Renaissance." These words declare the film to be less a biography than an exemplification of a form which, in its traditional Christian deployment, involves an apprehension-through-complication. Similarly, the film's title promises a search without a discovery or conclusion, a looking which is more akin to browsing than to detection. However, the activity foregrounded in the words "Looking for Langston" indexes more even than this browsing or cultural cruising. It designates Langston as he on whose behalf a certain kind of looking is solicited. That visual transaction is synonymous with what Benjamin calls "*Belehnung,*" and Lacan calls "the active gift of love."

It is not merely through its title that *Looking for Langston* makes this connection; in a crucial scene within the film, Alex, the character who bears the name "Langston" in the original script, actively confers the gift of love on another black man. Thus, Julian's text not only wraps Langston in an associational aura, but also makes the look which is most associated with him the model for that libidinal transaction through which the subject affirms both the ideality and the alterity of another.

Looking for Langston begins with a series of documentary shots, first, of a train moving at night across a Manhattan bridge, then, of visitors to the funeral of Langston Hughes. The faded quality of these images, as well as what they show—cars and clothes from an earlier epoch—locate them firmly in the past. Both because they provide the record of an historical event, and because they do so in an overtly documentary style, they are permeated with that evidentiary value which Benjamin attributes to a certain kind of photograph.

This brief sequence gives way to a strikingly antithetical series of images, which lift the death of Langston Hughes out of the real and into an overtly theatrical frame. The camera pans slowly and elegiacally across the faces of fictive mourners clustered around a casket in which a black man lies. Although the dead man ostensibly represents Hughes, he is played by Julien himself, as if to heighten the unreality of the scene. The fourth wall is even more emphatically marked in the final shot in this sequence. The mourners stand together in an artfully composed long shot, surrounded by flowers [figure 23]. All that moves within this sumptuous black-and-white image are the smoke from incense and the flames from many commemorative candles. The camera then cranes down, without a cut, to the nightclub below, where a wake celebration is in progress [figure 24]. The room is illuminated with a secular but nonetheless celestial form of light—with "stars" refracted onto the wall from a mirror ball hanging from the ceiling. The drinkers and dancers are all frozen in theatrical positions

figure 23   figure 24

that are paradoxically suggestive of motion, much like the figures on Keats's famous Grecian urn. We are clearly no longer within what might be called "historical" time.

What is most striking about these images, apart from their hyperbolization of the representational "frame," is their overt solicitation of the look. The figures within them both offer themselves up to visual scrutiny, and turn that scrutiny back on itself. At the same time, there is no one within the fictional world inscribed within this sequence to whom its images might be attributed. Consequently, it can only be the spectator's look to which these images are addressed, and which they interrogate. I say "look" rather than "gaze" because almost every image which follows this sequence is somehow anchored to a pair of fictional eyes which dramatize either what it means to look "for" or "against" Langston. Let us examine some paradigmatic instances of this scopic principle.

The sequence concluding with the immobile dancers is immediately followed by some documentary footage produced during Riverside Radio's tribute to Hughes after his death. The sound from this broadcast continues as *Looking for Langston* cuts, first, to a shot of Manhattan streets taken from inside a train moving across elevated tracks some time in the 1920s, then, to a glossy close-up of a record playing on a phonograph. The camera now reverses its earlier direction and pans elegantly to the left, first showing the gramaphone trumpet and more of the "stars" cast by the mirror ball against the black of the nightclub walls. It finally comes to rest on the thoughtful face of Alex (Ben Ellison), the forty-year-old black man to whom the original script of the film gives the name "Langston" [figure 25]. This close-up lasts for several emphatic seconds, connecting what follows to his look.

Significantly, the sounds and images which proceed as if from Alex's imagination culminate in two shots which not only are dramatically idealizing in function, but also announce themselves as such. Leading up to these shots is a montage consisting of, first, the neon names of nightclubs, then, a series of shots of black musicians, and finally, a cluster of still photographs of Hughes himself in various situations. These images are accompanied by the song "Blues for

figure 25

Langston." Then come two extraordinary staged images. In each of these images, a black angel stands in a nocturnal graveyard holding a large photograph. These photographs have been unrolled, as if they were sacred texts written on parchment. The first shows Langston Hughes, the second, James Baldwin [figures 26, 27]. The effect is precisely what Benjamin would call a "ceremonial image." Hughes and Baldwin are rendered dramatically distant through the doubling of the representational frame from which their faces look out at us; they are given to us not only as cinematic representations, but also as cinematic representations of photographic images. As such, they have none of that illusory three-dimensionality for which cinema is celebrated.[58]

figure 26

figure 27

Hughes and Baldwin are also "lit up" or exalted, both by the light which falls onto their photographs in the darkness of the night and the illumination cast by the angels' wings, and by the preceding montage, which weaves that network of metaphoric associations that Benjamin and Lacan associate with idealization. Significantly, the photograph of Hughes appears first in a much more mundane guise; it is simply part of the montage that precedes the appearance of the angels. In effect, then, Julien's film suggests that the later, irradiated version of that photograph is what results when its quotidian counterpart is read through the preceding montage of music and image.

This is not the only way in which the ideality which attaches to the illuminated photographs is shown to be more a gift than an essence. The angels are very obviously actors wearing constructed wings—light bulbs have even been attached to the wings. The angels also exalt without being exalted themselves. Thus, they dramatize a capacity inherent in every human subject—the capacity to confer upon another an ideality which he or she does not possess.

What it means to bestow this gift is made strikingly evident slightly later in the film. During the second nightclub sequence, which begins with another image of dancers frozen in position, Alex is shown looking from his perch at the bar toward Beauty (Matthew Baidoo), a black man who sits drinking at a table with a white man. Beauty, who initially has his back to Alex, turns and smiles at him with answering desire. Significantly, only at this moment does *Looking for Langston* have recourse to the traditional reverse shot formation. Earlier it moves from a close-up of Alex looking to a shot that encompasses both the bar and the table where Beauty sits. Now, it provides a reverse shot of Beauty, but only to show that he returns Alex's look [figure 28]. As is made evident by the jealousy of Beauty's white companion, here, that return look has very much the force that Benjamin attributes to it in his essay on Baudelaire; it means, precisely, to be a (desiring) subject.

figure 28

There is, of course, no doubt that this status is enjoyed by every sane human being, black or white, male or female. However, the subject who relates to the other only through the logic of "self-sameness" refuses to acknowledge as much with respect to that other. He or she either responds to the bodily coordinates of that other with the "horror" and "contempt" that Freud suggests can be a normative male response to the female genitals[59]—a psychic reaction which is far from being always incommensurable with sexual attraction, but which reduces that other to the status of a pure object—or he or she assimilates the other to him- or herself, and so denies the former's separate existence. When Julien shows Beauty energetically returning Alex's look, he therefore emphasizes not only that Beauty, like Alex, is a desiring subject, but that Alex looks at Beauty in a way that accepts the distance which is an irreducible feature of a genuinely intersubjective relation.

Some time after the exchange of looks between Alex and Beauty, Alex is shown sitting at the bar with a glass of champagne, staring with an "inner" eye at an imagined scene. The camera cuts from this metaphoric look to a tracking shot of Alex lying on his stomach on a bed shrouded in a white sheet. As it moves slowly from his feet to his head, the sound of ocean waves is heard, and two other men are seen standing on the far side of the bed.

We are then provided with the first image of what can perhaps best be described as a dream within this dream: Alex walks in black tie and tuxedo across a marshland. Mysterious white flags flutter in the wind. A moment later, we are back in the bedroom, where Beauty and the white man stand facing each other in medium shot. Beauty, who has his back to us, is completely nude, the contours of his body idealized through the exquisite lighting of the shot. He reaches out and removes the white man's T-shirt. At one point in this shot, the "bulge" of the white man's genitals can be clearly discerned through his underwear, but we see Beauty only from the back, as if to deny to us access to that part of the black male body through which it has been most stereotypically apprehended.[60]

figure 29

Looking for Langston returns to the marshland, across which Alex walks in slow motion. The landscape is bereft of trees or plants. The camera then cuts to a medium close-up of Beauty's legs and feet [figure 29]. He is surrounded by white lilies. As the camera tilts up the back of his body, in a shot which evokes the earlier one of Alex on the bed, Beauty is shown standing in the middle of the marshland, facing Alex. A male voice-over utters the following words from Bruce Nugent's "Smoke Lilies and Jade":

He was in a field—a field of blue smoke and black poppies and red calla-lilies. He was searching on his hands and knees.... Then he saw two strong legs—dancer's legs. The contours pleased him. His eyes wandered on past the muscular hocks to the firm thighs, the rounded buttocks, then the lithe narrow waist, strong torso, and broad deep chest. The brown eyes looking at him. His hair curly, and black, and all tousled. It was Beauty, who just smiled, and looked at him, and smiled and said: "I'll wait."

The images which initially accompany this text use the shot/reverse shot formation once again to inscribe not so much a look and its object as two reciprocal looks. *Looking for Langston* provides a close-up of Alex smiling at Beauty, and then a medium close-up of Beauty smiling back. Alex reaches out and touches the other gently on his chest.

But although physical contact has been established between Alex and Beauty, the words that follow immediately ("He was searching…") once again establish distance between them, as do the words Beauty finally speaks. The shot of Alex and Beauty in the marshland gives way to a close-up of Beauty in profile, a conch-shell held to his ear [figure 30]. Two other images slowly dissolve in and out of this one: a sunset and a pool of water with lilies in it. After this shot, Alex smiles again at Beauty in close-up. Once more, Beauty returns the look, now in an extreme close-up which emphasizes precisely those particular classically black features which have been for centuries most subjected to a violent cultural dei-dealization: his nose, and then—a moment later—his mouth. As the camera tilts down to the latter, Beauty speaks the words: "I'll wait." The dream sequence thus asserts Beauty's subjectivity most energetically at precisely that moment when it shows an image which would, in a more conventional text, be used to assert the contrary.

figure 30

Apart from the moments at which the male voice-over speaks about the two men looking at each other, an exchange which the film again chooses to empha-size, there is a striking disjuncture of sound and image throughout this entire sequence. The landscape in which Alex ostensibly searches for Beauty is in dra-matic contrast to the one in which he is shown standing, and as the voice-over describes Beauty's body, we look at him in close-up, with the conch shell at his ear. There are other points of disjuncture as well. The conch shell shot itself marks a break with the marshland shots, suggesting as it does other, lusher land-scapes; and, in the image in which we first glimpse Beauty's feet, there are flow-ers on the ground, in spite of the fact that he ostensibly stands on the marshland. All of these disjunctures emphasize that what Alex "sees" when he thinks about Beauty is somehow in excess of that figure himself. It does so, of course, not in that pejorative sense in which we customarily comment on the incommensu-rability of an object to the desire it ostensibly arouses, but rather to foreground once again the investitory potential of the look.

What I am attempting to suggest is that although the body is here the focal point for the process of idealizing Beauty, it—like the figure of Langston Hughes himself—is not intrinsically ideal, but is rather exalted via the context into which it is inserted. That context is openly fantasmatic, and dramatically defamiliariz-ing. The first textual component which overtly contributes to its production is the image of Beauty's feet and legs surrounded by lilies. But after the camera has tilted up to reveal the rest of Beauty's body, and has directed its attention to the exchange of looks between him and Alex, the process of contextual idealization is pushed much further. Alex now imagines discovering Beauty in "a field of blue smoke and black poppies and red calla lilies." And as the voice-over begins its itemization of the parts of Beauty's body, those corporeal elements are further enriched through a series of visual metaphors, which themselves intercommu-nicate complexly via the lap dissolve until the sequence as a whole seems to "light up." The close-up of Beauty evokes warm summer days and the sound and smell of ocean and sand. The sky ablaze with a brilliant sunset evokes not only radi-ance, but also the celestial. And the pool of water, in which lilies are floating, brings to three the references to that flower, and associates Beauty with clarity, coolness, and the power to quench thirst.

A sequence somewhat later in the film dramatizes a look which is the very opposite of that attributed to Alex—a look which, far from identifying at a dis-tance from itself, represents the veritable apotheosis of "self-sameness." The sequence in question begins with a close-up of a white man, Karl (John Wilson), earlier shown sitting with Beauty in the nightclub. He looks ahead of himself at an unspecified object. Smoke passes between him and what he sees, as if to sug-gest that his look is somehow mediated. He raises a glass of champagne to his lips, and continues to stare. A male voice-over reads an excerpt from Essex Hemphill's "If His Name Were Mandingo" to the accompaniment of music:

> He speaks good damn English to me. I'm his brother, Carver. He doesn't speak the "dis" and "dat" bull I've seen quoted. Every word he speaks rings clear in my head.

The camera then cuts to a dark room illuminated with blown-up images from Robert Mapplethorpe's *Black Book* projected onto hanging panels. Karl walks among these panels, touching them appropriatively, yet negligently, as if they were familiar possessions [figure 31]. As he does so, the voice-over continues the text begun a moment ago:

I don't suppose you ever hear him clearly?
You're always busy seeking other things of him.
His name isn't important, it would be coincidence if he had a name
A face, a mind.

If he's not hard on, then he's hard up
And either way you watch him.
You want cross-over music,
You want his pleasure without guilt or capture.

You don't notice many things about him,
He doesn't always wear a red ski cap,
Eat fried chicken, fuck like a jungle,
He doesn't always live with his mother or off the streets
Or off some bitch as you assume.

You appear to be concerned, you offer him $20
Telling him it's cab fare, and discharge him from your home.
Your paths cross the next day, you don't acknowledge him but
He remembers his semen dilutes in your blood,
He doesn't dance well but you don't notice,
To you he's only visible in the dark.

figure 31

With the words "To you he's only visible in the dark," the camera cuts to Karl reclining in underwear on a chaise longue in a heavily shadowed room. A black man stands on the other side of the chaise longue, wearing only shorts. Karl reaches into the cushion behind him, detaches a bill, and hands it to the black man. As the black man takes the money, he stares with an eloquently inexpressive face at Karl for a moment, before walking away.

I suggested a moment ago that the "horror" and "contempt" with which the normative subject might respond to bodily parameters other than his or her own are by no means incompatible with sexual desire. On the contrary, this repudiation often provides the very bedrock of male, heterosexual desire. This sequence from *Looking for Langston* suggests that the same principle may also come into play in the relationship of the white gay man to his black counterpart. Through the offhanded gesture with which Karl gives the $20 note to his sexual partner, the film shows him withholding from the other that acknowledgment which every subject requires to function socially as such.

The voice-over text suggests that Karl not only apprehends the black men who command his sexual interest exclusively through the intervening agency of the screen (foregrounded here through the smoke which mediates his vision), but that he also comfortably inhabits the viewing position that has been culturally assigned to him with respect to those men. Those with whom he goes to bed are consequently synonymous for him with a series of stereotypical attributes ("dis" and "dat," fried chicken, red ski cap) indicative of a retarded cultural development, and with that appendage with which the black male subject is so often conflated. Although Karl eroticizes the black male body, his relation to his sexual partner and the men in the Mapplethorpe photographs is nevertheless exclusively that of a subject to an object. Consequently, if a black man doesn't have a "hard-on," he is, quite simply, "hard-up."

I have commented already on the "stars" which illuminate the nightclub, and on the two shots of "angels" with which the first montage about the Harlem Renaissance concludes. Both of these tropes recur repeatedly in *Looking for Langston,* always in an idealizing context. However, most of the subsequent contexts featuring stars or angels serve to underscore a point which I have not yet sufficiently emphasized: the "distance" that separates the actively loving look from the other has no more to do with physical remoteness in *Looking for Langston* than it does in "The Work of Art in the Age of Mechanical Reproduction." In fact, Julian's film is at pains to establish that this distance can coexist with the most extreme sexual intimacy.

In the sequence given over to the elaboration of Alex's "dream," the caresses which he and Beauty give each other are almost ritualistic in nature. However, somewhat later in the film, a male voice-over reads a Hemphill poem about cruising while the images show a gay pick-up in a leafy nocturnal landscape ("Stalking./The neighborhood is dangerous/But we go there./We walk the long way./Our jangling keys/Mute the sound of our stalking./To be under the sky, above/Or below a man,/This is our heat"). These images are once again associated with a particular look: that of a wake reveller who goes for a walk in the dark. However, even more central to the organization of the sequence are four cut-away shots to statues of angels on pedestals, silently affirmative spectators of the sexual events which this sequence depicts [figures 32, 33]. These shots work to render something profoundly terrestrial—something which is, within the popular imagination, the very epitome of the "fleshly"—somehow celestial.

figure 32   figure 33

Two subsequent, interlocking sequences clarify more precisely the terms of this seemingly oxymoronic idealization, while at the same time carrying it further. The first of these sequences begins with a shot of two shadow figures dancing together in a beam of light [figure 34]. They separate, and the camera cuts first to an overhead pan of couples dancing in the dim illumination of the nightclub, and then to the figure whose look is responsible for the unusual angle of vision— a black angel smiling and watching from a lofty perch, and swaying to the music [figure 35]. This paradigm is repeated, now with another black angel, who also smiles. An overhead shot follows of two naked figures in an erotic embrace on a bed, which is attributed to a white angel [figure 36]. The camera cuts once again to an overhead pan of the nightclub, then to yet another black angel, and finally to an overhead shot of Karl flipping through the pages of Mapplethorpe's *Black Book* while reclining on a rotating chaise longue. The sequence ends with a shot of the white angel, another overhead pan of the nightclub, and a second shot of

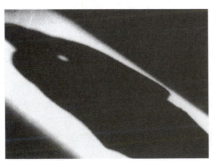 

figure 34   figure 35

figure 36

the first black angel. During this sequence, a male voice slowly speaks the words to Hughes's "Stars" against a background of music:[61]

Oh sweep of stars over Harlem Streets
Oh little breath of oblivion that is night.
A city building to a mother's song
A city dreaming to a lullaby.

Reach up your hand dark boy and take a star
Out of the little breath of oblivion that is night.
Take just one star!

As in the sequence concluding with the photographs of Hughes and Baldwin, the conjunction of the nightclub dancers with angels serves to exalt the dancers. Indeed, like the photographs, the dancers are "lit up" by that conjunction: a spotlight plays across the room of the nightclub in each of the overhead pans [figure 37]. However, here, the angels do not so much display as *look*. The moving spotlight is the implicit trace of their eyes roaming around the room, and conferring an aura of radiance on whatever they see. Although angels are somehow associated with the process of idealization earlier in the film, it is only in this

figure 37

sequence that they explicitly emerge as the dominant representatives for Benjamin's attentive observer. To confer the active gift of love, *Looking for Langston* now explicitly suggests, is to be an angel.

Although the angels remain in their elevated position throughout this sequence, the film holds out the possibility of intercourse between earth and heaven not only through the beam of light which plays across the room of the nightclub, but through the Hughes poem, which exhorts the "dark boy" to "take one star." The next sequence suggests that the path leading from earth to heaven is heavily traversed in both directions, and it equates that path with gay sexuality. It thus radically redefines both "heaven" and "earth," showing them to represent less regions within the Christian cosmology than positions which can be subjectively assumed. "Heaven" now means simply "the place from which ideality is dispensed." "Earth," in turn, signifies "the depository of ideality." Ideality is itself decisively disarticulated from the values with which Christianity associates it—values like "purity" and "spirituality"—and defined as the end result of an exchange which is simultaneously ennobling and frankly carnal.

The first shot of this sequence shows a formally attired black man climbing a flight of stairs, holding a pole with a banner in his right arm. The latter is reminiscent of the white flags in the dream sequence. The bannister is illuminated with a string of light bulbs. On the platform at the top of the stairs await a group of angels. During this shot, a male voice-over speaks the following words from Hemphill's "The Edge, Third Movement":

> You left me begging for things
> Most men thought they had below their belts.
> I was reaching higher.
> I could throw my legs up like satellites
> But I knew I was fucking fallen angels.
> I made them feel like demigods.
> I believed my mission
> to be a war zone duty:

In the next shot, a black angel walks at night in a half-lit forest toward an undisclosed goal. The camera tracks with him as he moves. He arrives at last at his destination: a black man. As he tenderly touches the man's face, the camera moves into a medium close-up of their faces. The male voice-over continues:

> Don't create casualties,
> Heal them.
> But I was the wounded almost dead,
> Helping the uninjured.

Men whose lusty hearts
Weakened in the middle of the night
And brought them to tears, to their knees,
For their former lovers.
They could look at me and tell
What beauty love's scars give me.
So touch me now—
Hannibal to Toussaint
I am a revolution without bloodshed.

In the last shot in this sequence, a black angel stands motionless in the darkened woods, only the edges of his wings and his right side illuminated. Several other angels mill around him, and finally exit left-frame. He remains standing alone for several seconds as the voice-over finishes the Hemphill poem. The words he speaks would now seem to derive from a second speaker, who addresses the first:

I can change the order of things
To suit my aspirations. You can raise your legs,
Almost touch heaven.
I can be an angel,
Falling.

The three shots which comprise this sequence dramatize the two tropes around which Hemphill's poem revolves: ascendent man and the fallen angel. Through their sexual congress, the one moves heavenward, the other toward earth. Significantly, as they do so, the man becomes the agent of the angels' exaltation—"I knew I was fucking fallen angels," says the first speaker in Hemphill's poem, "[But] I made them feel like demi-gods"—and the angel comes to occupy the position previously occupied by the man. This sequence thus dramatizes the reverse movement of the transaction to which this chapter is devoted; it is not only the angel who confers ideality upon the man, but also the man who confers ideality upon the angel. The last two sequences give new meaning to the notion of reciprocity which is so central to Benjamin's theory the aura: they show both angels and humans actively bestowing the gift of love upon each other.

The notion of reciprocity is taken further in the next and final sequence, which begins with another image of bodies frozen in mid-dance in the nightclub, and concludes with a second clip from the memorial radio broadcast. In between these two "bookends," the camera cuts back and forth between the wake celebration and the police and thugs, who first pound on the door of the building in which the celebration is taking place, then break in and climb the steps, and finally vainly search the premises of the nightclub for traces of the revellers. During this montage, two male voices speak the words to Hemphill's "The Brass Rail," which the script to *Looking for Langston* characterizes as "a call response duet for two men." This verbal text is repeatedly anchored to the image-track through an echoing gesture, sound, or visual detail, and it references both in its opening and closing lines the failure of the police and thugs to find the wake revellers:

C: I saw you last night
R: Many occupants are never found.
C: In the basement
C: Many canoes overturn
R: Of the Brass Rail.
C: Your dark diva's face, a lake.
R: Lushing and laughing.
C: I hear the sea
R: Your voice falling from the air.
C: screaming behind your eyes.
R: Dancing with the boys on the edge of funk.
C: Twilight.
R: The boys danced, darling,
C: My tongue
R: touching you indiscreetly.
C: walks along your thighs like a hermit.
R: Your body a green light
C: I have been naked with you.
R: urging them.
C: Dear Diva, Darling: You were in the mirrors,
R: the light,
C: their arms.
R: The boys whispered about you
C: Singapore slings toasted you.
R: Under the music pumping from the jukebox.
C: They were promises chilled by ice cubes.
R: The boys whispered about you.
R: The sloe gin fizzes
C: under the music pumping from the jukebox.
R: and Singapore Slings toasted you.
C: You were in the mirrors
R: the light
C: their arms.
R: Your body a green light.
C: Dear Diva, Darling:

R: The boys danced darling,

C: I have been naked with you.

R: touching you indiscreetly.

C: My tongue has walked along your thighs.

R: Dancing on the edge of funk.

C: I have found the scent.

R: Your voice

C: Twilight.

R: falling from the air.

C: I hear the sea screaming behind your eyes.

R: Lushing and laughing.

C: Your dark diva's face,

R: I saw you last night

C: a lake.

R: in the basement

C: Many canoes overturn.

R: of the Brass Rail.

C: Many occupants are never found.

The Hemphill poem comprises two different texts, but they are imbricated in such a way that each transforms the significance of the other. Each speaker might thus be said to surrender his poem to his counterpart. Because in doing so he allows his words to be carried away from the meaning he would otherwise impart to them, this surrender must be understood in the most radical sense; it is nothing less than a self-expropriation.

The inclusion of "The Brass Rail" in *Looking for Langston* is also significant because of the centrality which it gives to the signifier "you." In *Problems in General Linguistics,* Benveniste maintains that the first-person pronoun confers subjectivity on the one who uses it ("'Ego' is he who *says* 'ego,'" he writes).[62] But it could also be argued that by referring to one's interlocutor with the second-person pronoun, one acknowledges him or her as a subject, or—in the Benjaminian sense—invests him or her with the capacity to look back. One accepts the distance of the other from oneself, while at the same time addressing him or her as an equal. In effect, one says to that other, "You are not me."[63]

Because this linguistic *Belehnung* does not work to diminish or negate the speaker, "The Brass Rail" dramatizes a relationship which is very far removed from that murderous binarism of "you" or "me" I discussed in Chapter 2, in which each flourishes only at the other's expense. At the same time, that relationship is far from being purely symbolic, in the Lacanian sense of that word. Each speaker illuminates the other with the "stars" of ideality, or, to state the case slightly differently, adorns him with a necklace of metaphors.

Not surprisingly, then, the final sequence of Julian's film once again moves the spectator toward the conclusion that to look "for" Langston is to transfer to the bodily coordinates of another the luster which in the Lacanian account of the mirror stage attaches only to one's own visual imago—to identify, in other words, at a manifest distance from the proprioceptive body. Interspersed throughout this sequence is an important series of non-diegetic shots which serve, in conjunction with the voice-over commentary, to make the mirror the locus no longer of self, but of the other.

figure 38

figure 39

figure 40

In one of these shots, a man of indeterminate ethnicity lies on a mirror which simulates the pool in which Narcissus admired his image [figure 38]. However, his head is turned away from his reflection; he is, in effect, "asleep" to himself. Another of these shots seems at first to serve a contrary function, since, in it, a black man sitting in profile in front of a mirror turns to look at his image [figure 39]. However, in a second variant of this shot, he turns toward the mirror, but does not actually look at his reflection. And in a third, he finally turns altogether away from the mirror [figure 40]. The mirror now frames not "me," but the reciprocal "you" of the Hemphill poem. "You were in the mirrors/the light/their arms," the two male voices declaim. One of the speakers then gives utterance to words which, perhaps more than any others, work to envelop the black, gay, male body in an aura of iridescence and, in so doing, to produce it as as a locus for pleasurable identification, even in the case of the spectator whose proprioceptive coordinates are strikingly divergent: "Your body a green light."

The Visible World

4

The Gaze

Camera and Eye

It has long been one of the governing assumptions of film theory that the cinema derives in some ultimate sense from the Renaissance, via intervening technologies like the camera obscura, the still camera, and the stereoscope, and that its visual field is defined to a significant degree by the rules and ideology of monocular perspective. Since, within cinema, as within photography, the camera designates the point from which the spectacle is rendered intelligible, the maintenance of the perspectival illusion is assumed to depend upon a smooth meshing of the spectator with that apparatus. Both times that Christian Metz invokes quattrocento painting in *The Imaginary Signifier,* he immediately goes on to speak about the importance of what he calls "primary" identification, or identification with the apparatus.[1] Jean-Louis Baudry also maintains that, within cinema, the ideological effects of perspective depend on identification with the camera.[2] And Stephen Heath explicitly states that "in so far as it is grounded in the photograph, cinema will…bring with it monocular perspective, the positioning of the spectator-subject in an identification with the camera as the point of a sure and centrally embracing view."[3]

For both Metz and Baudry, there is a certain inevitability about this identification. Thus, Metz writes that "the spectator can do no other than identify with the camera…which has looked before him at what he is now looking at and whose stationing…determines the vanishing point" (49). And Baudry represents primary identification as the necessary preliminary to other identificatory relations (295). Significantly, a successful imaginary alignment with the camera is seen as implying not only an access to vision, but an access to a seemingly *invisible* vision; Metz remarks that "the *seen* is all thrust back on to the pure object" (97). The spectator constituted through such an alignment seemingly looks from a vantage outside spectacle. Primary identification also implies a vision which is exterior to time and the body, and which yields an immediate epistemological mastery. Although both Metz and Baudry are quick to denounce this invisible, disembodied, timeless, and all-knowing vision as an ideological construction, they nevertheless see its illusory pleasures as an almost unavoidable feature of the cinematic experience. The viewing subject is constituted in and through this fiction.

Feminist film theory has qualified the claims of Metz and Baudry somewhat by suggesting that classic cinema makes primary identification more available to certain spectators than to others. Laura Mulvey and others have argued that Hollywood not only enforces an equation between "woman" and "spectacle," but effects a closed relay between the camera, male characters, and the male viewer.[4] However, even while showing that the equation of camera and eye is qualified in complex ways by gender, feminist film theory still implicitly assumes that the "ideal" or "exemplary" cinematic spectator is constructed through an identification with the camera, and, hence, with transcendent vision.

But the theoreticians of suture articulate a more disjunctive and even antipathetic relation between camera and eye.[5] Spectatorial pleasure, they maintain, depends on the occlusion of the enunciatory point of view, and the seeming boundlessness of the image. But the enunciatory activities of the cinematic text cannot be entirely concealed. Even so simple a device as the implied frame around a given shot can serve as a reminder of those activities. And at the moment that the frame becomes apparent, the viewer realizes that he or she is only seeing a pregiven spectacle, and the *jouissance* of the original relation to the image is lost.

The theorists of suture also thematize the camera as an "Absent One," thereby further emphasizing the distance that separates it from the spectatorial eye. It represents that which is irreducibly Other, that which the subject can never be. Not only does the Absent One occupy a site exterior to the spectator, but it also exercises a coercive force over the spectator's vision. The spectator is consequently, as Hitchcock would say, a "made-to-order-witness."[6]

And although Metz and Baudry insist perhaps more than any other film theorists on the capacity of the eye to accede imaginarily to the place of the camera, there are elements within each of their writings which belie that capacity. As Mary Ann Doane has recently pointed out, the argument advanced by Baudry in "The Apparatus" posits a very different spectator than that assumed by

"Ideological Effects of the Basic Cinematographic Apparatus."[7] Whereas the earlier essay presents cinema as an instrument for the perpetuation of the idealist illusion of a transcendental spectator, the later essay stresses the permeability of the boundary separating the spectator from the spectacle. The viewer described by "The Apparatus" is no longer situated at a distinct remove from the image, but is enveloped by it, even undifferentiated from it. Baudry stresses that, at the cinema, as in our dreams, there is "a fusion of the interior with the exterior,"[8] or—to state the case slightly differently—a crossing of the eye over into the field of vision.

And Metz begins the section of *The Imaginary Signifier* titled "The All-Perceiving Subject" with an analogy between cinema and the mirror stage, an analogy which once again calls into question the firm demarcation between spectator and spectacle. Although he subsequently distinguishes this kind of identification from that which the viewer ostensibly forms with respect to the camera, he also stresses that it is only as a result of first passing through the actual mirror stage that the subject can form such an identification (45–49). Primary identification is thus implicitly routed through the image, according to a kind of retroactive logic.

Geoffrey Nowell-Smith suggests that it is not only extra-cinematically that the mirror stage might be said to enable identification with the camera, but within the cinema itself. "So-called secondary identifications," he writes, "…tend to break down the pure specularity of the screen/spectator relation in itself and to displace it onto relations which are more properly intra-textual—i.e., relations to the spectator posited from within the image and in the movement from shot to shot."[9] A particularly striking instance of this displacement would seem to be the articulation of shot/reverse shot relationships along the axis of a fictional look, which gives identificatory access to vision from within spectacle and the body. The theoreticians of suture argue that it is only through such specular mediations that the viewer can sustain an identification with the camera.

But within film theory, it is probably Jean-Louis Comolli who has insisted most strenuously on the nonmatch of camera and spectatorial look. "At the very same time that it is thus fascinated and gratified by the multiplicity of scopic instruments which lay a thousand views beneath its gaze," he writes, "the human eye loses its immemorial privilege; the mechanical eye of the photograph machine now sees *in its place,* and in certain aspects with more sureness. The photograph stands as at once the triumph and the grave of the eye. There is a violent decentering of the place of mastery in which since the Renaissance the look had come to reign."[10] Comolli argues that the photograph represents the "triumph" of the eye because it confirms the perspectival laws which have for so long constituted the Western norm of vision—because it shows what we have learned to accept as "reality." It represents the "grave" of the eye because it is produced by an apparatus capable not only of "seeing" this reality more precisely than it can, but of doing so autonomously.[11] In this respect, the camera might be said not so much to confirm as to displace human vision from its ostensible locus of mastery.

Jonathan Crary has recently expanded upon and enormously complicated Comolli's argument. In *Techniques of the Observer,* he calls into question perhaps the most fundamental assumption about cinema's visual organization, an assumption which even Comolli does not challenge: the notion that an uninterrupted series of optical devices lead from the camera obscura to the camera. Crary argues convincingly that the nineteenth century witnessed the shift from a "geometrical" to a "physiological" optics.[12]

Techniques of the Observer employs the camera obscura as the privileged example of geometrical optics because, unlike a conventional perspective construction, it does not prescribe a fixed site for the spectator, but allows a certain degree of physical mobility, thereby fostering the illusion of spectatorial freedom. Since the viewer must physically enter the camera obscura in order to see the images it produces, it also implies "a spatial and temporal simultaneity of human subjectivity and [optical] apparatus" (41), and an emphatic sequestration of the eye from the world (39). It consequently provides a figure not only for a "free sovereign individual" (39), but for a vision which is unburdened by the body, and sharply differentiated from what it sees (55).

While the camera obscura is Crary's primary metaphor for the geometrical optics of the seventeenth and eighteenth centuries, the stereoscope is his emblematic apparatus for the physiological optics which emerged in the nineteenth century. The stereoscope enjoys this status not only because it provides a heterogeneous and planar apprehension of space rather than one which is homogeneous and perspectival, but because it foregrounds the difference between its own principles of organization and those of human vision. The stereoscope contains two images, one of which addresses the left eye and another one which addresses the right. However, the stereoscopic spectator sees neither. Instead, his or her bipolar sensory apparatus conjures forth a fictive image—a composite of the two actual images, with an apparent depth of field. The stereoscope thus positions the spectator in a radically different relation to visual representation than that implied by the camera obscura or perspectival painting.

More is at issue here than the dramatic disjunction of eye and optical apparatus. The stereoscope calls into question the very distinction upon which such mastery relies, the distinction between the look and the object. What the eye sees when peering into the stereoscope is not a specular order from which it is detached, but "an undemarcated terrain on which the distinction between internal sensation and external signs is irrevocably blurred" (24). The stereoscope thus precipitates a referential crisis. This referential crisis has less to do with the displacement of the real by the simulacrum than with a loss of belief in the eye's capacity to see what is "there." Relocated within the "unstable physiology and temporality" of the body (70), human vision no longer serenely surveys and masters a domain from which it imagines itself to be discrete.

Within Crary's argument, the stereoscope is also emblematic of nineteenth-century ways of thinking about the eye in that it is in a sense "about" that organ; it is a direct extension of the discovery that the human subject has binocular rather than monocular vision. *Techniques of the Observer* suggests that from the 1820s on, vision increasingly functioned as the object rather than as the subject of optical knowledge. This investigation of the eye worked to further diminish belief in its supposed objectivity and authority. Not only was a blind spot uncovered at the point at which the optic nerve opens onto the retina (75), but visual apprehension was shown to fluctuate over time (98). Color came to be understood less as an inherent attribute of the object than as an extension of the viewer's physiology (67–71). And the discovery of the afterimage, which feeds directly into cinema, suggested once again that the human eye is capable of a counterfactual perception.

Although the invention of the stereoscope postdates that of the camera, Crary argues that the camera is part of the same epistemological rupture as the stereoscope (5). Photography, like the stereoscope, is "an element of a new and homogeneous terrain of consumption and circulation in which an observer becomes lodged" (13). "Observer" is the term Crary consistently uses to designate a viewer who no longer regards the world from an ostensibly transcendent and mastering vantage point, a viewer whose unreliable and corporeally circumscribed vision locates him or her *within* the field of vision and knowledge. Presumably, then (although he does not argue this case in any specificity), Crary means to suggest that because of its autonomy from the human eye, and its capacity to "see" differently from the latter, photography also dislodges that organ from the seemingly privileged position it occupies within the camera obscura.

Later in *Techniques of the Observer*, Crary proposes that the stereoscope was doomed to extinction because it makes too manifest the disjuncture of camera and look. Photography—and later cinema—prevailed because it maintained earlier pictorial codes, particularly those of perspective, making it an apparent extension of human vision, and resecuring the viewer in a position of visual authority (136). Like Comolli, then, Crary suggests that the photographic image affords the eye an illusory "triumph."

However, there is a strange way in which, even within photography, the maintenance of the referential illusion—or the attribution to the image of a "truthful" vision—overtly depends on the isolation of camera from human look. In a crucial passage from early film theory, Andre Bazin suggests that knowledge of the discreteness of camera and human look may be tolerable provided that the photograph seems synonymous with the "real," since the photograph thereby gives the spectator retroactive access to what he or she would otherwise lack. But, he also maintains that such knowledge may seem at moments the necessary condition for sustaining the belief in the equivalence of photograph and referent—that only when the camera is established as being independent of the eye can we trust it. "For the first time," he writes in "The Ontology of the Photographic Image," "between the originating object and its reproduction there intervenes only the instrumentality of a nonliving agent. For the first time an image of the world is formed automatically, without the intervention of man.... The objective nature of photography confers upon it a quality of credibility absent from other picture-making...we are forced to accept as real the existence of the object reproduced."[13]

And, of course, one of the privileged textual sites out of which cinema might be said to develop is Muybridge's series of sequential photographs of trotting horses, images which were produced precisely to dispel an illusion of the eye—the illusion that a horse in motion always maintains at least one foot on the ground.[14] Here, the camera manifestly sees what the look cannot. We are thus obliged to consider the possibility that the codes of perspective may survive in cinema and photography without anything approximating the close identification of eye and optical apparatus that was implied in the case of the camera obscura.

The relation between the camera and the human optical organ might now seem less analogous than prosthetic: the camera promises to make good the deficiencies of the eye, and to shore up a distinction which the eye alone cannot sustain—the distinction between vision and spectacle. However, even this formulation suggests that the camera entertains a more benign relation to the eye than is always the case. The camera is often less an instrument to be used than one which uses the human subject; as Crary suggests, the camera is more of a machine than a tool (131). And Vilem Flusser, another recent theorist of the camera, proposes that the photographer is at best a "functionary" of that apparatus.[15]

The concept of the "observer" thus implies not only an embodied and spectacularized eye, but one whose operations have been subjected to a complex rationalization—an eye which has been rendered socially productive. "Almost simultaneous with this final dissolution of a transcendent foundation for vision emerges a plurality of means to recode the activity of the eye," Crary writes,

> [means] to regiment it, to heighten its productivity and prevent its distraction. Thus the imperatives of capitalist modernization, while demolishing the field of classical vision, generated techniques for imposing visual attentiveness, rationalizing sensation, and managing perception. (24)

In the wake of the camera, the eye can clearly be seen to be the site for the induction of a specific kind of vision, one which is not only socially "useful," but also predetermined. In the next chapter, I will elaborate in considerable detail upon this last point through the category of the "given-to-be-seen."

I have dwelt at such length on *Techniques of the Observer* for three reasons. First, it profoundly problematizes the still-dominant assumptions within film theory that the look—or at least the male look—can be easily aligned with the camera, and that the relation of camera and look always works to the credit of human vision. Second, it provides a very rich and multifaceted account of the actual relation between those two terms. Finally, its discussion of the camera coincides at crucial points with that offered in Harun Farocki's *Bilder der Welt und Inschrift des Krieges,* a film to which I will turn in a few pages.

But even though *Techniques of the Observer* offers invaluable assistance in articulating the relation between the camera and the eye, it omits a crucial term from that equation: the gaze. Crary does not account for the underlying field of vision onto which the camera/eye opposition is mapped. He approaches his topic through such an exclusively historical lens that he fails to discern that the camera derives many of its powers to coerce and define through its metaphoric connection to a term which is much older than it. Indeed, in some larger sense, he neglects to distinguish what is socially and historically relative about the field of vision from what persists beyond one social formation to the next.

Let us now turn to a text about which the opposite could be said, a text for which the visual domain would seem to be absolutely timeless: Lacan's *Four Fundamental Concepts of Psycho-Analysis.* As we will see, Lacan offers a powerful transhistorical model for theorizing the relation of gaze and look. He also uses the camera as a metaphor for the first of those terms. However, he never properly interrogates the relation between camera and gaze, or proposes that it might be central to our present field of vision. Having brought Lacan into the discussion as a way of clarifying what might persist within the visual domain from one epoch to another, I will then be obliged to critique him for ignoring what does not.

The Gaze and the Camera

In *Four Fundamental Concepts of Psycho-Analysis,* Lacan also insists emphatically upon the disjunction of camera and eye, but instead of deploying the camera as an independent optical apparatus, he uses it as a signifier of the gaze. The passage in which he introduces this metaphor locates the subject firmly within spectacle, and attributes to the camera/gaze a constitutive function with respect to him or her: "What determines me, at the most profound level, in the visible, is the gaze that is outside. It is through the gaze that I enter light and it is from the gaze that I receive its effects. Hence it comes about that the gaze is the instrument through which light is embodied and through which…I am *photo-graphed.*"[16]

However, although Lacan emphasizes the exteriority of the camera to the look, his use of that apparatus as a metaphor for the gaze works to erase the kinds of historical demarcations drawn by *Techniques of the Observer.* He associates the gaze not with values specific to the last century and a half, but rather with illumination and "the presence of others as such" (91, 84). Within the context of *Four Fundamental Concepts,* the gaze would thus seem to be as old as sociality itself. Even in his deployment of the photographic metaphor, Lacan resists historical periodization. He divides the word "photograph" in half, thereby suggesting that, if the camera is an appropriate metaphor for the gaze, that is because it models or schematizes its objects within light. This is a definition of photography which strips it of most of its apparatic specificity.

Since I have discussed the Lacanian model at considerable length elsewhere,[17] I will reiterate here only its primary features. Lacan elaborates the field of vision through the three diagrams reproduced below:

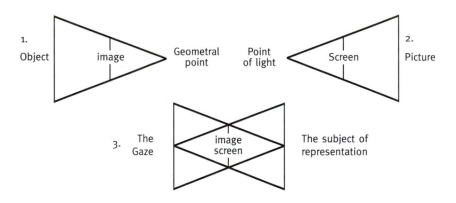

The first diagram represents the preliminary step in Lacan's exhaustive deconstruction of the assumptions behind the system of perspective. In it, the subject is shown looking at an object from the position marked "geometral point." He or she seemingly surveys the world from an invisible, and hence transcendental, position. However, the intervening "image," which coincides with the "screen" in diagram 2, immediately troubles this apparent mastery; the viewer is shown to survey the object not through Alberti's transparent pane of glass, but through the mediation of a third term. He or she can only see the object in the guise of the "image," and can consequently lay claim to none of the epistemological authority implicit in the perspectival model.

Diagram 2 situates the subject at the site marked "picture," and the gaze at that marked "point of light." It thus locates the subject within visibility. It also dramatically separates the gaze from the human eye. Consequently, both the subject-as-spectacle and the subject-as-look are situated outside the gaze. As I suggested earlier, the gaze represents both the point from which light irradiates, and the "presence of others as such" (84). In this second respect, it can perhaps best be understood as the intrusion of the symbolic into the field of vision. The gaze is the "unapprehensible" (83) agency through which we are socially ratified or negated as spectacle. It is Lacan's way of stressing that we depend upon the other not only for our meaning and our desires, but also for our very confirmation of self. To "be" is in effect to "be seen." Once again, a third term mediates between the two ends of the diagram, indicating that the subject is never "photographed" as "himself" or "herself," but always in the shape of what is now designated the "screen."

The last diagram superimposes the second over the first, suggesting that diagram 1 is always circumscribed by diagram 2; even as we look, we are in the "picture," and, so, a "subject of representation." The gaze occupies the site of the "object" in diagram 1, and that of "point of light" in diagram 2. In this double capacity, it is now at an even more emphatic remove from the eye. Indeed, it would seem to "look" back at us from precisely the site of those others whom we attempt to subordinate to our visual scrutiny—to always be where we are not. Once again, the relation between the terms on the left and those on the right is mediated, in this case by something that could be called the "image," the "screen," or the "image/screen," but which I will henceforth designate simply the "screen."

Thus, Lacan provides a transhistorical account not only of the gaze, but also of the entire field of vision, which for him includes the look and the screen. *Four Fundamental Concepts* offers an invaluable corrective to the extreme historical relativism of *Techniques of the Observer*. It suggests that there might be a "deep structure" to the psyche and the socius which is indifferent to many temporal demarcations—something which we might, for instance, designate as "libido" in the case of the psyche and "interrelationship" in the case of the socius. Consequently, certain elements of each may stubbornly persist from one specular regime to another. However, Lacan's model errs too far in the other direction. Its elaboration of the field of vision is finally as untenable in its ahistoricism as one which can acknowledge only historical difference.

I will now attempt to bring together Crary's account of the camera/eye relation with Lacan's account of the gaze/eye relation by advancing a provisional formulation of what is and is not historically variable within the field of vision. I will also attempt to give back to the camera—which Lacan uses as a metaphor for the gaze—some apparatic specificity, and to consider some of the implications of that metaphor. I propose to perform the first of these tasks through a revisionary reading of the paradigm put forward by *Four Fundamental Concepts*, which lends itself in some surprising ways to a historical elaboration. I will undertake the second of these tasks by removing the hyphen from "photo-graph," by taking Lacan's allusion to the camera much more seriously than he intended.

Lacan seems to me correct when he suggests that the gaze and the look are in certain respects ahistorical. If the gaze is to be connected to illumination and "the presence of others as such"—as I agree that it should—then it would seem to represent an inevitable feature of all social existence. Indeed, it would seem to be the registration within the field of vision of the dependence of the social subject upon the Other for his or her own meaning. It is thus necessarily independent of any individual look, and exterior to the subject in its constitutive effects.

As human, the look would seem, by contrast, to be always finite, always embodied, and always within spectacle, although it does not necessarily acknowledge itself as such. Since, as I will argue in the next chapter, the look is a psychic as well as a visual category, it would also seem unavoidably marked by lack. It would consequently seem to be propelled by desire, and to be vulnerable to the lures of the imaginary.

At the same time that I make these concessions to the Lacanian model, I remain convinced that acute variations separate one culture and one epoch from another with respect to at least three dimensions of the field of vision. These variations pertain to how the gaze is apprehended; how the world is perceived; and how the subject experiences his or her visibility. As should be evident, to factor variability into the visual domain at three such crucial sites is to indicate that this domain can assume extremely divergent forms.

I would like to propose that the screen is the site at which social and historial difference enters the field of vision. In *Four Fundamental Concepts*, Lacan elaborates the screen exclusively in terms of the determining role it plays in the visual articulation of the subject. However, in the diagrams included above, it intervenes not just between the gaze and the subject-as-spectacle, but also between the gaze and the subject-as-look, and between the object and the subject-as-look. Since Lacan characterizes the screen as "opaque" (96), it does not merely "open," like a door or a window, onto what it obstructs, but rather substitutes itself for the latter. It must consequently determine how the gaze and the object, as well as the subject, are "seen." But what is the screen?

Although Lacan does not really define this component of the field of vision, he offers a few suggestive remarks about it. In specifying its effects with respect to the subject-as-spectacle, he comments on the possibility open to the latter of manipulating the screen for purposes of intimidation, camouflage, and travesty. He also maintains that it is through the "mediation" of the screen, or "mask," that "the masculine and the feminine meet in the most acute, most intense way" (107). On the basis of these two observations, I some years ago attributed to the screen a representational consistency. However, I elaborated this argument in terms which are quite alien to the intent of *Four Fundamental Concepts*. I attributed to the screen a constitutive role with respect to a series of social categories which do not concern Lacan. "It seems to me crucial that we insist upon the ideological status of the screen by describing it as that culturally generated image or repertoire of images through which subjects are not only constituted, but differentiated in relation to class, race, sexuality, age, and nationality," I wrote in *Male Subjectivity at the Margins* (150).

Now, I would like to put an even greater distance between myself and *Seminar XI,* and define the screen as the conduit through which social and historical variability is introduced not only into the relation of the gaze to the subject-as-spectacle, but also into that of the gaze to the subject-as-look.[18] The screen represents the site at which the gaze is defined for a particular society, and is consequently responsible both for the way in which the inhabitants of that society experience the gaze's effects, and for much of the seeming particularity of that society's visual regime.

I would also like to suggest that Lacan invokes the camera in the context of discussing the gaze not just because the camera, like the gaze, "graphs" with light, but also because the connection between the two terms is so powerfully overdetermined. Indeed, I will go so far as to claim that due to its association with a "true" and "objective vision," the camera has been installed ever since the early nineteenth century as the primary trope through which the Western subject apprehends the gaze. Its elevation to that position has precipitated the crisis in human vision so compellingly documented by Crary, and has worked to foreground the disparity of look and gaze concealed by the camera obscura.

In advancing this formulation, I want both to bring history to the Lacanian paradigm, and to explain how the camera assumes the enormous significance Crary imputes to it. Not only does the camera work to define the contemporary gaze in certain decisive ways, but the camera derives most of its psychic significance through its alignment with the gaze. When we feel the social gaze focused upon us, we feel photographically "framed." However, the converse is also true: when a real camera is trained upon us, we feel ourselves subjectively constituted, as if the resulting photograph could somehow determine "who" we are.

In claiming that the camera is the primary metaphor for the gaze, I am obliged to complicate enormously the definition which I earlier offered of the screen—to conceptualize it as more than a repertoire of ideologically differentiating images. At the time I was writing *Male Subjectivity at the Margins,* I had already grasped that the screen must work to determine how we experience the gaze, as well as how we are seen. However, my primary concern in theorizing the screen as a mediation between us and the gaze was to find a way of accounting for how the gaze, which is itself unlocalizable and "unapprehensible," has for so long seemed to us masculine. I understood that in order for the gaze to be perceived in this way, the male eye had necessarily to be aligned with the camera. I also saw that the endless subordination of woman-as-spectacle was necessary to the establishment of this alignment. Nevertheless, it did not occur to me to ask the question which now poses itself with a certain urgency: "What is a camera?"

As soon as that question is asked, it becomes evident that it is not enough to suggest that the screen through which we mainly apprehend the gaze is synonymous with the images by means of which a given society articulates authoritative vision. At least since the Renaissance, optical devices have played a central role in determining how the gaze is apprehended, and such devices cannot simply be reduced to a set of images.

The camera is less a machine, or the representation of a machine, than a complex field of relations. Some of these relations are extrinsic to the camera as a technological apparatus, others are intrinsic. Some follow, that is, from its placement within a larger social and historical field, and others stem from its particular representational logic. Crary's remarks about the camera obscura are thus equally applicable to the camera. "What constitutes the camera obscura," he writes,

> is precisely its multiple identity, its "mixed" status as an epistemological figure within a discursive order *and* an object within an arrangement of cultural practices. The camera obscura is…"simultaneously and inseparably a machinic assemblage and an assemblage of enunciation," an object about which something is said and at the same time an object that is used. It is a site at which a discursive formation intersects with material practices. (30–31)

An analysis of the camera both as a representational system and a network of material practices would thus seem the precondition for understanding the primary screen which presently defines the gaze. It would also seem to constitute the necessary first step in a historical conceptualization of the screen.

Harun Farocki's 1988 film, *Bilder der Welt und Inschrift des Krieges (Images of the World and the Inscription of War)* not only offers an extended meditation on the representational logic of the camera, but also conceives of it as an intricate and constantly shifting field of social and technological relations. It is consequently to this text that I will now turn in an attempt to arrive at a clearer understanding of what it means to represent the gaze as a camera. An examination of *Bilder* will help to clarify both the points of continuity and those of discontinuity between that apparatus and earlier visual technologies. It will thus facilitate a further elaboration of the ways in which a fundamentally atemporal gaze is culturally and historically specified.

As we will see, Farocki insists as strenuously as Crary upon the disjunction of camera and eye, and in ways that almost uncannily echo Lacan. Not only does the camera emerge in *Bilder* at a site equivalent to the gaze in *Four Fundamental Concepts*, but human vision is once again situated manifestly within spectacle. But Farocki is not content merely to disassociate camera/gaze and eye, and to establish the placement of the human subject within the purview of that apparatus. He also interrogates another of the camera/gaze's functions—what might be called both its "memorializing" and its "mortifying" effects. Together these two functions serve to define, at least in part, the representational system proper to the gaze. In addition, Farocki scrutinizes the social as well as the psychic field of relations with which the camera is synonymous, and some of the ways in which the social impinges upon the psychic. He looks, that is, at some of the exemplary material practices through which the camera/gaze's disjunction from the eye, the articulating role it plays with respect to human subjectivity, its memorializing function, and its mortifying effect have been historically exploited and discursively specified.

Not surprisingly, gender and race also come into play in *Bilder* in complex ways. Although Farocki reiterates again and again in that text that it is only through the hyperbolic specularization of the female subject that the disjunction between the camera and the male eye can be masked, he also shows how this paradigm can be complicated by other forms of cultural difference. Finally, he attempts to indicate what, if not the domain of the camera/gaze, might be said to represent the province of the look. An analysis of *Bilder* will consequently provide the occasion not only for a further elaboration of how the gaze is figured within the social field, but also for a provisional theorization of the look.

The Look as Spectacle

Bilder der Welt und Inschrift des Krieges begins with a series of images of a laboratory built in Hannover for the study of the movement of water. These images are not easily assimilated into the complex montage that follows, since they seem at first glance outside the associative network the film weaves. However, the commentary accompanying a later repetition of one of these images will connect it to Auschwitz under the mutual sign "laboratory." And the first words uttered by the disembodied female voice-over immediately introduce the issue of seeing, encouraging us to find a relation between vision and the images of controlled water. "When the sea surges against the land, irregularly, not haphazardly," she observes, "this motion binds the look [*den Blick*] without fettering it and sets free the thoughts. The surge that sets the thoughts in motion is here being investigated scientifically in its own motion—in the large wave channel at Hannover."

This brief text establishes an opposition not only between regularity and irregularity, fettering and setting free, but between scientific observation—which is here shown to involve a whole range of visual technologies—and the look, which, far from mastering its object, is itself implicated or "tied up" with it.

An extraordinary series of shots follows the Hannover sequence, and further diminishes the authority of the look by dislocating it from the gaze, and placing it within spectacle. This series begins with a shot of a drawing from Dürer's *Instruction in Measurement* which conforms closely to Lacan's first diagram, except in one extremely important detail. In it, a human figure is shown looking from one end of a triangle at an object which stands at the other end [figure 41]. However, the eye is located not at what Lacan calls the "geometral point," but rather at the wide end of the triangle, where he situates the gaze.

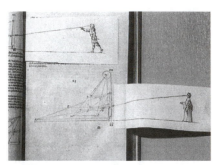

figure 41

The Dürer drawing is used here to represent a different model of vision from the one with which we are familiar, one providing a potent metaphor for the delusory supremacy of the eye—a model of vision, available to the Greeks and operative in the West until the thirteenth century, in which light was assumed to proceed from the look rather than object, much like a projector or flashlight.[19] As this image comes onto the screen, the female voice-over says: "Enlightenment—that is a word in the history of ideas—in German '*Aufklärung.*'" The word "*Aufklärung*" will accrete additional meanings over the course of the film, but here it is literally the first word spoken by the voice-over after the text quoted above, a text which ends with the word "light." It thus establishes a close analogical connection betwen the rationalism and humanism of the Enlightenment project, and the notion of human vision as an agent of illumination and clarification, which the Dürer drawing is made to figure.

But at the moment the voice-over utters the word "*Aufklärung,*" the Dürer drawing gives way to a radically different image. On the right side of the drawing, where the human figure stood in the preceding image, a dot is drawn, reminiscent of what Lacan calls the "geometral point" [figure 42]. (I will be arguing that within all of the diagrams and drawings used by *Bilder* to figure the place of

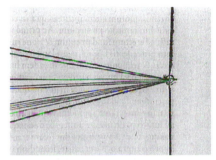

figure 42

the human subject within the field of vision, that subject is always situated on the right, in another echo of *Four Fundamental Concepts.*) Lines forming a triangular pattern converge toward this point, but we are not shown where they lead; the other end of the triangle is occluded. This drawing would seem to schematize that model of vision with which we are more familiar, in which light emanates not from the eye, but from the object of vision.

Because *Bilder* equates the earlier model of vision so strongly with the aspiration toward mastery and knowledge, the reconfiguration of the site occupied in it by the human eye as a geometral point cannot help but effect a diminution of that organ's powers. This is particularly the case because the eye is now positioned more as the object than as the agent of vision; we are not even shown the site at which it ostensibly comes to rest. With the third image in this series of shots, the look is even more overtly specularized. That image shows the left eye of a white model, whose face is being elaborately made up [figure 43]. Her eyelids are weighted down with powder, and she blinks as the make-up man rubs around her eye with a cotton puff. This is an eye which is less seeing than seen.

figure 43

Through this shot, and through the many other images of women woven into its discourse, *Bilder* makes clear that the human eye is no sooner differentiated from the camera/gaze than it is gendered "female." The female subject, in other words, is obliged to bear the burden of specularity so that the look of her male counterpart can be aligned with the camera. We need only remember that it is most typically at the level of spectacle—classically through the shot/reverse shot formation—that woman is subordinated to the male look to realize how precarious or even impossible this alignment is.

This three-shot sequence is followed by a story about the discovery of scale photography, a story which further severs eye from gaze, and which figures the gaze through the camera. In 1858, the voice-over explains, a local government building officer named Meydenbauer almost lost his life while performing scale measurements of a cathedral from a basket suspended from the roof. It subsequently occurred to him that it might be possible to effect scale measurement through photography. "The idea of obtaining measurements through photography came to Meydenbauer after he was suspended between life and death," the voice-over adds. "That means: it is dangerous to hold out physically on the spot.... Arduous and dangerous, to hold out physically on the spot. Safer to take a picture and evaluate it later, protected from the elements, at one's desk." Human vision is thus not only isolated from the camera/gaze, but also associated with danger and mortality.

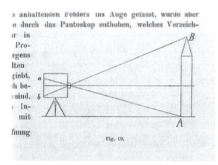

figure 44

As we listen to this narrative, we look again at the geometral point and the model's eye, two additional reminders of the immanence of the look to the domain of spectacle. Another of the images which accompanies the Meydenbauer narrative also warrants mention in this context, since it positions the camera so overtly in the place where Lacan situates the gaze. That image shows a triangle pointed in the same direction as the Dürer drawing, but put to very different uses. On the left side, where the object is located in the Dürer drawing [figure 41], and where the triangle narrows to a point, stands the camera [figure 44]. It photographs an object located on the right, where the human figure stands in the Dürer drawing, suggesting that, insofar as the camera is concerned, each of us is less subject than object. This point is driven home by another detail as well. The wide end of the triangle coincides with the site which has by now been established as the human locus, as it does in the Dürer drawing. But to be situated at the wide end of the triangle no longer means to be the source of light, but rather to be lit up by an illumination which has its origin elsewhere, an illumination which is perhaps better metaphorized by the projector than the camera. It thus signifies not visual mastery, as it does in the Dürer image, but rather "to be in the picture," "photographed" by the camera/gaze. In effect, then, this image performs the same deconstruction of the Dürer drawing as Lacan's second diagram performs with respect to his first, indicating that even as we look, we are within spectacle.

Later, *Bilder* will repeat this deconstruction twice in quick succession. As the female voice-over remarks, "Enlightenment—*Aufklärung*—that is a word in the history of ideas," we are asked to look at a Leonardo drawing of the human eye, replete with humanist significance [figure 45]. This is an eye which says not only "I think, therefore I am," but "I think, therefore the world is"—an eye which is still unshaken in its claim to be the gaze. However, the immediately preceding shot focuses once again upon the model's eye, even more heavily made up than before [figure 46], and the following shot reveals a blue computer cross-section of an eye, which is now not merely specularized, but measured and quantified [figure 47]. By the time we arrive at the fourth image in this sequence, which shows a Renaissance artist producing a picture with the aid of a perspectival grid, again occupying a position on the right side of the image [figure 48], its celebration of man's visual mastery can only be read as a radical *méconnaissance* of the field of vision.

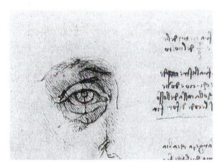

figure 45

figure 46

Some found footage later in the film suggests even more forcefully than the computer cross-section of the eye that the eye is situated irreducibly within spectacle. Taken from a film about ergonomic research, this found footage shows a male pilot wearing a device designed to record the movements made by his eyes during a short flight [figure 49]. Those movements manifest themselves as white marks moving across the terrain at which the Caucasian pilot looks [figure 50], in a veritable collapse of the distinction between the eye and what it sees.

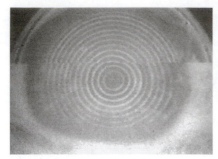

figure 47

figure 48

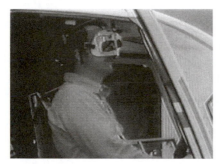

figure 49

figure 50

After the Hannover sequence, *Bilder* is thus given over for some time to a series of shot clusters which work both to align the camera with the gaze, and to isolate the camera/gaze from the eye. The eye is, in the process, shorn of its Cartesian pretensions. It is shown to look not from a site exterior to the field of vision, but from one fully inside. Indeed, the eye itself emerges as an object of visual investigation. Finally, in this series of shot clusters, *Bilder* dramatizes and ultimately reverses the sexually differentiating displacement whereby woman is made to bear the burden of specularity—to function as image, so that her male counterpart can align himself with the camera/gaze, and so regain his lost humanist heritage.

The Camera as Social Apparatus

As I have already indicated, one of the material practices through which *Bilder* shows the disjunction of camera/gaze from eye to be socially specified is scale photography. In the Meydenbauer story, scale photography represents the deployment of the camera for purposes of quantification. However, *Bilder* is careful to note that if it can be used for such ends that is because the images it produces are themselves numerically based. The "rules of projective geometry," as the voice-over at one point emphasizes, precede "depiction by photographic means…Leonardo depict[ed] the whole earth, projected onto the surface the level of the two-dimensional picture. Dürer, again, took measurements of objects, from the study of nature he obtained numbers and rules. The calculating machines of today make pictures out of numbers and rules. Here Piero della Francesca, then pictures into measurements, today measurements into pictures." The camera/gaze thus emerges within *Bilder* as an apparatus for the production of quantified and quantifiable images. From this vantage point, the invention of the camera represents less a moment of rupture with earlier visual technologies than the moment at which their implicit disjuncture from the eye becomes manifest. (As I will indicate later in this chapter, *Bilder* repeatedly associates the eye with a highly subjectivized and nonquantifiable vision.)

figure 51

The use of aerial photography during World War II provides another of the material practices through which *Bilder* defines the camera, and through which it dramatizes its autonomy from the look. The second time the female commentator utters the words "'Enlightenment'—'*Aufklärung*'—that is a word in the history of ideas," she adds, "In German, '*Aufklärung*' also has a military meaning: reconnaissance. Flight reconnaissance." Over a series of shots showing airplanes on a bombing mission, a camera strapped to a pigeon, a map designating the itinerary of a bombing mission, an aerial photograph of Auschwitz, Farocki looking at the latter, military figures studying war photographs, and an aerial view of a war production plant, the voice-over recounts the story behind the production of the Auschwitz photograph [figure 51], an image to which the film will repeatedly return:

American aircraft had taken off in Foggia, Italy, and flown towards targets in Silesia—factories for synthetic petrol and rubber…. On the flight over the IG Farben company factory still under construction, a pilot clicked his camera shutter and took photographs of the Auschwitz concentration camp…. The pictures taken in April 1944 arrived for evaluation in Medmenhan, England. The analysts discovered a power station, a carbide factory, a factory under construction for

Buna and another for petrol hydrenation. They were not under orders to look for the Auschwitz camp, and thus they did not find it.

Not only does the camera/gaze here manifestly "apprehend" what the human eye cannot, but the eye also seems strikingly handicapped by its historical and institutional placement, as if to suggest that military control extends beyond behavior, speech, dress, and bodily posture to the very sensory organs themselves. This sequence indicates, in other words, that military discipline and the logic of warfare function to hyperbolize the distance separating look from camera/gaze, and to subordinate the former completely to the latter. The voice-over adds that the photograph of Auschwitz remained imperceptible to the human viewer until 1977, when it was studied by two CIA employees, whose historical and institutional vantage finally rendered it legible.

Slightly later in *Bilder,* one of the images from this aerial montage is repeated, as the voice-over probes more deeply into the ways in which the military establishment both exploited and helped to define the autonomy of the camera/gaze from the eye during the twentieth century. Over a photograph recording some of the destruction effected during a bombing mission, the commentator observes, "Because bomber pilots cannot properly estimate whether they have hit their target and to what effect, in World War II they began to equip bomber planes with cameras." A moment later she adds, "The bomber pilots had the first workplace in which a camera was employed to control effectivity," indicating again that at the point where the camera/gaze intersects with the military establishment it is not only distinct from, but antinomic to, the eye. If cameras were placed in World War II bomber planes, *Bilder* suggests, it was as much to "observe" the pilots as to record what they could not see. The next sequence, which shows a computerized camera checking the specifications of a factory-produced door, also stresses the usefulness of the camera as a mechanism for controlling worker efficiency, now not merely in bomber planes, but in industrial sites as well.

But *Bilder* is not content merely to analogize war and industrial production. Immediately after commenting on the inability of the Allied analysts to see Auschwitz in the aerial photographs taken on April 4, 1944, the voice-over remarks, "How close the one is to the other: the industry—the camp." As these words are spoken, Farocki shows with his thumb and forefinger how little geographical and political distance separates the IG Farben plant from Auschwitz on an aerial photograph. *Bilder* thus connects the camera/gaze not only to scale measurement and modern warfare, but also to mass production. And once again that connection is enabled by the disjunction of optical apparatus and look, to which it in turn gives new meaning.

A lengthy meditation on metal pressing follows the sequence devoted to the aerial photographs of Auschwitz. Like the Hannover footage, this meditation does not at first seem related to the rest of the film. However, it ultimately permits *Bilder* to articulate the antinomy of camera/gaze and eye in terms which make evident photography's intimate relation to industrial production, and which tighten the linkage between industry and modern war.

At first, the voice-over stresses the apparent affinities between photography and metal pressing; coexisting for over a century, both are forms of reproduction. Moreover, during World War II, metal sheets were pressed "for searchlights to show up aircraft in the sky." The airplanes, in their turn, "threw light bombs, like a lightning flash, to illuminate the earth for a photo." However, the voice-over makes clear these were only apparent convergences, made possible by what Marx would call "uneven development." Although not much older than photography, metal pressing is shown to represent a radically different form of reproduction. "The skill of metal pressing traces back to the trades of belt-maker and armoury smith," the voice-over remarks. The still photographs over which the commentator speaks, moreover, stress the intimate connection between the metal presser and the object he produces [figures 52 and 53]; they attest to the subordination of hammer and metal press to the human hand and eye, and reveal the traces left on the end product by the force of each blow. Although contemporaneous with photography, metal pressing was originally artisanal, and even today employs the hand in a quasiartisanal capacity. It is hence inimical to twentieth-century war production, which is—*Bilder* insists—"mass production."

figure 52   figure 53

The camera/gaze is consequently shown to represent a very different form of reproduction from metal pressing. First of all, as we have already seen, it inverts the hierarchy implicit in the relation of worker to tool. Whereas the metal presser's hammer is subordinate to his arm, the camera might be said to "use" the pilot who is obliged to click its shutter every time he drops a bomb. Moreover, precisely because of its autonomy from the human eye—because, as Benjamin would say, it constitutes a *mechanical* form of reproduction[20]—the camera can be used not only for the surveillance of pilot and target, but also for the *mass production* of images, a production in excess of both the human worker and the human consumer. As if further to emphasize this last point, the voice-over twice maintains that "more pictures of the world [were taken during World War II] than the eyes of the soldiers [were] capable" of "consuming" or "evaluating."

Bilder suggests that the field of vision implied by the camera/gaze has also been shaped in part by the uses to which the institution of the police has put that apparatus, uses which again capitalize on the latter's autonomy from the eye. However, since what is at issue in police photography is less its capacity to quantify, participate in mass production, or regulate efficiency, than its capacity to name and identify, it situates the subject much more hyperbolically within spectacle than do the other material practices that *Bilder* studies. The moment when *Bilder* introduces police photography is consequently the moment when it first shifts attention dramatically away from what it means to photograph, to what it means to be photographed.

How to Face a Camera

At the beginning of the section in which *Bilder* first addresses the issue of police photography, the commentator asks: "How to face a camera?" Not surprisingly, even the partial answer which the film gives to this question immediately necessitates an engagement with those two forms of social difference which are most dependent upon a visual articulation: gender and race. As the question is posed, we are shown a medium close-up image of an Algerian woman in native dress and jewelry [figure 54], followed by a series of others [figures 55–58].

figure 54

At first glance, these images seem fully compatible with the sequence that begins with the Dürer drawing, and concludes with the image of the Dior model. As I have already indicated, through the attention *Bilder* lavishes upon the heavily made-up eye of that model, it makes clear that, although every subject depends upon the "affirmation" of the camera/gaze, visibility is differentially distributed within the domain of representation. Woman is often obliged to "live" hers much more fully than is her male counterpart, who is within many discourses and material practices aligned with the camera/gaze. Consequently, within certain cultural contexts the female subject might be said to signify not only "lack," but "spectacle." By focusing on another female face at the point that the voice-over asks: "How to face a camera?" *Bilder* appears intent upon reiterating that point.

figure 55

figure 56

figure 57

figure 58

However, it becomes almost immediately apparent that, in the case of the Algerian women, things are not so straightforward. The image which accompanies the question "How to face a camera?" reminds us that although Western society maintains a close connection between the terms "woman" and "spectacle," sexual difference can manifest itself in other ways within the field of vision, and can be complicated by other kinds of culturally constituted differences—in this case, most manifestly, by race.

The images of Algerian women around which this sequence is organized are eventually shown to derive from the pages of a book. The voice-over explains that these images are identity photographs, produced for the French colonial authorities in 1960 by a conscript soldier, Marc Garanger, for policing purposes. For the French, to rule is to render visible and "legible." Again, the word "*Aufklärung*" comes into play, now in the sense of "clearing up the case." French rule also implies the imposition of a Western system of sexual differentiation, for the camera/gaze clearly functions to constitute these Algerian women not merely as colonial subjects, but also as subjects who are, within a Western context, manifestly female. However, *Bilder* is at pains to show that the enactment of this imperative violates the terms through which Algerian culture itself constructs sexual difference; "femininity" there demands the veil, and hence signifies public invisibility.

Bilder does not adjudicate between these two systems of sexual differentiation, but it does work to challenge the popular Western assumption that removing the veil from the face of the Algerian woman would in all situations represent a "liberation." The voice-over suggests that, in addition to rendering its wearer publicly invisible, the veil provides a kind of shield. It provides protection not so much from the gaze—which is itself both "unapprehensible" and neutral, and is, in some guise, necessarily already a part of these women's lives—as from that experience of it which is mediated by the colonial deployment of the camera, a deployment which can only be characterized as a violation and subjugation. "The horror of being photographed for the first time," the commentator observes over the second image in this sequence. "The year 1960 in Algeria: women are photographed for the first time. They are to be issued with identity cards. Faces which up till then had worn the veil. Only those close have looked on these faces without the veil—family and household members." Thus, although within the context of Algerian culture the veil is obviously one of the primary signifiers of woman's subordinate status, it performs a very different function within the context of French colonialism.

A moment later, the commentator suggests that when attempting to account for the "horror of being photographed for the first time" it is necessary to take into account not only the material practices in which the camera/gaze is embedded, and through which it derives its value, but the representational logic specific to that apparatus. She approaches this logic by differentiating the camera once again from the eye. "When one looks into the face of an intimate," the commentator observes, "one also brings in something of the shared past. The photograph captures the moment and thus crops away past and future."

The commentator also draws attention to another of the camera's intrinsic properties, one which makes it such a potent metaphor for the gaze. She suggests that the photograph severs a moment from the temporal continuum and "carries" it away to another domain. She thus comments on that feature of photography which most distinguishes it from other representational systems—the fact that it conventionally requires the physical presence of an object in order to produce an image of it. This feature has inspired many paeans to the "realism" of photography and its sister art, cinema, but *Bilder* presents a very different argument. It suggests that photography intervenes in a real in which it

paradoxically cannot participate, a real which it can, in fact, only work to derealize. It is, consequently, precisely an antirealist representational system.

Bilder thus accounts for photography in terms very similar to those suggested by Metz in "Photography and Fetishism." In that text, he characterizes photography as "a cut inside the referent," by which he means that it produces images
only by seizing upon the real. This capture permits a piece of the real to escape
the vicissitudes of time, but only at the cost of a kind of death. "The snapshot,
like death," Metz writes, "is an instantaneous abduction of the object out of the
world into another world, into another kind of time…. the photographic *take* is
immediate and definitive…. Photography…cuts off a piece of [the referent], a
fragment, a part object, for a long immobile travel of no return."[21] Although the
photograph might be said to immortalize the moment it depicts, Metz suggests,
it does so only through a devitalizing sublation, by lifting that moment out of life
into the frame of representation. The preservation photography affords is thus
simultaneously a destruction, a point upon which—as we will see—*Bilder* also
insists more than once.

Between the first and second parts of the Algerian sequence is a set of images
suggesting another way in which photography acts destructively upon the real,
and one which provides a more direct answer to the question of what it means
to face the camera/gaze. A woman's face appears on a blue video screen, and has
superimposed upon it, first, the spectacles and eyes of two other people, then, the
hair and mouth of another [figure 59]. Ostensibly a demonstration of the
process whereby a composite police "sketch" is produced for purposes of apprehending a suspect, this sequence brilliantly illustrates the projection of the screen
onto the subject by the camera/gaze.[22] It consequently serves as an important
reminder that the camera/gaze intervenes in the real not only by abducting it, but
also by installing the image in its place.

figure 59

If Metz's "Photography and Fetish" provides an exemplary gloss of *Bilder*'s
first account of the relationship of photograph to referent, a passage from
Barthes's *Camera Lucida* offers the definitive commentary on that implied by

the composite "sketch." Perhaps because Barthes is concerned here less with the relation of the camera/gaze to the object than with the *subject's* relation to the camera/gaze—because, that is, he attempts to answer precisely the question "How to face the camera?"—the screen comes into focus for him in a way that it does not for Metz. Barthes stresses that when the subject faces the camera/gaze something is conjured into existence which was not there before, something which he calls "an other body," and "myself as other." "Once I feel myself observed by the [camera] lens," he writes, "everything changes: I constitute myself in the process of 'posing.' I instantaneously make another body for myself, I transform myself in advance into an image…. I feel that the Photograph creates my body or mortifies it…. the Photograph is the advent of myself as other, a cunning dissociation of consciousness from identity."[23]

In this passage, Barthes articulates the relation of subject to camera in ways that enable us to see why the camera has survived for a century and a half as a privileged figuration of the gaze. Like the camera, the gaze confers identity only through an irreducibly exterior image which intervenes between it and the subject. And like the camera, the gaze provides the subject with a specular body at the same time that it abolishes his or her existential body. Death, in other words, is something that happens to the real within which the camera intervenes, as well as to the real that it carries away. In this respect, the photograph resembles the screen, which confers identity upon the subject only at the expense of his or her "being."[24]

Of course, I am far from suggesting that the Algerian women whose photographs *Bilder* shows us came into existence as subjects only at the moment that the colonial camera was trained upon them, and provided them with a specular image. What is perhaps most immediately striking about the faces shown by these photographs is how fully culturally inscribed they are. Indeed, in several cases those faces are so elaborately tattooed that it almost seems as though the screen has been directly grafted onto them, in a literalization of that three-dimensional photography which Roger Caillois mentions in his essay on mimicry.[25] So how then are we to understand the "cut inside the referent" in relation to the Algerian sequence?

I would like to propose a two-fold answer to this question and, in so doing, to indicate further how the representational logic of the camera can be both exploited and inflected by a material practice—in this case, colonialism. Insofar as none of us can ever be fully "inside" either language or the images which define us, each utterance and each specular captation might be said to induce all over again the "fading" of our being. To face the camera/gaze is, then, always to experience a certain "horror" or "mortification," even as we embrace its constitutive effects. However, there is also a way in which the French colonial camera might be said to repeat the same drama at another level, this time by installing its own screen in place of the Algerian screen. With the "clicking" of Garanger's camera shutter, the Algerian screen "fades" away, and is replaced by one connoting "exoticism," "primitivism," "subordinate race," and a European notion of femininity ("woman as spectacle"). The one image, emblematized by the veil, must "die" in order for the other to prevail.

Just as *Bilder* is not content merely to dramatize the disjunction of camera and eye, but insists on showing some material specifications of that disjuncture, as well, so it not only foregrounds the photograph's memorial function and mortifying effect, but also draws attention to some of the extrinsic uses to which they have been put. The film repeatedly focuses on the military deployment of the camera/gaze as one which literalizes these two features of photography. Thus, we learn that in addition to being the first to use the camera for scale measurement Meydenbauer also "initiated the establishment of memorial archives [for the military], which creates a correlation, in the sense that the military destroy and the curators of monuments act to preserve." Subsequently, we are shown an extraordinary image of a World War II bomb approaching its target, a moment before its destruction [figure 60]. The voice-over comments, "The preserving photograph, the destroying bomb—these two now press together." *Bilder* thus suggests that the photograph's memorial function is so closely imbricated with its mortifying effect that it becomes the ideal agent for representing all that has fallen under the sentence of death.

figure 60

The question "How to face a camera?" gives rise to a second meditation on a photographic image of a woman. Because that photograph shows a Jewish prisoner immediately after her arrival in Auschwitz, and presumably shortly before her death, it again marks the point of conjunction for a literal memorialization and mortification. "The camp run by the SS shall bring her to destruction and the photographer who captures her beauty for posterity is from this same SS," observes the voice-over. "How the two elements interplay, preservation and destruction!"

As in the sequence involving the Algerian women, questions of sexual and racial difference are once again complexly at the forefront of this meditation upon the subject's relation to the camera/gaze. The image, which is interrogated both by the voice-over and by Farocki's camera,[26] which frames it in three different ways, shows, in its fullest exposure, the figure of a woman wearing a star of David moving in medium shot in front of a line of Jewish men being inspected by a Nazi soldier [figure 61]. She occupies the center of the frame, and looks toward the camera/gaze which photographs her. This image gives way to two others, produced through a reframing of the same photograph. The first of these variants relocates the Jewish woman on the right side of the image [figure 62], in a position occupied by the human eye in the various drawings and diagrams schematizing the field of vision. It thereby differentiates her look—which organizes the image—from the gaze. The second variant centers her in close-up [figure 63], making her drama the focal point of the photograph. Over these three images, the commentator utters these words:

figure 61

figure 62

figure 63

A woman has arrived at Auschwitz; the camera captures her in movement. The photographer has his camera installed and as the woman passes by he clicks the shutter—in the same way he would cast a glance at her in the street, because she is beautiful. The woman understands how to pose her face so as to catch the eye of the photographer, and how to look with a slight sideways glance. On a boulevard she would look in the same way just past a man casting his eye over her at a shop window, and with this sideways glance she seeks to displace herself into a world of boulevards, men, and shop windows. Far from here.

At first, this text is shocking in its imputation to the Jewish woman and her Nazi photographer of viewing relations which we associate with "normality," and which seem unthinkable within a context like Auschwitz. However, one of the primary functions of this sequence is to stress that, although the male subject is at most a "functionary" of the camera/gaze, the camera is defined as a masculine extension through a whole confluence of institutional, discursive, and representational determinants. At least in the West, the same determinants posit the female subject as the specular object par excellence. Given how over-determined these relations are, there would seem to be no context—even one as given over to death as Auschwitz—in which they could not be somehow inscribed.

The star of David specularizes the Jewish woman in a second way, as well, reminding us that Auschwitz, like other Nazi concentration camps, subjected its inmates to a hyperbolic visibility, stripping them of their clothes and possessions, and maintaining those who were not immediately consigned to death under an unceasing surveillance. This surveillance is but a further extension of the ideology of "detection" through which the Nazis attempted to root out the Jewish body; within this ideology, "Jewishness" was defined as a compelling series of visual signifiers.

At first, these two kinds of visibility would seem to compound or magnify each other. However, as with the sequence devoted to the identity photographs, things are not so simple here. The narrative through which *Bilder* reads the photograph of the Jewish woman defines the specular relations by means of which sexual difference conventionally manifests itself within the Western field of vision as a refuge from those implied by Auschwitz. It thereby suggests that Nazism not only placed the Jewish body hyperbolically within spectacle, but also interposed between it and the camera/gaze a much more profoundly dei-dealizing screen than that through which "femininity" is conjured into existence—or, to state the case more precisely, one without femininity's erotic equivocations.

In the sequence devoted to the Jewish woman, how one is seen becomes literally a matter of life or death. The critical problem faced by the Auschwitz inmate is how to be "photographed" differently—how to motivate the mobilization of another screen. But *Bilder* narrativizes this crisis in a way that once again troubles our usual ways of thinking about visuality and sexual difference.

In the interpretation of the photograph offered by the commentator, the Jewish woman attempts to situate herself elsewhere, in a world "far from here," by soliciting the male look and the screen of "femininity," rather than, for instance, asserting her "Germanness." In this imagined situation, racial difference preempts sexual difference; the inscription of "Jewishness" works to cancel out gender. *Bilder* thus suggests that the screen of "femininity" is always more available to certain female subjects than to others. Although we have grown accustomed to thinking of that screen in terms of the disadvantages it imposes, it also implies certain limited privileges, and those privileges may be precluded by race, class, age, nationality, and other forms of social discrimination.

In addition to *Bilder*'s invocation of sexual difference in the context of Auschwitz, audiences are sometimes disturbed by its superimposition of a narrative on the image of the Jewish woman. We are invited to "see" something which is not "in" the photograph. The voice-over performs a similar function later in the film. As we look at a detail from another photograph taken by a Nazi camera—this time, a close-up of a Jewish girl standing in an Auschwitz line [figure 64]—the voice-over remarks, "Among the shaven heads, a girl who smiles. In Auschwitz, apart from death and work, there was a black market, there were love stories and resistance groups." To object to the commentary for imputing to these two photographs meaning which was not available to the camera/gaze, and which cannot be historically documented, is to overlook another crucial feature of *Bilder*'s interrogation of the visual field—its discourse on the human look.

figure 64

The Resistant Look

As I indicated earlier, I derive my distinction between the gaze and the eye from Lacan. However, *Seminar XI* is much more expansive about the gaze than the eye. In passing, Lacan comments there on a passage from Sartre's *Being and Nothingness* which suggests that the look is perhaps most likely to experience the exteriority of the gaze and to feel shame in relation to it from a keyhole position (84).[27] Lacan also proposes that the eye experiences its dislocation from the gaze as castration (73). These few references to the economy of the look led me to propose in *Male Subjectivity at the Margins* that, unlike the gaze, the look is within desire. I also suggested that it is inscribed by lack, with which it is centrally concerned (130). While these few remarks still seem to me to touch upon something fundamental about the look, they constitute only the most preliminary form of a definition. However, the textual matrix that has made possible this attempt at a historical specification of the gaze, and its more precise differentiation from the human eye, also facilitates a somewhat fuller elaboration of the look.

As we have seen, the first of the triangles from *Four Fundamental Concepts* places what it calls the "image" between the eye and the object, indicating that our apprehension of the world is always mediated by representation. While still insisting upon this mediation, I now want to emphasize more than previously the "errant" nature of the look, by which I mean not only its susceptibility to *méconnaissance,* but also its resistance to absolute tyranny by the material practices that work to determine how and what it sees. Although human vision always occurs through the frame of representation, it is not always easy to control which frame is mobilized in a given viewing situation. As Norman Bryson has eloquently suggested, "The life of vision is one of endless wanderlust, and in its carnal form the eye is nothing but desire."[28]

In *Techniques of the Observer,* Crary argues against the absolute opposition that is usually maintained between photography, on the one hand, and late romanticism and modernism, on the other—an opposition made on the basis of the one's ostensible objectivity, and the other's manifest subjectivity. He suggests that both dramatize the dislocation of eye from gaze, but to different ends. In the case of photography, the separation of look from camera works to buttress the camera's claims to a truthful and scientific vision. In the case of romanticism and early modernism, the reverse is true; freed from its alignment with the optical apparatuses which define objective vision, and firmly rooted in a body which often threatens to overwhelm it, the eye can abandon its vain project to see what the camera sees, and instead see what it cannot. As Crary puts it at one point, "Once vision became relocated in the subjectivity of the observer, two intertwined paths opened up. One led out toward all the multiple affirmations of the sovereignty and autonomy of vision derived from this newly empowered body.... The other path was toward the increasing standardization and regulation of the observer that issued from knowledge of [the] visionary body" (150).

But even as I draw upon Crary's excellent formulation, I want once again to soften the severity of its historical demarcations. While it is indisputable that romanticism and early modernism exploited and celebrated subjective vision to a hitherto unprecedented degree, we cannot impute to those movements the inception of such vision. If, as I have been arguing, the look has never coincided with the gaze (although certain optical technologies might have worked to deny the distance which separates them), then the look has never possessed the mastering and constitutive functions that have traditionally been attributed to it. The body to which it stubbornly belongs has also always been positioned within spectacle. Finally, the look has all along possessed the capacity to see otherwise from and even in contradiction to the gaze. The eye is always to some degree resistant to the discourses which seek to master and regulate it, and can even, on occasion, dramatically oppose the representational logic and material practices which specify exemplary vision at a given moment in time.

The commentator of *Bilder* repeatedly associates the look with the capacity to see things that the camera/gaze cannot see. The first occasion on which it does so provides a startlingly direct dramatization of Crary's suggestion that late romanticism and modernism celebrated the independence of the eye from the optical devices which earlier defined it. Coming immediately after the sequence beginning with the Dürer drawing and concluding with the model's eye is a sequence showing art students sketching female nudes. Although they are all ostensibly drawing the same model, a black woman, there is no consistency of representation from one easel to another. As *Bilder* emphasizes when it returns later to more footage from the same modeling session, each student "sees" something different from every other student [figures 65–67] and—even more dramatically—from the camera [figure 68]. *Bilder* focuses at length on the motions of a

figure 65

figure 66

figure 67

figure 68

hand which repeatedly blurs and shifts the outer boundaries of the human form it is in the process of drawing. Not only does it thereby suggest the impossibility of fixing those boundaries once and for all, but it also inscribes the hesitations and passions of the drawing hand itself, as if to insist upon the corporeal locus of the eye.

When the commentator distinguishes the eye from the camera/gaze in the meditation on the Algerian photos, she stresses that whereas the camera/gaze "captures the moment and thus crops away past and future," the eye is capable of putting the present once again in contact with what went before. "When one looks into the face of an intimate," she observes, "one also brings in something of a shared past." *Bilder* thus proposes that if the camera/gaze performs a memorial function, the look is allied to something which is ostensibly related to that function, but is in fact very different: memory. Whereas photography performs its memorial function by lifting an object out of time and immortalizing it forever in a particular form, memory is all about temporality and change. It apprehends the other less as a clearly delineated object than as a complex and constantly shifting conglomeration of images and values.

The commentator makes this point even more forcefully later in the film. As we look at more of the identity photographs of Algerian women taken by Marc Garanger, she differentiates "the picture of a human being"—by which she seems to map out the domain of the eye—from what the camera/gaze can "see" in terms of the instability and uncertainty of the eye's object of vision. Significantly, she also valorizes the indeterminacy of that "picture" over the determinacy of the identity photograph:

> The police, here and elsewhere, [have] on file photographs of millions of people, criminal suspects. How can the face of a human be described with certainty so that it can be recognized by everyone? By everyone—also a machine. How to describe a face? The police [are] not yet able to register the characteristics of a human face that remain the same, in youth and old age, in happiness and in sorrow. The police [do] not know what it is, the picture of a [human being].

Elsewhere, *Bilder* reiterates the connection between the look and recollection, while extending the semantic range of memory. At one point, as the camera shows us some drawings by Alfred Kantor, a concentration camp survivor, the commentator associates the look with what might be called the "memory trace." "Alfred Kantor, who survived three concentration camps, including Auschwitz, drew these pictures immediately after the Liberation," she remarks. Some were "based on sketches kept by fellow-prisoners, [but] most [were] based on his own visual imprints." To associate the look with memories or visual imprints is to attest once again to its ever-changing relation to a given object. It is also to make evident once again its subjective basis. In *The Interpretation of Dreams,* Freud suggests that the flow of perceptions across the psyche leaves behind memory "traces" or imprints. These memory traces are far from providing a registration of the "real."[29] As perceptions flow across the psyche, prior to arriving at consciousness, they are worked over in all kinds of ways by censorship and fantasy, and this process is a continuing one at the level of memory.

Given its unrealiability as a gauge of external reality, the look might seem a strange site at which to locate resistance, but *Bilder* does not hesitate to do so. Late in the film, over a series of concentration camp photographs, the voice-over tells a story which those photographs manifestly fail to dramatize. That story involves two Auschwitz inmates who escaped from the camp, reached Slovakia, and wrote a report about the "final solution." The commentator remarks on the riskiness of their enterprise in terms which link it directly to an embodied, mortal, yet nevertheless resistant look. She first suggests as a general principle that "it was dangerous to be an eyewitness" to events at Auschwitz, and then twice characterizes the testimony offered by the two escapees as "[giving] witness." And once again, memory plays a central role in this specular revolt; Wetzler, the voice-over notes, "had worked in the clerical office" of Auschwitz, where he "committed to memory the date, country of origin and the number of the new arrivals."

At one point, the commentator stresses the "factual" nature of the visual imprints that certain concentration camp survivors carried away from Auschwitz, and hence the capacity of those imprints to substitute for photographs. However, almost immediately, she once again foregrounds the incommensurability of the imprints with photographs. Kantor's visual imprints show a place "which cannot possibly be conveyed by photographic images." They communicate a "truth" which the camera/gaze could never capture, precisely because it "sees" with a mechanical and decorporealized lens—a truth which is inseparable from the subjective and embodied experience of being a Jewish inmate in a Nazi concentration camp.

Although this "truth" lacks temporal stability and formal coherence, and although it cannot be "objectively" verified, it is elsewhere shown to provide the basis for a political revolt. *Bilder* concludes with an account of an uprising on the part of a group of Auschwitz inmates which resulted in the partial destruction of a crematorium, and it overtly links this uprising to its larger disquisition upon spectacle and vision. As the camera focuses on a photograph showing lines of handwritten numbers, each separated from the others by a comma [figure 69], the voice-over induces us to visualize once more what that apparatus cannot show: "Numbers once again. These numbers are coded messages from Auschwitz prisoners who belonged to a resistance group. They set the date for an uprising." A close-up of this photograph provides the penultimate image of *Bilder*

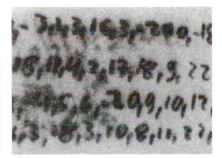

figure 69   *figure 70*

[figure 70], and as it materializes the commentator links its numbers, like those which underpin the system of perspective, to the production of an image: "Despair, and a heroic courage," she concludes, "made out of these numbers a picture." However, the numbers serving as coded messages for a prisoner revolt have nothing whatever to do with mathematical systematization and quantification; what they permit us to "see" is something inapprehensible by the camera/gaze.

As should be evident by now, the disjunctive and oppositional relation between the camera/gaze and the look is often materialized in *Bilder* through the disequivalence of photographic image and word. As we have seen, the commentator speaks "over" the photographs of the Algerian women and the Jewish concentration camp inmate. She thereby attempts to apprehend and to make us apprehend something the photographs themselves cannot show: the subjective experience of being "inside" those particular bodies, as a camera/gaze, caught in a particular representational system, and embedded in certain material practices, was trained upon them.

In the Algerian sequence, this process is taken even further. Farocki's hand literally reveils the face of one Algerian woman [figure 71] as the commentator says, "The veil covers mouth, nose and cheeks and leaves the eyes free." He then covers first the mouth and nose of another woman, and later her eyes [figure 72], as the commentator adds, "The eyes must be accustomed to meet a strange gaze. The mouth cannot be accustomed to being looked at." The voice-over is thus at moments closely aligned with the look. It articulates or bears witness to what the photograph might be said actively to repress—the corporeal and psychic "reality" of being female and Algerian in a French colony in 1960, or female and Jewish in Germany in the early 1940s.

Thus, *Bilder der Welt und Inschrift des Krieges* does more than specify some of the intrinsic and extrinsic relations which constitute that apparatus which, more than any other, still defines the gaze within Western culture, and thereby facilitate a better understanding of what is both historical and transhistorical within

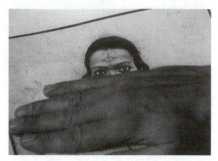

figure 71

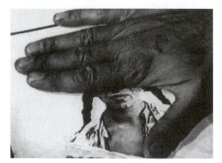

figure 72

the field of vision. It also does more than show that the look is within spectacle, and that it is coerced in all kinds of ways by the material practices and representational logic through which the camera/gaze makes itself felt. Farocki's film also indicates that precisely because the look is located within desire, temporality and the body, it can reanimate and open to change what the camera/gaze would both mortify and memorialize. It can consequently provide the locus for a resistant and even transformative vision.

The final shot of *Bilder* attests precisely to that transformative potential. It shows an image of Auschwitz taken after the partial destruction of Crematorium 4 (figure 73). Although it is ostensibly a product of aerial photography, one of the material practices which Bilder has shown to define the camera/gaze, it is not legible within the terms of that representational system; it resembles an abstract painting more than a photograph. Moreover, because the last words spoken by the commentator ultimately refer to this image, it might be said to emerge out of very different numbers than those underpinning perspective—out of those shown in the penultimate shot. Since there is a cause-and-effect logic implicit in the juxtaposition of that shot's ink-spotted notations with the photograph of the damaged crematorium, the one making possible the other, *Bilder* here suggests both the oppositional potential of the look, and its capacity to intervene within the field of vision. In other words, it underscores the capacity of the look not merely to see what is inapprehensible to the camera/gaze, but also to alter what that apparatus "photographs." The words with which Sally Potter concludes *The Gold Diggers* might thus serve as a second epigraph to the "picture" generated by the handwritten numbers: "I know that even as I look and even as I see, I am changing what is there."

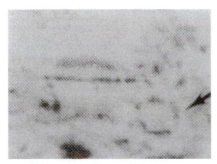

figure 73

5

The Look

In the previous chapter, I distinguished the look from the gaze on the basis of the look's emplacement within spectacle, the body, temporality, and desire. I also argued that although this emplacement is limiting in certain respects, it is enabling in others. Some very strong claims were advanced on behalf of the look's consequent capacity to circumvent the directives placed upon it to see in certain ways. However, these claims were made without theoretical "collateral." Because I was primarily concerned with the gaze in Chapter 4, I dealt with the look there only within the localized context of *Bilder der Welt und Inschrift des Krieges*. The moment has now come for a more paradigmatic account of that visual agency, along with the forces that coerce it.

The human eye cannot simply be taken at face value. In addition to being the locus of visual perception, it is the faculty through which the image is appropriated in the guise of "self." It also represents one of the primary axes along which projection occurs, and the most classic perceptual locus of disavowal. Finally, the look regularly imputes to itself powers which do not belong to it, powers which reside elsewhere in the field of vision, and which restrict what it can see. My account of the eye will consequently begin not where the previous chapter left off, with a triumphant affirmation of that organ's contestatory capabilities, but with a deconstruction, via Sartre and Lacan, of its fantasy of mastery and transcendence, and a specification of the social and psychic limitations which constrain it. Only then will I embark upon the difficult task of elaborating something which is to be found in neither *Being and Nothingness* nor *Four Fundamental Concepts of Psycho-Analysis*—something that I will call the "productive look." It is my contention that if that concept is to have any theoretical validity, it must emerge *inside* rather than *outside* the discursive space of psychoanalysis. Consequently, although psychoanalysis is notoriously inhospitable to the notion of "agency," it is there that I propose to elaborate the productivity of the look.

Sartre and Le Regard

In *Being and Nothingness,* which was first published in French in 1943, Sartre isolates and critiques the fantasy which is most specific to the look *as look*. In the process, he strips the look of a number of attributes which it often falsely imputes to itself. He then relocates those attributes elsewhere—at the site of what he calls "*le regard.*" Sartre begins his account of the visual field by drawing a comparison between two very different acts of looking. In the first, a voyeur peers through the keyhole of a door. He[1] is so completely engrossed in the act of seeing that he is devoid of self-consciousness—so absorbed in the spectacle in front of him that his "very being" escapes him. As Sartre explains it, "There is nothing *there* but a pure nothingness encircling a certain objective ensemble and throwing it into relief outline upon the world."[2] This "nothingness" is paradoxically synonymous with a certain transcendence—a transcendence of spectacle, of the body, and, ultimately, of self.

But, suddenly, the voyeur hears footsteps in the hall or the rustle of leaves on the ground, and the first visual tableau gives way to a second. He is conjured out of nothingness into existence in the guise of an image for that Other who is evoked by the footsteps or the leaves. The voyeur now vibrates with an awareness of himself-as-spectacle, and through that awareness a consciousness of self is produced in him. This "being seen" is precipitated in the voyeur by what Sartre calls "*le regard.*"

Sartre associates this experience of specularity with a whole series of psychic "symptoms," all of which are somehow indicative of the condition of being in a relation of exteriority to one's self. These symptoms are then imaginarily converted into a list of directly antithetical values to produce *le regard.* The subject of whom the voyeur is emblematic suffers his specularity initially as the loss of transcendence (262–63). His experience of himself as a "pure" look, exterior to the field of vision, gives way to the disquieting realization that he is himself immanently in that field, "on-view." And his assumption of his own look as the point in relation to which the world is ordered yields to the disorienting realization that the world assumes its coherence in relation to a radically other position, one which is inaccessible to him. His transcendence is consequently, as Sartre puts it, "transcended" (263), and the world flows away from his look (261).

The voyeur's apprehension of his own specularity also leads to the discovery that he has his "foundations" outside himself, and that he "exists for the Other" (260, 261). The fact that this apprehension is conducive for Sartre primarily to "shame" suggests that to exist for the Other implies for him not only a state of dependency, but also a condition of guilt. To be seen is to be judged and found wanting, says Sartre at one point (261). A later passage from *Being and Nothingness* introduces an even more insistently Christian thematics. To function as spectacle, and so to exist for the Other, is to lapse into a "fallen" state (288–89).

Finally, to apprehend one's own specularity is to find oneself in circumstances which are inimical to the illusion that one is "master" of the "situation" (265). As this last characterization would suggest, Sartre imports into the field of vision a Hegelian, as well as a Christian, thematics. To be seen is to be "the object of values which come to qualify me without my being able to act on this qualification or even to know it" (267);[3] to be "the instrument of possibilities which are not my possibilities"; and to be constituted "as a means to ends of which I am ignorant." It is thus to be stripped of mastery, and reduced to the condition of a slave (267–68).

The Other for whom the voyeur exists designates not only the position from which he is seen, but also the site toward which the world flows when it flows away from his look. This Other represents the limit of the voyeur's freedom, but is characterized by Sartre as himself infinitely free (270). Sartre also imputes to the Other an absolute autonomy. The voyeur, he suggests, cannot derive this Other from himself since the Other is self-present and self-conceiving, a kind of "I am who I am." He is the God (266) whose judgment induces shame (267), and who causes the world of which the voyeur is a part to be (271). Finally, this Other is the master to whom the voyeur is enslaved.

Although the oppositions of God and sinner and master and slave constitute centrally structuring terms within Sartre's account of *le regard*, another opposition is even more pivotal. At the heart of *Being and Nothingness* is the antithesis between subject and object, or, to be more precise, between the "pure" or "absolute" subject and an object which is its absolute opposite. "The Other is present to me everywhere as the one through whom I become an object," writes Sartre (280).[4] Both here and in a somewhat earlier passage from the same text, he not only insists on the impossibility of halting that ceaseless process of self-expropriation whereby I am referred outside of myself in the guise of an object, but also suggests that I can only be an object to a "pure subject," i.e., to someone who is himself incapable of becoming an object in turn. This subjectivity is somehow implied by my own objectivity, or, to be more precise, read off the latter as its precondition. "The Other is first the being for whom I am an object," writes Sartre, "the being *through* whom I gain my objectness. If I am to be able to conceive of even one of my properties in the objective mode, then the

Other is already given. He is given not as a being of my universe but as a pure subject" (270).

Sartre characterizes this "pure subject" in terms that are so in excess of human capacities that it ultimately becomes a phantom category, one which cannot be associated with an actual pair of eyes. Any attempt to effect that condensation has one of two results: either *le regard* seems somehow to float in front of the eyes with which it is confused (258), or the eyes come into focus and *le regard* evaporates, only to take up residence elsewhere (282). When Sartre finally suggests that it can best be defined as "the prenumerical presence of the Other," since although it can only be represented as a "One," it implies "the presence of an unnumbered reality of men" (281), he attests eloquently to the impossibility of punctually locating *le regard*—to the fact that it is at the same time everywhere and nowhere. This specular agency is finally specifiable more through its effects than its tangible properties. It could indeed be characterized as an "empty cause"—as an agency which is fantasized into existence on the basis of the voyeur's apprehension of his emplacement within the field of vision.

But although Sartre repeatedly stresses that *le regard* radically exceeds human possibilities, he consistently attributes to it human or at least anthropomorphically inflected functions—looking, creating, judging, dominating. He also suggests more than once that the voyeur's disempowerment is somehow simultaneous with the empowerment of the Other to whom he imputes *le regard;* the transcendence which is evacuated from one site is simply reinstated at the other, according to the logic of that by-now familiar "either you or me" binarism. The Other who is conjured into existence through the rustle of leaves or the sound of footsteps thus finally figures within Sartre's account less as a symbolic abstraction than as the imaginary rival, whose fabled attributes are as much a product of *méconnaissance* as were those originally claimed by the voyeur.

Valuable as Sartre's distinction between the eye and *le regard* is, and compelling as is the voyeuristic allegory through which he actualizes that distinction, his account of the visual field still remains far too "personalistic," a kind of fight to the death of looks. Also, although his insistence upon the eye's embodiment and specularity is of inestimable value to all feminist attempts to divest the male look of its false claim to be the gaze, Sartre reduces that organ to the status of a lackey or slave, devoid of power. He consequently makes it very difficult to attribute to the eye even a limited agency. In addition, Sartre imputes to *le regard* everything that he subtracts from the voyeur's look. He might thus be said not so much to deconstruct as to relocate the notion of a transcendental eye. Finally, Sartre misses the crucial opportunity implicit in the concept of the looked-at look—the opportunity to theorize it in relation not to objectivity, but to subjectivity. He fails to understand that latent in the voyeur's apprehension of the exteriority of *le regard* is the possibility of both coming to an awareness of the lack upon which the look pivots, and—in accepting this lack, which not only limits, but opens the door to the infinitude of desire—emerging as a subject in the strongest sense of that word.

I have so far avoided translating "*le regard.*" French has only this one word for vision, whereas English has two: "look" and "gaze." In *Four Fundamental Concepts of Psycho-Analysis,* the work to which I will turn next, Lacan, too, relies heavily on the only noun the French language provides for designating the activity of seeing. However, he distinguishes *le regard* insistently from the eye, and so from human vision. In his translation of *Four Fundamental Concepts,* Alan Sheridan translates "*le regard*" throughout as "the gaze," presumably because "gaze" is not so narrowly tied to actual seeing. In the pages that follow, I will be reserving the word "look" for the activity implied by the human eye, and counterposing it in a variety of ways to the gaze. However, because *Being and Nothingness* does not consistently differentiate the gaze from the look, but repeatedly "subjectivizes" the gaze, it was not possible to account for the Sartrean *le regard* through only one of those categories. I therefore attempted to signal their imbrication by preserving the French noun in my text.

Lacan and the Field of Vision

Although *Four Fundamental Concepts,* which was first published in France in 1973, directly engages with *Being and Nothingness* only once, it begs to be read in tandem with that text. Indeed, in some respects, Lacan's formulation seems to follow directly from Sartre's. As in *Being and Nothingness,* the Lacanian gaze is somehow at the same time everywhere and nowhere. It is simultaneously ubiquitous and "unapprehensible."[5] Moreover, once again, the gaze manifests itself more through its effects than through its source. It impresses itself upon us through the sensation each of us at times has of being held within the field of vision, of being given over to specularity.

But there are a number of ways in which Lacan's account of the gaze differs dramatically from Sartre's account of *le regard.* In fact, *Four Fundamental Concepts* often reads as a thoroughgoing reconceptualization of the Sartrean field of vision. Although in the one passage in which Lacan alludes to *Being and Nothingness* he refers to the double scenario in which the voyeur first looks through the keyhole and then experiences himself as a spectacle in relation to an unseen Other (84), he does not articulate the relation between the two parts of that scenario in terms of a simple displacement. Nor does he define that relation in terms of a reified subject/object opposition. Rather, he emphasizes the asymmetry of the *look* with which the voyeur peers through the keyhole, and the *gaze* with which he is surprised. He also provides a very different account of subjectivity.[6]

First, Lacan makes clear that the gaze—which represents for Sartre a "pure" or "absolute" subject—itself escapes altogether the category of the subject. Although he defines it at one point as "the presence of others as such" (84), he so relentlessly deanthropomorphizes it as to associate it in one passage with the "pulsatile, dazzling and spread out function" of light, and in another passage with the "function of *seeingness*" (89, 82). This "function" precedes any individual act of looking, and is that out of which the look somehow emerges (81–82), much as language might be said to preexist the subject and provide him or her with his or her signifying resources. The gaze is, in this respect, the manifestation of the symbolic within the field of vision.

Second, the category through which Lacan concretizes the gaze is not God or the master, but the camera (106). The camera, like God and master, represents one of the persistent screens through which we have traditionally apprehended the gaze. As I argued in the previous chapter, it has for over a century and a half provided the gaze with its primary metaphor. However, Lacan's choice of "camera" rather than "God" or "master" does not speak only to his contemporaneity. Nor does it attest either to a thoroughgoing secularism or a determined anti-Hegelianism. Rather, Lacan's metaphorization of the gaze as a camera represents that gesture through which he most energetically disassociates it not only from such psychoanalytically specific signifiers of subjectivity as "lack" and "desire," but also from such conventional designators of the human as "psyche," "spirit," or "soul."

Finally, Lacan desubjectivizes the gaze by stripping it of all of the qualitative functions which Sartre attributes to it. For Lacan, the gaze does not judge, create, or dominate. It does not even "look," in any real sense of the word, although the paucity of the English language sometimes obliges us to fall back upon that verb to signify its activity. Lacan metaphorizes the gaze as a camera so as to characterize it as an "apparatus" whose only function is to put us "in the picture." It does not determine what that "picture" will be, nor what it will mean for us to "be" there. Nor is it possessed of any intrinsic properties whereby we might truthfully "know" it. How we are "photographed," and the terms under which we experience our specularity, are the result of another agency altogether, as are the values which we impute to the gaze. They are the result of the cultural screen.[7]

Lacan's account of the field of vision also differs from Sartre's in its characterization of the look. Lacan insists that the gaze by which the voyeur is "surprised" not only constitutes him as spectacle, and divests his look of its illusory mastery, but reveals to him that he is a "subject sustaining himself in a function of desire" (85). Lacan thus imputes a self-conscious *subjectivity* rather than a self-conscious *objectivity* to the voyeur at the moment at which he is made aware of himself, and severs the connection between subjectivity and transcendence.

A later passage works even more decisively to isolate those two values from each other. There, with specific reference to the act of looking, Lacan reiterates one of the fundamental tenets of his psychoanalysis: desire within the scopic field, as elsewhere, is necessarily grounded in castration (88–89). *Four Fundamental Concepts* thus suggests not just that the look is one of the primary trajectories through which subjectivity is routed, and that it is always libidinally sustained, but also that it is predicated upon lack.

I would like to suggest that the productivity of the look—its ability to conjure something new into existence—depends in part on its acknowledgment and acceptance that the void upon which it depends is the irreducible condition of all subjectivity. However, lack is socially codified in ways that turn it into an unwanted burden, and the normative psyche consequently attempts to free itself of that burden through an externalizing displacement. In so doing, it works to constitute as alien and external what it cannot accept about itself—lack, but also (as in Sartre's story about the voyeur) those terms through which it is visually specified: specularity, embodiment, and subordination to the gaze. Significantly, as Freud makes clear, vision and hearing are the two faculties most at the service of projection, which operates at the behest of sexual, racial, and class "difference."

Lacan indicates in *Seminar XI* and in his texts on the imaginary[8] that the look also comes into play in a range of other activities whereby the conventional subject fortifies him- or herself against lack, activities which are also constitutive of "difference." Most classically, the subject procures for him- or herself a fantasmatic identity, whereby he or she attempts to fill the void out of which desire proceeds. The mirror stage gives us, of course, our primary model for conceptualizing this particular visual misrecognition, which denies the alterity and exteriority of the constituting image.

The subject may also reconstitute the erotic object in his or her own image, through a corporeal colonization. Fetishism supplies the most paradigmatic model for conceiving this form of *méconnaissance*.[9] Finally, the subject often assumes a proprietary relation to the world, making the look the punctual source of all that he or she sees. Lacan indicates what is involved in the last of these visual deformations when he speaks of the "*belong to me* aspect of representations, so reminiscent of property."[10] This misrecognition figures dramatically in the narrative that *Four Fundamental Concepts* appropriates from *Being and Nothingness*. It is not surprising, then, that when Sartre's voyeur apprehends the gaze behind his look, he experiences the world flowing away from the look to the gaze.

In general, these acts of projection and introjection are not only enacted at the behest of the self, but are also culturally facilitated. Although indicative of subjective vision, they consequently cannot be said to be "productive," in any real sense of that term. The eye which conjures something new into existence operates according to a different set of imperatives. It attempts, first of all, to apprehend the otherness of both the gaze and the constitutive image by foregrounding (rather than disavowing) those signifiers through which they sometimes mark their presence within the field of vision. This eye also scrutinizes those forms of *méconnaissance* to which it is most prone, and seeks to rearticulate the terms of the self/image or self/other relationship. Instead of assimilating what is desirable about the other to the self, and exteriorizing what is despised in the self as the other, the subject whose look I am here describing struggles to see the otherness of the desired self, and the familiarity of the despised other. He or she attempts, that is, to grasp the objectivity of the *moi*, and to recognize him- or herself precisely within those others to whom he or she would otherwise respond with revulsion and avoidance.

I have devoted a great deal of attention in this book to the first of these possibilities—to the political potential implicit in the assumption of "identity-at-a-distance." But it is equally important that we learn to recognize ourselves within the images through which we have helped to constitute the "alien" or "other," through one of those deformations of the eye that underpin "difference." Although Rosalind Krauss is not explicitly concerned with either of these potential ways of looking, she provides an extended discussion in *The Optical Unconscious* of a work by Marcel Duchamp that has enormous relevance to the present discussion. As Krauss notes, this work provides a hyperbolic dramatization of the exteriority of the gaze. But this is not the extent of its project. The Duchamp work also situates the male eye in an identificatory relation with what it conventionally repudiates as radically "other." It can thus serve as a partial demonstration of what I mean by the productive look.

Toward an Ethics of the Look

The work in question is *Etant donnés,* a life-size diorama on which Duchamp worked from 1946 until his death, but which he never assembled. In *The Optical Unconscious,* Krauss illustrates this diorama through two images, one from Duchamp himself, and one from Jean-François Lyotard's discussion of it in *Les TRANSformateurs DUchamp.* The first of these images shows a naked but strangely shapeless female body with spread legs and one outstretched hand holding a lamp [figure 74]. She lies at a diagonal angle in a field, behind which extends a landscape so foreshortened that it does not have a vanishing point. Through this foreshortening, the spectator is made aware that the vanishing point in this image is to be found somewhere other than on the horizon. The woman's head and feet are obscured by the edges surrounding a large, jagged opening in a brick wall, through which we apprehend the rest of her body. Her genitals occupy the lower middle half of the frame.

figure 74

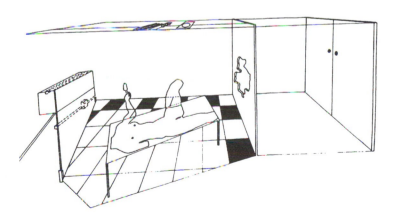

figure 75

The second image represents Lyotard's attempt to diagram the space of the diorama. In it a headless, footless female form with only one arm lies on a table in a room [figure 75]. The table is positioned at an angle to the irregular opening in the wall through which it is seen, and raises the female body to the height of the opening. The woman's outspread legs and exposed vulva are the nearest points in this figure to the opening in the wall. The room in which the "woman" lies is itself enclosed within a larger room, which was meant to be the public space of a museum.

In her analysis of these two images of *Etant donnés,* Krauss suggests that the Lyotard version simultaneously solicits the viewer to look through the hole in the wall at the female figure, and—by virtue of its location within the museum—puts this act of looking "on stage." It could thus be said to dramatize the moment in which the Sartrean voyeur becomes aware of being himself observed by *le regard.* For Krauss, this looked-at-look is representative of that subterranean modernism to which *The Optical Unconscious* is devoted. She writes that "to be discovered at the keyhole is…to be discovered as a body; it is to thicken the situation given to consciousness to include the hither space of the door, and to make the viewing body an object for consciousness." It is also to be put in a mirror relation to what is seen, which is here—above all—the female genitals.[11]

In his own discussion of *Etant donnés*, Lyotard comments on the implicit equation of the vanishing point and the point at which the observing subject is encouraged to stand in front of a perspective representation; he suggests that in Duchamp's work this implies an alignment of eye and vulva. "In this type of organization," Lyotard writes, "the viewpoint and the vanishing point are symmetrical. Thus if it is true that the latter is the vulva, this is the specular image of the peeping eyes; such that: when these think they're seeing the vulva, they see themselves. *Con celui qui voit.* He who sees is a cunt."[12]

For Lyotard, the significance of Duchamp's diorama is that it works to corporealize the male eye. Krauss goes further, pointing out that the diorama exposes the voyeur as much to the public look as it exposes the woman to his look. But the Duchamp work also effects a remarkable deconstruction of the grounding opposition upon which sexual difference is based. The male look at the female genitals is emblematic of that exteriorizing displacement through which the male subject repeatedly situates his lack at the site of the female body, and naturalizes it as essentially (i.e., anatomically) "other." The additional oppositions which the Duchamp diorama works both to articulate and collapse—carnality/transcendence, spectacle/eye—are built upon this foundational antithesis. When the male voyeur who is caught within the machinery diagrammed by Lyotard—a machinery which is itself the product of Duchamp's own transformative act of seeing—finds his look put in a mirror relation to the female genitals, he is given the opportunity to acknowledge as his own what he is accustomed to throw violently away, and, so, to renegotiate the relation between his ego and the object.

But how realizable is such a renegotiation in everyday life? Can it result from a simple act of will? If that renegotiation is assumed to involve unconscious as well as conscious processes, the answer is clearly "no." No look can extricate itself in any absolute way from the snares of the self. It can only work ceaselessly, with that all-too-limited knowledge to which consciousness has access, to undo the projections through which it rids itself of lack, and the incorporations through which it arrogates to itself what does not belong to it. Over and over, this struggle will end in failure, or, at most, partial and transitory success. However, the impossibility of ever finally achieving these goals does not liberate us from the ethical necessity of renewing the project of which they are a part every time it fails.

But whether or not we entertain an ethical relation with a particular other may finally have less to do with our immediate, largely involuntary reactions to him or her than with how we subsequently reinscribe those reactions at the level of consciousness. It may very well be, as I will suggest in the next chapter, that there is nothing we can consciously do to prevent certain projections from occurring over and over again, in an almost mechanical manner, when we look at certain racially, sexually, and economically marked bodies. That does not, in and of itself, signify the failure of the ethical. The ethical becomes operative not at the moment when unconscious desires and phobias assume possession of our look, but in a subsequent moment, when we take stock of what we have just "seen," and attempt—with an inevitably limited self-knowledge—to look again, differently. Once again, then, the moment of conscious agency is written under the sign of *Nachträglichkeit,* or deferred action.[13]

Even while I insist upon the importance of this revisionary rereading, I must also concede that consciousness is a precarious site from which to launch so uncompromising an assault on the delusions of the self as that which I have associated with productive looking. The experience of being a subject is so intimately connected to those delusions that when they are momentarily disabled, as in Sartre's scenario of the voyeur, one feels oneself psychically reduced to the condition of a pure object. Consequently, we need somehow to engage unconscious desire as well in the battle against our selves, and for that we need textual assistance. That is why I have devoted so much of the first half of this book to the formulation of an aesthetic practice capable of assisting us in the difficult task of living at a distance from the mirror. For the same reason, I have introduced the example here of Duchamp's *Etant donnés,* a work which facilitates the viewer's inverse and equally important acknowledgment of the familiarity of what has been cast violently away. Later, I will have more to say about the assistance visual texts can give us in the task of effecting not only a conscious but an unconscious renegotiation of our relation to the other.

Unfortunately, formidable as this task sounds, I have provided only a partial account of the obstacles standing in the way of the look's assumption of a radical subjectivity. It is not only the self or the *moi* which works to impair the look's productivity, but also a category which is so far removed from Sartre's conception of the field of vision that it cannot be even retroactively factored into the story of the voyeur—that is the category which Lacan calls the "given-to-be-seen" (74).[14]

In the three diagrams from *Four Fundamental Concepts* which I reproduced in the previous chapter, a mediating grid—which Lacan calls the "image" in the first, the "screen" in the second, and the "image/screen" in the third—intervenes between three sets of terms. It mediates the relation between the gaze, or "point of light," and the subject-as-spectacle, whom it puts in the "picture"; the relation between the gaze and the subject-as-look; and, finally, the relation between the object and the subject-as-look.[15] The screen, in other words, gives shape and significance to how we are seen by "others as such," how we define and interact with the agency to whom we attribute our visibility, and how we perceive the world.

In *Seminar XI,* Lacan deals almost exclusively with the mediation between the gaze and the subject-as-spectacle. He stresses both the "opacity" of the screen, and the constitutive role it performs with respect to the subject. As he puts it, "If I am anything in the picture, it is always in the form of the screen" (96–97). Although Lacan thereby forecloses the possibility of the subject ever being entirely self-defining or directly accessible to the gaze, he nevertheless maintains that the subject need not have a strictly passive relation to the screen. In fact, Lacan celebrates the human subject's capacity—a capacity which, he insists, is available to him or her alone—for "playing" with the screen (107).

Lacan has nothing to say about the second set of relations outlined above. Although the third diagram from *Four Fundamental Concepts* clearly shows the image/screen—or what I have been simply calling the "screen"—intervening between us and the gaze, the text in which the diagram appears never comments on what that intervention might entail. In the preceding chapter, I attempted to supply this missing commentary. I argued that the screen separating the gaze from our look provides one of the points at which historical and social variability is introduced into the field of vision, which is in certain other respects invariable. The screen encompasses the particular representational logic and range of material practices through which a given society at a particular moment in time apprehends something which is itself unchanging.

My concern in this chapter is with the last of the mediations enumerated above: the eye's relation to the screen through which it "perceives" its object. Lacan's observations about this relation manifest none of the guarded optimism which surfaces elsewhere in *Four Fundamental Concepts.* He does not speak about the possibility of manipulating the screen which defines the object in the way that one might manipulate the screen defining the subject. Instead, he stresses only that the look apprehends what is already given to be seen, and he comments wryly on the self-deluding gesture with which it then claims this pregiven spectacle as its own (80).

Several times, Lacan attributes to the gaze the faculty of showing (75)—of constituting the world as a spectacle to be apprehended by the eye (74). He also suggests that objects dictate how they are seen—that "perception is not in me," but rather "on the objects that it apprehends" (80). With both formulations, Lacan stresses the passivity of the look—its apprehension of a pregiven spectacle. However, he never really explains what he means by this predetermination of the look. In the next section of this chapter, I will attempt to theorize the crucial concept of the given-to-be-seen, though not necessarily in ways that directly follow from *Four Fundamental Concepts*.

Lacan not only refines Sartre's distinction between the gaze and the look, he deanthropomorphizes the gaze. And, at the same time, he strips the gaze of many of the functions which *Being and Nothingness* mistakenly imputes to it. He thereby encourages us to think of the gaze more as the symbolic third term, or Other, than as an imaginary rival. Lacan also introduces the invaluable category of the screen, which makes possible a historical and social specification of gaze, subject, and object, and opens the way for an account of the subject's limited agency with respect to the representations through which he or she is apprehended. Finally, Lacan defines the look not as the mark of a servile objectivity, but as the evidence of a desiring subjectivity. However, he places so much more emphasis on the given-to-be-seen than on the look's creative capacities that his account of the look is almost as pessimistic as Sartre's.

A series of interlocking questions consequently pose themselves with considerable force at this juncture: Is it possible, from a position within the specular model outlined in the last few pages, to impute to the look any creative potential, or must its province be assumed to be as completely laid out for it in advance as *Four Fundamental Concepts* would imply? Are there conditions, in other words, under which the eye can resist the solicitation of the screen, or at least see in ways which are not entirely predefined? If so, what are these conditions, and how might they be realized?

The Given-to-Be-Seen

A central section of Lacan's discussion of the field of vision in *Four Fundamental Concepts of Psycho-Analysis* is titled "Anamorphosis," and the last few pages of that section are given over to a discussion of a particularly famous instance of that form of visual manipulation—Hans Holbein's *The Ambassadors* (1533). This painting, which also adorns the cover of the French edition of *Seminar XI*, shows two men standing on either side of a two-tiered table on which are clus-

figure 76

tered a range of objects evocative of the arts and science of the times—two globes, books, a sundial, a decagon, a square, a pair of compasses, a lute [figure 76]. The men are, as Lacan puts it, "show[ily]" dressed (88). Indeed, their clothing proclaims their social importance; the man on the left is a French knight and ambassador, the one on the right is another French ambassador, later a bishop. In the foreground is a strangely distorted object, which is impossible to decipher when one stands directly in front of the painting—the customary position for viewing a perspective image. Only by standing far to the right of the painting can the viewer recognize the strange object as a human skull, or death's head.[16]

Lacan puts this painting to many uses. He points out, first of all, that the position in relation to which the conventional perspectival image comes into focus—the geometral point—is closely connected, historically and philosophically, to a Cartesian notion of subjectivity (86). Since, when we occupy that point, everything seems to radiate out from our look, any painting organized in relation to it encourages us to enact that form of *méconnaissance* which is, for Lacan, the visual equivalent of the *cogito*—to equate our look with the gaze, and to impute to it a mastering relation to the world. However, *The Ambassadors* undoes this *méconnaissance* by rendering part of the image unavailable to our vision. It prevents our look from effecting an imaginary mastery of its contents by dramatizing what might be called our "blind spot."

But it is not only because Holbein's painting prevents the eye from enacting a fantasy of "all-seeingness" that Lacan speaks at such length about it. For him, the death's head in the foreground is the product of an inversion of the geometry used to paint the rest of the image (87). Viewing the skull requires a reversal of the implicit triangle linking the geometral point, from which we look at the table and men, to them. Rather than occupying the position of the "object" in the first of the diagrams with which *Four Fundamental Concepts* illustrates the field of vision, the skull occupies the position of "point of light" in diagram 2— the position which I have shown to be indicative of the gaze. And rather than positing us as viewer, it puts us in the "picture." The presence of the death's head thus marks the alterity of the gaze in relation to our look, and our emplacement within the field of vision. As Lacan puts it, the anamorphic skull "makes visible for us here something that is simply the subject as annihilated—annihilated in the form that is, strictly speaking, the imaged embodiment of the *minus-phi* of castration, which…centres the whole organization of the desires through the framework of the fundamental drives" (88–89).

Read this way, *The Ambassadors* effects a deconstruction of normative vision which is analogous to that offered by *Being and Nothingness*. However, in thinking about the Holbein painting in relation to Lacan's three diagrams, it occurred to me that it also provides a model both for understanding normative vision, and for imagining how it might be possible to see in a way which is not entirely given in advance. It shows that the same image can look very different depending upon the vantage-point from which it is observed.

The Holbein painting is organized according to two competing systems of intelligibility—one perspectival, one anamorphic. The conflict between these two systems of intelligibility is so acute that when one stands in the position from which the perspectival part of the painting can best be seen, the rest of the image is indecipherable. Conversely, when one occupies that position to the extreme right of the image from which the death's head can be seen, the human figures and the table are decentered and distorted. The two parts of the painting are also thematically incommensurate: whereas the perspectival section celebrates earthly power and accomplishment, the human skull decrees these values to be the purest "vanitas."[17]

The first of the two vantage points projected by Holbein's painting is easily assimilable to what Lacan calls the "geometral point," since it represents the site from which the perspectival image is legible. The second vantage point is somehow oppositional to the first; it calls its rules into question. *The Ambassadors* thus suggests that the geometral point is only one site from which to apprehend an image—or, by extension, the cultural screen—and that the screen can appear very different depending upon where one "stands." But what is really seen from each of these two vantage points? What does it mean to look according to each of the systems of intelligibility made available by the Holbein painting?

In one case it means to affirm and in the other to negate the "world," or that which generally passes for reality.[18] Significantly, not only do the objects on the table symbolize all of human knowledge, and not only do the two men represent the possibility of a harmonious relationship between Church and State, but—as I have already mentioned—there are even two globes resting on the two-tiered table. This "world" was what Holbein's contemporaries were given to see. It was what most readily interposed itself between their look and the social field.

Elsewhere, I have theorized what passes for reality in a given society as the "dominant fiction."[19] Parts of the dominant fiction are in constant fluctuation, historically and culturally. Other aspects have a much greater longevity and persist from one culture to another, even though they may be dependent for their survival on a perpetual reiteration, within which local variations inevitably find expression.[20] In *Male Subjectivity at the Margins,* I suggested that the dominant fiction's most rudimentary binary opposition is that distinguishing masculinity from femininity; its most fundamental equation is that of penis and phallus; and its most central signifier is the family. All of the other elements of a given dominant fiction are articulated in relation to these core terms. Although generally prone to a more frequent historical variation, racial categories almost always have a crucial part to play in the constitution of the dominant fiction; there, class and other forms of social difference also find their most insistent formulations.

The dominant fiction can sustain itself only so long as the larger society affirms it. This affirmation does not involve only—or even primarily—conscious belief. It involves, rather, the activation of certain desires and identifications. Those desires and identifications are first and foremost those produced through the positive Oedipus complex, but they are always also carriers of more directly social values, such as race and class.

I have invoked the dominant fiction in the context of the present discussion because the notion of the given-to-be-seen cannot be understood without it. The upper portion of *The Ambassadors* shows us more than Holbein's "world." It also shows us our own. In addition to earthly accomplishment, the painting validates "masculinity," "whiteness," "monarchy," and "God," and it places all of these terms in a close metaphoric relation with one another. In so doing, it also effects that equation upon which the dominant fiction still depends, and upon which our sense of "reality" is consequently most dependent: the equation of penis and phallus. The upper part of *The Ambassadors* thus provides the allegorical provocation for defining the given-to-be-seen as the operation within the field of vision of the system of intelligibility which is synonymous with the dominant fiction.

As the Holbein painting shows, this system of intelligibility does not go unchallenged at the site of the screen or cultural image-repertoire. It figures there more prominently than any other system of intelligibility, but it is often sharply contested by competing views of "reality." Indeed, I will go so far as to suggest that the screen conventionally consists not only of normative representations, but also of all kinds of oppositional and subcultural representations.

The upper portion of the Holbein painting exercises its reality-effect only so long as the viewer occupies the geometral point. The given-to-be-seen similarly depends for its hegemonic effects on the slotting of the eye into a particular spectatorial position—into a metaphoric geometral point. The latter can then best be defined as *the position from which we apprehend and affirm those elements of the screen which are synonymous with the dominant fiction.* But how is it that we come to do so? And under what conditions might we occupy a different viewing position with respect to the screen?

In *Male Subjectivity at the Margins,* I made much of the fact that the dominant fiction "invites" subjects to validate it by saturating the field of family relations with eros. However, in so doing, it not only works to promote a certain "reality," but also opens the door to its dissolution. The Oedipus complex ideally inducts the male subject into desire for the mother and identification with the father, and the female subject into desire for the father and identification with the mother. It thereby secures their libidinal investment in the central elements of the dominant fiction. However, the Oedipus complex has a homosexual as well as a heterosexual form, and it can consequently precipitate libidinal transactions which negate rather than affirm the dominant fiction.[21]

I still believe the positive Oedipus complex to be the primary psychic mechanism for interpellating the subject into the dominant fiction, and, by extension, for affirming the given-to-be-seen. I would also still argue that the double nature of the Oedipus complex works to complicate enormously the subject's relation to the dominant fiction. However, I am now concerned to broaden my conception of libidinal resistance beyond the transgressive possibilities implicit in that psychic structure. I would like to formulate the terms under which even a subject whose desires and identifications have been organized through the positive Oedipus complex might have access to the productive look. In other words, I would like to define the conditions under which we might step away from the geometral point, and see something other than the given-to-be-seen. The category through which I propose to do so is memory.

The Productive Look

In *The Interpretation of Dreams,* Freud provides a topographical model with rich implications for the present discussion.[22] In that model, visual stimuli enter the psyche from the "side" of the unconscious, and are processed in complex ways before arriving at a state of conscious perception. As these stimuli traverse the imaginary "space" of the psyche, they pass through two mnemic reserves, one unconscious and one preconscious. At the level of the preconscious a process of classification occurs, whereby the stimulus in question is "recognized" through its paradigmatic grouping with other, similar, stimuli.

When I look at a red chair, for instance, it is classified at the level of my preconscious, at the very least, under the categories "chair" and "red object," permitting me to apprehend it, in a seemingly automatic and unmediated way, as a "red chair." Since the preconscious also performs various screen functions, it may classify the chair in more overtly evaluative ways as well. Before even becoming aware of seeing a red chair, I may, at the preconscious level, reject it as "cheap" or "only appropriate for children," or recognize it as the work of a famous designer, and elevate it to the category of "art."

However, it is not only what transpires between my glance at the red chair and my seemingly instantaneous conscious perception of seeing it which determines what it means in this case to have "looked." Before I even register that perception, it has been been put in communication with my unconscious memories, and, so, worked over in certain ways. And during the rest of the day, this red chair, which now persists in my psyche as a memory-trace in its own right, may also undergo a much more complex semanticization. Through its shape or its color, it may become connected with the chair my mother used to sit on while rocking me to sleep, and, through that association, with a dense, libidinally resonant signifying network.

Through displacement, then, the red chair may partake of some of the value which emanates outward from those wishes which eternally persist and insist at the level of my unconscious. Perhaps it will become a prop in the night's restaging of my unconscious fantasmatic—in the reminting of what Freud calls the "stereotype plate," which underpins my dreams, my fantasies, and my object-choices.[23] When this happens, my look at the red chair has assumed that affirmative function I spoke of earlier.

The attribution of psychic value to the red chair may work in ways that consolidate the dominant fiction, but it should already be clear that the reverse is also possible. The unconscious manifests a striking indifference to the question of what is conventionally assumed to be important or worthless at the level of the cultural screen in the process of weaving its associative webs. It often transfers psychic value from one term to another on the basis of what would, in waking life, seem a completely inapposite analogy.

Freud problematizes the notion of objective vision through the delay which he insists obtains between the introduction of a stimulus into the psyche and its conscious perception. Equally deconstructive of that notion is his account of the dream-work, which integrates a day's perceptions into a complex network of interrelationships ready for unconscious deployment in the production of night dreams. A further challenge to the assumption that what the human look sees is what is really "there" is Freud's insistence upon the constant revision to which our memories are subject. Perhaps my glance at the red chair induces me to look again, in my mind's eye, at a whole concatenation of red things which I had stored away in my memory without deeming them of any consequence, and which now undergo a transvaluation, which will, in turn, affect the way I look at a traffic light next time.

In an attempt to forge some theoretical space for conceptualizing how we manage to see in ways that are to varying degrees independent of the given-to-be-seen, I have stressed only what is potentially transformative about the look's imbrication in memory. However, the complex signifying chains that are formed at the behest of unconscious desire do not operate merely or even primarily in the service of change. They are formed, rather, to permit the indirect and disguised expression of the desire for an object or a scene which cannot be named directly. They are thus governed by the imperative to return, by the imperative to get back to those images that provide the fantasmatic grounding for all of our fantasies and object choices.

The potentially productive uses to which the remembering look can be put reside not in the imperative to return, but, on the contrary, in the interlocking imperative to displace. Because the backward path ostensibly leading to gratification is blocked, as Freud puts it in *Beyond the Pleasure Principle,* we have no choice but to move forward; repression dictates that the desired object can only be recovered or "remembered" in the guise of a substitute.[24] There can thus be no return or recollection which is not at the same time a displacement, and which, consequently, does not introduce alterity. The productively remembering look is one in which the imperative to displace has come to supersede the imperative to return. It is a look which has developed such an appetite for alterity that it is capable of seizing upon even the most fleeting metaphoric or metonymic connection so as to facilitate the transfer of psychic value from one term to another, otherwise radically divergent, term. The productively remembering look, in other words, is one in which the movement forward is no longer at the service of a return, but has developed an independent momentum.

Roland Barthes's *Camera Lucida* provides a brilliant dramatization of both this appetite for visual alterity, and the resistance which such a remembering eye can exercise when confronted with the given-to-be-seen. In that book,

Barthes distinguishes between two looks, the "studium" and the "punctum." He says that the studium is "ultimately always coded";[25] it is the result of a "contract" between the creators and the consumers of culture to perpetuate those "myths" which are synonymous with normative representation (28). It is what we see when we apprehend the world not only through a particular image-repertoire, but from the position which is assigned to us in advance—the position indicated by the geometral point in Lacan's first diagram, by the keyhole in Sartre's story, and by the perspectival grid which gives me access to an undistorted view of the two human figures in *The Ambassadors.* The studium, in other words, designates the given-to-be-seen.

Barthes contrasts the studium to the punctum. The punctum, he says, is that "wound" or "prick" experienced by the subject when he or she directs his or her look away from those elements within an image which speak with the "voice" of "knowledge" and "culture" (51) and toward those which are decentered.[26] As examples of the punctum, Barthes cites Tristan Tzara's "large hand whose nails are anything but clean" in a portrait of him taken by André Kertész in 1926 (45), and the strapped pumps worn by the sister or daughter in a photograph of African Americans produced by James Van der Zee in the same year (43). Later in *Camera Lucida,* Barthes associates the punctum with the movement of the desiring look beyond the "frame" or "picture" of the given-to-be-seen toward what lies "outside." The example Barthes uses here is Mapplethorpe's "Young Man with Arm Extended," a self-portrait which shows only his head, naked chest, and outstretched left arm, the rest of his body having been cropped by the left edge of the frame (59).

Barthes suggests several times that the eye's transformative potentiality—its capacity for looking from a position which is not assigned in advance, and for affirming certain ostensibly marginal elements within the screen at the expense of those that are culturally valorized—somehow resides in memory. The punctum can perhaps best be defined as the "prick" one feels when an otherwise insignificant component of the screen comes into contact with one's own mnemic reserve. Barthes provides us with two examples of this representational intersection. He writes that the dirt road in a Kertész photograph from 1921 showing a boy leading a blind gypsy violinist made him "recognize," not only rationally, but "with [his] whole body," the "straggling villages [he himself] passed through on [his] long-ago travels in Hungary and Rumania" (45). Similarly, the necklace worn by a black woman in a Van der Zee photograph evokes one worn by someone in his own past:

> it was this same necklace (a slender ribbon of braided gold) which I had once seen worn by someone in my own family, and which, once she died, remained shut up in a family box of old jewelry (this sister of my father never married, lived with

her mother as an old maid, and I had always been saddened whenever I thought of her dreary life). (53)

Barthes suggests that to embed a detail in this kind of associational matrix is to confer new significance upon it—to illuminate it with a little "star" (49). His text bears out this contention. Over and over again, *Camera Lucida* succeeds in irradiating otherwise insignificant—or even culturally devalued—details in photographs which Barthes studies with a keen, remembering eye.

The look Barthes brings to bear on the photographs reproduced in *Camera Lucida* is one in which the imperative of displacement seems to reign supreme. It is a wayward or eccentric look, one not easily stabilized or assigned to preexisting loci, and whose functioning is consequently resistant to visual standardization. Moreover, although, as always, the repressed term or scene which initiates displacement exercises considerable control over the libidinal connections which it is capable of making, that psychic process often pursues a startlingly unorthodox trajectory. Even though it is anchored in the unconscious to so conventional and insistent an object of desire as the mother, its itinerary cannot be charted in advance. Who could predict, for instance, that in the case of the Van der Zee photograph, Barthes's remembering look would come to rest on the thin gold necklace around the neck of an African-American woman, and thereby assimilate that woman (through the intervening figure of his father's sister) to what might be called the "mother complex"?

The look can develop an even more insatiable appetite for alterity than that manifested by *Camera Lucida's* authorial eye. It can develop a predilection for the eccentric or unusual association; for the diversity which persists within metaphor; and for the heterogeneity which undoes the compulsive repetition through which every recollection is made to attest to the same unconscious desire. When it does so, it embraces the drift and discontinuity implicit in the imperative of displacement. However, it may, at the same time, deploy memory primarily for the purpose of making a representational element its "own," or as a validation of the *moi*. The remembering look is not truly productive until it effects one final displacement—the displacement of the ego. It does not fully triumph over the forces that constrain it to see in predetermined ways until its appetite for alterity prevails, not only over sameness, but also over self-sameness.

Barthes fails to effect this last, all-important displacement. *Camera Lucida* dramatizes the possibility of apprehending the image-repertoire from an unexpected vantage point. However, it also makes evident the limited nature of the gains to be realized when this revisionary act of looking does not involve at the same time a realignment of self and other. One is left with the disquieting sense that whereas Barthes consistently apprehends the photographs about which he writes from a viewing position which is radically divergent from that indicated by the metaphoric geometral point (associating an African-American woman, for instance, with his aunt), his own sovereignty vis-à-vis the object remains unquestioned.

Indeed, he seems, in general, less motivated by the desire to shift the terms through which we apprehend the world than by that more conventionally aesthetic wish to assert the superiority of his own look and the uniqueness of the sensibility which informs it. Barthes claims that he not only eschews "culture" and "knowledge," but also that he "refuse[s] to inherit anything from another eye" (51). He maintains that what he sees when he looks at a photograph refers to "a value buried in [himself]," i.e., that it is something inaccessible to any other viewer (16).

In another very disturbing way, *Camera Lucida* attests to the unquestioned primacy of the *moi*. When Barthes apprehends a photograph in the way he celebrates, his own past is victorious over the photograph's assertion of a "this has been." The figures depicted in the photograph serve only to activate his own memories, and so are stripped of all historical specificity. Barthes's recollections might thus be said to "devour" the images of the other.

This would seem the juncture to reiterate, once again, that productive looking necessarily requires a constant conscious reworking of the terms under which we unconsciously look at the objects that people our visual landscape. It necessitates the struggle, first, to recognize our involuntary acts of incorporation and repudiation, and our implicit affirmation of the dominant elements of the screen, and, then, to see again, differently. However, productive looking necessarily entails, as well, the opening up of the unconscious to otherness.

None of us can effect this project merely through good intentions, since we cannot voluntarily direct the process whereby a visual detail comes to be resemanticized through its incorporation into our memory reserve (or, conversely, how our memory reserve is reconfigured through its assimilation of what is alien to it). So, how precisely is our look to become productive in all of the senses I have outlined here? How is it to affirm—not only at the conscious level but also at the unconscious level—what is other, both from the given-to-be-seen, and from the term or terms whose repression initiates displacement? And through what prompting can it be brought to accept as its own what it would otherwise throw violently away, and to acknowledge as other what it conventionally claims as its self?

As I indicated in Chapter 3, the aesthetic work is a privileged domain for displacing us from the geometral point, for encouraging us to see in ways not dictated in advance by the dominant fiction. The conscious and unconscious faculties "lose their mutual exclusiveness" during the act of artistic creation.[27] The works resulting from such an act consequently often engage us in more "primarized" forms of mental activity than are normal in daily life—forms of mental activity in which the pleasure principle predominates, and in which desire is given lavish expression.[28]

Such texts are capable of implanting in the viewer or reader "synthetic" memories—libidinally saturated associative clusters which act like those mnemic elements which, as a result of a psychic working over, have been made the vehicles for the expression of unconscious wishes. Because these "synthetic" memories are so psychically resonant, they generally move immediately into the orbit of those other, more "indigenous" memories through which such wishes find expression. They are thus in a position to put marginal elements of the cultural screen in contact with what is most meaningful to a viewer or reader, and thereby to validate what would otherwise be neglected or despised.

But the visual text for which I am arguing would displace me from my self, as well as from the geometral point. It would do so by enlisting me in an act of "heteropathic recollection." It would factor into my mnemic operations not only what resides outside the given-to-be-seen, but what my *moi* excludes—what must be denied in order for my self to exist as such. It would, in short, introduce the "not me" into my memory reserve.

The constitution of the representational terms under which the spectator can be brought to identify at a distance with bodily coordinates which are both culturally devalued and markedly divergent from his or her own is a crucial component of this textual enterprise. However, the concern of this chapter is not so much with the corporeal ego per se, as with the larger domain of human relations. The issue, then, is not merely how we might be textually encouraged to confer ideality upon the face and lineaments of another, but how, through discursively "implanted" memories, we might be given the psychic wherewithal to participate in the desires, struggles, and sufferings of the other, and to do so in a way which redounds to his or her, rather than to our own, "credit."

I want to devote the remainder of this chapter to an analysis of a text which works to bring about this final displacement—Chris Marker's film *Sans Soleil* (1982). Like *Camera Lucida*, *Sans Soleil (Sunless)* is centrally concerned with the remembering look, which it also associates with a "wound." However, Marker's film promotes a very different kind of remembering from that enacted by Barthes. As we will see, although conceived in ways which are at all times psychically specific, memory implies in *Sans Soleil* less a biographical recuperation than the perpetually repeated recovery in an always transfigured guise of a past which does not "belong" to the spectator any more than the fictional narrator, but which, nevertheless, reverberates within him or her in ways that provide a new access to the screen. In the process, *Sans Soleil* effects a renegotiation of the relation between the Western self, and the African and Asian other.

The Disembodied Wound

Most of the images in *Sans Soleil* are documentary in origin, but many have been fed through a synthesizer, which radically denatures them; combined with still photographs and the credit sequence from *Vertigo;* and juxtaposed in a series of complex graphic montages. Even more importantly, they are often combined with a voice-over text which alternates between the first- and third-person, and which purports to consist of letters written by a filmmaker named Sandor Krasna during his journeys to the various locations depicted, but which is entirely fictional. In their formal qualities, the images are almost ethnographic and they show cultures which would conventionally qualify as "foreign"—most importantly, Japan and Guinea-Bissau. However, *Sans Soleil* does not attempt to "penetrate" these cultures, like a traditional ethnographic film. It also declines to offer an "anthroplogy" of these cultures. Rather, it opens itself up to "penetration" by them, and it repeatedly registers and retransmits the shock of that encounter. It provides an extended dramatization of and meditation upon the operations of memory, which it puts to highly unusual purposes. It "remembers," and encourages the viewer to "remember," what might best be characterized as "other people's memories." In the process, it both radically revises what it means to look at Japan and Africa, and engages the Western viewer in an exemplary self-estrangement.

This "remembering" of other people's memories is built into the very narrative structure of the film. A female voice (which, in the English version of *Sans Soleil,* belongs to Alexandra Stewart), reads from and sometimes paraphrases letters ostensibly sent to her by Krasna. Her voice, in other words, speaks his memories, often with the first-person pronoun, and on occasion in direct discourse. However, rather than "possessing" Krasna's words, and subordinating his memories to her own, she might almost be said to be possessed by them.

Although she is internal to the film's diegesis, inhabiting the same world as its images, the female narrator is not semically specified; she is present only as the reader of letters which address her, but which speak about a range of other cultures. Krasna, in turn, describes a series of gestures, actions, and events, sometimes quotidian and sometimes "historical" in nature, which "belong" to someone else's or to another nation's "past." Each time, this act of heteropathic recollection mediates our relation to a particular set of images, indicating the point from which the film "looks" at them, and the point from which it invites us to do the same. As a result, these images, many of which might serve an unproblematically ethnographic function in another context, are here given a totally different resonance.

Sans Soleil begins with a strip of black leader, accompanied by the words: "The first image he told me about was of three children on a road in Iceland." Then, without commentary, the film shows us a hand-held shot of three blonde girls walking down a road in Iceland. The road is surrounded by green fields, the wind blows the girls' hair, and the image shimmers with refracted sunshine. Again over black leader, the voice-over continues: "He said that for him it was the image of happiness, and also that he had tried several times to link it with other images, but it never worked." Initially, it is unclear whose happiness is being referred to by the voice-over. But later in the film, we learn that the town in which the shot was taken was destroyed five years later by an erupting volcano. It thus becomes an externalization of the memory the three girls might cherish of life before that catastrophe; it is the textual "recollection" of their happiness.

A similar act of heteropathic remembrance occurs a moment later. Over a series of brief shots of various Japanese individuals sleeping, smoking, and reading on a ferry carrying them from Hokkaido to Tokyo, the voice-over says, "He wrote me: 'I'm just back from Hokkaido, the northern island. Rich and harried Japanese take the plane, others take the ferry. Waiting, immobility, snatches of sleep—curiously, all of that makes me think of a past or future war. Night trains, air-raids, fallout shelters. Small fragments of war enshrined in everyday life.'" Krasna's letter situates him in the same ferry as the Japanese travelers, and recounts what he saw when he looked around him. But, once again, this "seeing" has nothing to do with either his personal biography, or a normative apprehension of "Japaneseness." Instead, the images of the people sleeping and waiting in a public place serve to conjure forth for him what might best be described as "Japanese war memories." In this particular act of recollection, Krasna—who at one point identifies himself as French—opens himself not only to the memories of a stranger, but also to those of an ostensibly racial other.

Still later in the film, Krasna will "remember" the final moments in the life of a Japanese kamikazi pilot; the guerilla war against Portuguese colonialism in Guinea-Bissau; the trip to the cat temple in Tokyo of a woman whose cat had disappeared; the visit to a cemetery of a Japanese family on the Day of the Dead; the anguish felt by a Japanese man upon hearing the word "spring" after the death of his beloved wife; the indignation against injustice felt by many student radicals during the 1960s; and the words broadcast over loudspeakers to a group of Japanese girls during their coming-of-age celebration in Tokyo, telling them what society would expect from them. He also "remembers" Johnny's memory of Madeleine after her "death," during a long sequence devoted to Alfred Hitchcock's *Vertigo,* itself a film about a woman reputed to be haunted by someone else's recollections. Perhaps most extraordinarily, he "dreams" the dreams of a group of Japanese travelers, in a sequence which cross-cuts between them sleeping during a train journey, and the cinematic images which he imagines those dreams "recollecting" or reprising. The voice-over text which precedes this act of visionary looking makes explicit the alterity on which memory pivots in *Sans Soleil:*

One day he wrote to me: "Description of a dream. More and more my dreams find their setting in the department stores of Tokyo.... I begin to wonder if these dreams are really mine, or if they're part of a totality, a giant collective dream of which the entire city may be the projection. It might suffice to pick up any of the telephones that are lying around to hear a familiar voice, or the beating of a heart...all the galleries lead to stations. The same companies own the stores and the railroads that bear their names.... The train inhabited by sleeping people puts together all the fragments of dreams, makes a single film of them, the ultimate film. The tickets from the automatic dispenser grant admission to the show."

Sans Soleil not only dramatizes what it might mean to remember other people's memories, but it raises the act of doing so to the level of a metafiction. At one point, Krasna fantasizes Iceland as the landscape in which a man from 4001 would arrive in our own time. Over images of country roads, birds flying, a ship in a harbor, the streets of San Francisco, and an unspecified cityscape—images that attest in a variety of ways to the notion of "travel"—the voice-over reads aloud the letter in which this fantasy is narrated. Krasna's fantasy specifies that 4001 is "the time when the human brain has reached the era of full employment"—the era of total recall. But with the achievement of perfect memory, mankind has lost access to the experience of happiness and unhappiness, since "total recall is memory anaesthetized." A man from this period listens to a song cycle by Mussorgski, and vaguely understands from it that in the epoch in which it was written human beings suffered in a way he cannot grasp. He journeys back into the past in the hope of being able to experience and understand this unhappiness—to "remember" the unhappy memories of the people who were alive then. However, unlike Krasna and the viewer he solicits, this man is doomed to failure, since he cannot forget.

Sans Soleil twice counterposes the act of remembering not to forgetting—as I have just intimated, the kind of memory to which this film is committed is intimately connected with forgetting—but to what it calls "history," in the official and synchronic sense of that word. After the first sequence devoted to Guinea-Bissau and the revolutionary movement led by Amilcar Cabral, the voice-over quotes Krasna asking, "Who remembers all that? History throws its empty bottles out the window." Later, during a second sequence on the guerilla war and its aftermath in Guinea-Bissau, she says: "That's how history progresses—plugging its memories, as one plugs one's ears." At both of these moments, history signifies not revolution and change, but the eternal present implied by the dominant fiction. It extends the normative elements of the screen to include past and future, the denial of other possibilities.

In the sequence shot in the sex museum in Tokyo, Krasna suggests that history represents less the "hurt" with which Fredric Jameson has associated it[29] than the disavowal of what "hurts," the assertion of unity and wholeness over rupture and loss. However, although expelled from its human residence, the foreclosed wound of the past somehow persists. It languishes in the spiral of time, waiting once again to be granted a locus which is finally more psychic than corporeal. To remember is, in effect, to provide that psychic locus. As the camera cuts from one spotlit image of stuffed primates copulating to another, their genitals a visual evocation of "woundedness," the voice-over reads this extraordinary text:

> Who says that time heals all wounds? It would be better to say that time heals everything except wounds. With time the hurt of separation loses its real limits, with time the desired body will soon disappear, and if the desired body has already ceased to exist for the other then what remains is a wound, disembodied.

If to remember is to provide the disembodied "wound" with a psychic residence, then to remember other people's memories is to be wounded by their wounds. More precisely, it is to let their struggles, their passions, their pasts, resonate within one's own past and present, and destabilize them. Since the new mnemic matrix which weaves itself around the borrowed memory inevitably shifts the meaning of that memory, it is also to enter into a profoundly dialectical relation to the other, whose past one does not relive precisely as he or she lived it, but in a way which is informed by one's "own" recollections. Finally, to remember other people's memories is to inhabit time. For Marker, time signifies "drift" and discontinuity rather than "history," which implies the endless perpetuation of the "same."

At this juncture, the reader is likely to object that it is not possible to "remember" someone else's memories, and that—as I myself acknowledged a moment ago—any attempt to achieve such an act of recollection can only lead to a falsification. To this hypothetical objection, I respond that, for the fictional letter writer of *Sans Soleil*, there can be no accurate or authentic memory. The function of recollection, as he at one point suggests, is to transform, not to reproduce. "We do not remember," he writes, "We rewrite memory, much as history is rewritten." And implicit in this transformation or rewriting of our recollections is the possibility of also constantly reconfiguring the screen. To remember perfectly would be forever to inhabit the same cultural order. However, to remember imperfectly is to bring images from the past into an ever new and dynamic relation to those through which we experience the present, and in the process ceaselessly to shift the contours and significance not only of the past, but also of the present. For this reason, Krasna says in the same letter, forgetting is not the "opposite" of memory, but its "lining." It represents the possibility of seeing something other than what one saw yesterday or the day before: the possibility of apprehending the world under conditions other than those dictated in advance by the given-to-be-seen.

As *Sans Soleil* makes explicit, memory implies more than anything else the possibility of effecting change at the level of representation. The film demonstrates this point through two insistently deployed textual strategies. First, it shows a particular set of images, then "forgets" them by moving onto something else, and later "recollects" them once again, but now in the form of the new constellation which they form in relation to other images.[30] This constant recombination of familiar elements with new ones works at a formal level to dramatize the transformative process which results when the productively remembering eye transects the cultural screen. A second strategy *Sans Soleil* employs is to feed many of its images through a synthesizer, which serves to destabilize and to defamiliarize them. During the sequence about Narita Airport, for instance, Krasna comments that when visiting that location years after the original protests against it, the protesters were still there. Only one thing had changed in the interim: the airport itself had been built. As if in protest again this stasis, against the endless replay of the same images, the same scene, Krasna says: "If the images of the present don't change, then change the images of the past." And then he shows some footage of the original demonstrations transformed by a synthesizer. He attributes the idea behind these images to his Japanese friend Hayao Yamaneko, who views the synthesizer as a way of draining the reality out of the image-repertoire. Yamaneko maintains that synthesized images "are less deceptive…than those you see on television," since "at least they proclaim themselves to be what they are—images, not the portable and compact form of an already inaccessible reality."

Near the end of the film, Marker provides one last recombinatory montage, evoking again the cat cemetery, the sleeping Japanese on the train, the musical staircase, and a series of other, increasingly unintelligible images, but this time as a synthesized sequence. On this occasion, Krasna overtly associates the process of synthesization with forgetting. "Yamaneko showed me my images already affected by the moss of time," he remarks, "freed of the lie that had prolonged the existence of those moments, swallowed by the spiral." Significantly, a few moments later, he suggests that the same technical device can be read as a potent metaphor for memory, thereby linking it again to forgetting.

Krasna breaks open the category of memory to include not only the past, but also the future—or, to be more precise, a future other than the present, as if to suggest that it is above all this other future which the forgetting and subsequent recollection of the past would permit. As if to make this last point even more emphatically, he projects a temporal trajectory which includes every possibility but that eternal "now" which aspires to construct all of time in its own image: "Finally [Yamaneko's] language touches me," he writes, because he talks to that part of us which insists on drawing profiles on prison walls, a piece of chalk to follow the contours of what is not, or is no longer, or is not yet. The handwriting each of us will use to compose the list of things that quickens the heart, to offer or to erase. In that moment, poetry will be made by everyone, and there will be emus in the zone.

The notion of things that "quicken the heart" is introduced into *Sans Soleil* early on, via an anecdote about Shonagon, lady-in-waiting to Sadako at the beginning of the Heian Period in Japan. Krasna recounts that Shonagon was a famous compiler of lists—the list of elegant things, of distressing things, and, most importantly, of things that quicken the heart. "Not a bad criterion, I realize when I am filming," Krasna goes on to say, "I bow to the economic miracle, but what I want to show you are the neighborhood celebrations." An extended series of shots of Tokyo neighborhood celebrations follows, without commentary.

In this double sequence, Marker explicitly comments on the representational transformation to which the recollection of other people's memories leads in *Sans Soleil:* the shift of libidinal value away from the privileged nexes of the image-repertoire to its seemingly inconsequential elements. That film consistently manifests a preference for the marginal details of the cultures it depicts over those aspects which are more centrally featured at the site of the screen, or for what it at one point calls "banality" over "history."

In the letter in which Krasna tells his female reader about Shonagon, he offers a parable about how social change is effected. The parable is drawn from the Heian Period, during which political power was ostensibly concentrated in the hands of the regents, and the courtiers were left to amuse themselves harmlessly at court. It was, however, the courtiers rather than the regents who created a revolution. They who did so precisely through the sort of displacement Barthes associates with the punctum—through a shift of libidinal value from the "large" or "socially significant" to what was regarded as "small" and "socially insignificant." "By learning how to draw a sort of melancholy comfort from the contemplation of the tiniest things," writes Krasna, "the small group of idlers left a mark on Japanese sensibility much deeper than the mediocre thundering of the politicians."

Marker's camera also regularly deflects attention away from the great "tropes" about Japan which are endlessly reiterated at the site of the Western screen to seemingly incidental details of that culture. Thus, rather than telling us once again about Japanese efficiency, conformity, or ancestor worship, and Japanese rootedness in Confucianism and a feudal social structure, *Sans Soleil* shows us not only neighborhood celebrations, but also a bar where "every man is as good as any other—and knows it"; a ceremony for the souls of broken dolls; an inflatable saxaphone in a department store window; two leftist demonstrators collecting signatures; a family pouring a bottle of sake over a grave on the Day of the Dead; Japanese women in their furtrimmed winter kimonos; and an outstretched stockinged foot on the ferry from Hokkaido to Tokyo.

Insistently read through other people's memories, these details of Japanese life become, quite simply, "things that quicken the heart." Through them, "Japan" ceases to be an alien other, which must be colonized, exoticized, or phobically repelled, and becomes the thrilling prospect of another set of cultural possibilities. Not surprisingly, then, Krasna suggests that memory should involve a representational journey across geographical as well as temporal boundaries. He proposes at one point that memory as he conceives it "runs from camp to camp like Joan of Arc," and that it could be conceptualized as a short-wave announcement from Hong Kong radio picked up on a Cape Verde island and projected to Tokyo, or the recollection "of a precise color on the street" bouncing back "on another country, another distance, another music, endlessly." *Sans Soleil* is an extended dramatization of this space and time "travel," cutting back and forth between France, Guinea-Bissau, Iceland, Japan, San Francisco, and the island of Sal; and verbally evoking and visually reprising events as distant as the student movement of the 1960s, World War II, the Heian period in Japan, and the 1980s.

In one of his last letters, Krasna describes himself as no longer merely observing this other life, but, at least temporarily, living it. However brief this self-expropriation, it distances him not only from the imperatives of the self, but also from those of his own (French) screen. It thereby indicates that the renegotiation of the ego/other axis may often necessitate both a psychic and a cultural displacement, an estrangement from one's self, and from one's national coordinates. Only through this escape from national identity does Krasna finally, definitively, move through the keyhole to what lies on the other side. "I waited at the red light, Japanese style, so as to leave space for the spirits of the broken cars," he writes, during the final sequence of synchronized images,

> Even if I expected no letter I stopped at the general delivery window, for one must honor the spirits of torn up letters, and at the airmail counter to salute the spirits of unmailed letters. I took the measure of the unbearable vanity of the West, that has never ceased to privilege Being over Non-Being, what is spoken to what is left unsaid.

As my reading of *Sans Soleil* has suggested, Marker does not hesitate to associate the technology of cinema and video with the remembering look. In addition to evoking the operations of forgetting and recollection through montage and synthesization, he characterizes the television as a "memory box," and compares the operations of memory to the movement of film through a projector ("Memories must make do with their delerium, with their drift. A moment

stopped would burn like a frame of film blocked before the furnace of the projector"). *Sans Soleil* thus suggests that, far from being always subordinate to the
camera, the look can at times bend the camera to its mandates. In fact, it goes
further: it proposes that just as there is a cinema of the camera/gaze, so there is
a cinema of the productive look.[31]

I would characterize not only *Sans Soleil*, but also *Looking for Langston* and
Bilder der Welt und Inschrift des Krieges as instances of a "cinema of the productive look." *Sans Soleil* and *Bilder der Welt* indicate that, although the camera "sees"
what the eye cannot, the images it produces through this fictive act of "seeing"
can be retroactively worked upon in all kinds of transformative and destabiliz-
ing ways, and thereby stripped of their ostensible objectivity and authority. And
Sans Soleil and *Looking for Langston* indicate that the look can also interfere with
the camera's normative operations at the very moment of photographic "capture," leading to the production of films which, in addition to challenging the
complacencies of the self and the limitations of the given-to-be-seen, speak more
about desire, memory, and fantasy than about epistemological mastery. We need
more films of this kind.

6

The Screen

Ever since the publication of Guy Debord's *The Society of the Spectacle*, it has become fashionable to claim that we are more dependent on the image than were the subjects of previous historical periods. "Everything that was directly lived has moved away into a representation," asserts Debord, at one of the many points in his text where he imputes to our predecessors an existential immediacy that we ourselves lack.[1] I believe that this formulation is predicated on a radical misrecognition of what is historically variable about the field of vision. There can never have been a moment when specularity was not at least in part constitutive of human subjectivity. Lacan speaks as much for our medieval or Renaissance counterparts as for us when he remarks, "We are beings who are looked at, in the spectacle of the world."[2] And ever since the inception of cave drawing, it has been via images that we see and are seen.

What is specific to our epoch is not the specular foundation of subjectivity and the world, but rather the terms of that foundation—the logic of the images through which we figure objects and are in turn figured, and the value conferred upon those images through the larger organization of the visual field. It seems to me that three technologies play a preeminent role in both of these respects, all of which depend centrally upon the camera: still photography, cinema, and video. Perhaps surprisingly, it is the first of these technologies, rather than the second or third, that has the greatest import for how we experience our specularity.

In Chapter 4, I argued that the camera represents the screen through which we apprehend the gaze, and I attempted to answer the question: What is a camera? In this chapter, I will propose that the screen through which the *subject* is apprehended is also structured through its implicit relation to that representation of the gaze—that the camera is somehow internal to this screen in the sense that it represents the screen's imaginary source. It is no accident, then, that when Lacan seeks to clarify precisely how it is that the subject is put into the "picture," he should write, "The gaze is the instrument through which light is embodied and through which…I am *photo-graphed*" (106).

In this chapter, I will also pursue an answer to the question posed at one point by *Bilder der Welt und Inschrift des Krieges:* How does one face a camera, or anticipate one's "photographic" capture? This project will necessitate as dramatic a complication of the category of the screen as that provided in Chapter 4. It will require that we approach that category not only through the three diagrams of the field of vision provided in *Seminar XI*, but also through one of the other metaphors that Lacan uses to characterize the image-repertoire.

That text variably refers to the screen as a "stain," an "envelope," a "mask," a "double," a "semblance," and a "thrown-off skin."[3] I will argue that the first of these metaphors is crucial to any understanding of the photographic analogy with which Lacan illustrates his relation to the gaze. I will also attempt to show that it is central to the specification of the (once again, limited) agency available to the subject, who depends upon the camera/gaze for his or her specular affirmation. Finally, in this sixth and final chapter of *The Threshold of the Visible World,* I will engage with a series of images which together provide an extended commentary on the image-repertoire through which the late-twentieth-century subject sees and is seen, and which will further complicate the notion of the stain: Cindy Sherman's *Untitled Film Stills.*

The Photographic World Picture

Vilem Flusser reiterates Debord's lament about the disappearance of the referent into representation in his provocative book *Towards a Philosophy of Photography.* However, centrally informing this lament is the assumption that the images which intervene between us and the world are primarily *photographic* in nature. And, although Flusser manifests a naive nostalgia for a time when our representations enjoyed a more continuous relation to the real—somehow not only pointing us toward, but also taking us to the real—the passage in question is very reminiscent of the field of vision described in *Four Fundamental Concepts.* I will consequently take the liberty of quoting it in its entirety:

> Images are meant to render the world accessible and imaginable to man. But, even as they do so, they interpose themselves between man and the world. They are meant to be maps, and they become screens. Instead of presenting the world to

man, they re-present it, put themselves in place of the world, to the extent that man lives as a function of the images he has produced. He no longer deciphers them, but projects them back into the world "out there" without having deciphered them. The world becomes image-like.[4]

Flusser puts photographs in the very place Lacan reserves for the screen. He even deploys the word "screen" when attempting to specify the mediating role performed by photographic images in our culture. He, thus, implicitly underscores the fundamentally photographic "consistency" of the screen through which we apprehend the world. What this means is not that literal photographs block our access to objects and landscapes, but that when we look at those things it is more often than not through an imaginary viewfinder. This viewfinder organizes what we see in relation to the range and formal logic of culturally available photographic representations, in relation to what Flusser would call the "program" of the "black box."[5]

But it is not only that this imaginary camera lens intervenes between the world and our look, structuring what we see in photographic terms, but that we experience ourselves-as-spectacle in relation to it. As Susan Sontag observes, "We learn to see ourselves photographically: to regard oneself as attractive is, precisely, to judge that one would look good in a photograph."[6] Those moments at which we become conscious of our emplacement within the field of vision are precisely those at which we apprehend ourselves in the guise of a fantasmatic photograph. Conversely, it is when a real camera is trained upon us that we have our most acute awareness of being seen.

Roland Barthes is perhaps the greatest theorist of this particular variant of the experience of "being seen." For him, it entails, first of all, the "advent" of oneself as "other."[7] One apprehends oneself as emerging—or being made to emerge—as image. This is true of other forms of representational "capture" as well, but here the apprehension of oneself as image has a more profoundly self-alienating aspect than usual. The photograph is related to the body it depicts not only iconically but also indexically, and so is more closely tied to the profilmic referent. As Metz says, it effects a "cut" inside that referent.[8] It is as though our bodily *Gestalt* were itself suddenly objectified, transformed into a representation—and not for us, as in the mirror transaction, but for a visual agency radically exterior to our look. *Das Heimliche* suddenly becomes *unheimlich*.

There is something "mortifying" about the experience of being photographed by a real or metaphoric camera. This mortification involves not only that death which is the "*eidos* of [the] Photograph"[9]—an abduction from the realm of the vital into that of the image—but also the congealing of the body into a statue-like rigidity. Barthes literalizes this second meaning of mortification—immobilization, arrestation—through an example drawn from early photography:

Photography transformed subject into object, and even, one might say, into a museum object: in order to take the first portraits…the subject had to assume long poses under a glass roof in bright sunlight; to become an object made one suffer as much as a surgical operation; then a device was invented, a kind of prosthesis invisible to the lens, which supported and maintained the body in its passage to immobility: this headrest was the pedestal of the statue I would become, the corset of my imaginary essence. (13)

Since Barthes speaks here not so much about the camera in general as about the still camera in particular, the metaphoric applicability of this passage to the gaze might seem to be limited. However, I would like to suggest that, in fact, the opposite is the case. The still camera provides a more central metaphor for conceptualizing the gaze than does the film or video camera, particularly when it comes to constituting the subject-as-spectacle. The mobility of the moving image situates it symbolically on the side of vitality and movement, and those values make the film and video cameras less appropriate signifiers for the gaze, which in Lacan's account signifies death and immobilization. "The gaze in itself not only terminates the movement, it freezes it," he remarks in *Seminar XI*,

…it is that which has the effect of arresting movement and, literally, of killing life. At the moment the subject stops, suspending his gesture, he is mortified. This anti-life, anti-movement function of this terminal point is the *fascinum,* and it is precisely one of the dimensions in which the power of the gaze is exercised directly. (117–18)

The still photograph dramatizes more strikingly than the moving image both the advent of specular existence as the loss of flux and vitality, and that necessarily suspended state in which any body aspires to formal coherence. Movement disrupts the latter's "composition," in every sense of the word. It is synonymous with dehiscence, with a kind of unraveling of the *Gestalt.* And, in moving, the cinematic or video image not only undoes coherence, but also induces a certain amnesia. As Metz suggests, we see a new image only at the cost of a certain "forgetting" of the one which preceded it (158). There is, as it were, no "longevity" to the cinematic image. It is perhaps for this reason that we can remember a film better visually through the poster which represents it in the theater lobby than through any of its actual images, and that the video industry has felt impelled for memorial purposes to offer a machine for creating still images out of the flow of images constituting a home video. Whereas the moving image consigns what it depicts to oblivion, the still photograph gives us access to a stable and durable image of self.

The representational action of the still photograph also encroaches upon the referent more emphatically than does the moving image, and, thus, induces a more profound mortification there, as well. To cite the author of "Photograghy and Fetish" once again, whereas the all important relation in cinema is that linking one image to the next, the privileged connection in still photography is that tying the image to the object it depicts (156). What this means is that a still photograph of a given subject always designates him or her with a much more stubborn insistence than can a strip of film or video, which albeit also iconic and indexical, inevitably tilts in the direction of fictiveness.

Mortification, as Barthes uses it, also has a third meaning, one less specific to the still camera. The subject whose real or metaphoric photograph is in the process of being taken fantasizes that his or her sublation from life to the death of representation will at least work to preserve what would otherwise be vulnerable to the vicissitudes of time—that it will capture and immortalize his or her "essence." However, this subject undergoes over and over again the mortifying experience of being apprehended in ways which have nothing to do with any such essence or inner "truth," but are an effect rather of the screen. Only love, Barthes observes, can erase the often terrible meaning which the camera/gaze inscribes onto the frozen body (12). "Love" is here a signifier for that productive look about which I spoke in Chapter 5.

At the same time that the actual or imaginary photographic transaction kills, it also confers "reality" upon what it captures. As Sontag puts it, people in "industrialized countries"—people, that is, for whom the gaze is primarily figured as a camera—"seek to have their photographs taken" because they believe that they are "made real by photographs" (161). This is not only because they are thereby transformed into a psychically assimilable and affirmable image, but also because the clicking of the actual or metaphoric camera signifies that social "acknowledgment" or "recognition" upon which all subjectivity depends. The still camera simultaneously "kills" and affirms; it lifts the object out of life and into representation, and psychically and socially actualizes it. It would thus seem that what we generally think of as "reality" is on the side of "death" rather than "life," representation rather than being.

Pierre Bourdieu encourages us to extend this argument beyond the individual subject to the institution of the family. In his essay, "The Cult of Unity and Cultivated Differences," Bourdieu maintains that the family exists as such largely in and through the group photograph and photograph album, which confer upon it an actuality and a coherence which it would otherwise lack. Because of the social and psychic importance of the family, photographers—whether amateur or professional—devote themselves to this subject more than to any other. "Photographic practice only exists and subsists for most of the time by virtue of its *family function* or rather by the function conferred upon it by the family group," Bourdieu writes, "namely that of solemnizing and immortalizing the high points of family life, in short, of reinforcing the integration of the family group by [reasserting] the sense that it has both of itself and of its unity."[10]

Flusser remarks at one point that it is not only the subject and the family but also "events" which depend upon the camera for their actuality. He suggests that events have developed such a hyperconsciousness of their dependence on the camera that they go so far as to solicit its attention. "Every event aims at reaching the television or cinema screen or at becoming a photograph," he writes (14). In very different contexts, Siegfried Kracauer and Robert Smithson offer more extreme versions of the same argument. They both claim that the world in its entirety solicits the click of an actual or imaginary camera, and that it does so by making itself in advance into a "photograph." Kracauer writes that "the world itself has taken on a 'photographic face'; it can be photographed because it strives to be completely reducible to the spatial continuum that yields to snapshots."[11] And Smithson describes arriving at a location he planned to photograph, and finding that it had already assumed representational coherence before he even aimed his camera at it:

Noonday sunshine cinema-ized the site, turning the bridge and the river into an over-exposed *picture*. Photographing it with my Instamatic 400 was like photographing a photograph. The sun became a monstrous light-bulb that projected a detailed series of "stills" through my Instamatic into my eye. When I walked on the bridge, it was as though I was walking on an enormous photograph that was made of wood and steel, underneath the river existed as an enormous movie film that showed nothing but a continuous blank.[12]

Of course, in the passages I have just quoted, Flusser, Kracauer, and Smithson attest more to the thoroughness with which the photographic defines our contemporary field of vision than to some kind of intentionality inherent in objects and events. However, I have included these three passages here because they are displacements onto the nonhuman domain of a phenomenon which is a central feature of human subjectivity. Flusser's account of events, Kracauer's of the world, and Smithson's of a particular landscape make those three entities responsible for representing something which is familiar to all of us from the literal photo session, and which is also a feature of our everyday experience of the gaze. These examples dramatize the anticipatory congealing of the body confronted with a real or metaphoric camera into the form of what might be called a "pre-photographic photograph." They resituate onto a nonhuman category some of the gestures by which the subject offers him- or herself to the gaze already in the guise of a particular "picture."

Lacan devotes a number of pages in *Four Fundamental Concepts* to this phenomenon which he calls "mimicry," or, extrapolating from his major example, the "stain." Like Flusser and Smithson, he begins his account of mimicry with the natural domain, to which he imputes a similar intentionality. Drawing upon Roger Caillois's important deconstruction of the notion that natural selection precipitates all natural mutations,[13] Lacan advances as his primary instanciation of mimicry the behavior of certain species of insects, which adopt the shape or color of other natural objects. The example which interests him most is the crustacean called "caprella," which lives among the "quasi-plant animal" known as briozaires. In those surroundings, the caprella imitates the briozaires's intestinal loop, which assumes a stainlike shape. Like Caillois, Lacan quickly dispenses with the notion that this disguise serves a merely protective function by pointing out that it fails to deceive predators. Instead, he maintains that the caprella's disguise represents purely and simply its attempt to become part of a particular "picture":

> [The caprella] becomes a stain, it becomes a picture, it is inscribed in the picture. This, strictly speaking, is the origin of mimicry. And, on the basis, the fundamental dimensions of the inscription of the subject in the picture appear infinitely more justified than a more hesitant guess might suggest at first sight. (99)

Significantly, Caillois himself refers to this stain mimicry as "a reproduction in three-dimensional space with solids and voids: sculpture-photography or better *teleplasty*" (23). Although Lacan makes no reference to this striking metaphor, it is crucial to establishing the analogic link between the caprella, and the subject who occupies our contemporary field of vision. Like that crustacean, this subject does not always wait passively and unconsciously for the gaze to "photograph" him or her in the shape of a preexisting image. On the contrary, he or she may give him- or herself to be apprehended by the gaze in a certain way, by assuming the shape of either a desired representation or one that has come through less happy circumstances to mark the physical body. When this happens, the subject does not simply hold up the imaginary photograph in front of him or her, but approximates or attempts to approximate its form. In this sense, the mimicry which Lacan and Caillois discuss might be said to constitute three-dimensional "photography."

Lacan's recourse to the metaphor of a stain when accounting for the image in the guise of which we invite the gaze to affirm us suggests the need for a more supple understanding of the relation between our bodies and the representations which make up the cultural inventory than that suggested by the signifier "screen." The stain metaphor accounts for that relation in three-dimensional rather than two-dimensional terms, and it collapses the distance between the body and the image which defines it. This collapse facilitates a better understanding of the identificatory process at work in what Barthes refers to as the "cunning advent of myself as other." It designates, in a way the screen cannot, the transformation of actual muscles and flesh into a photographic representation, and it helps us to understand that this representation can implicate the postural schema and indeed the whole of what Wallon calls "proprioceptivity." It can thus involve precisely a corporeal assimilation of the image.

In *Seminar XI* Lacan also advances a number of other spatially suggestive metaphors for conceptualizing the relation of subject to image: "envelope," "double," "mask," and "thrown-off skin." "Envelope" suggests that the real or imaginary photograph may enclose the subject, contain him or her either protectively or entrappingly. "Double" indicates an identification opposite to that of the stain: rather than attempting to assimilate the image proprioceptively, the subject here identifies with it at a distance-from-the-self, heteropathically. "Mask" implies self-concealment behind something which is worn, but not psychically assumed. Finally, the notion of the image as a "thrown-off skin" connotes an excretion of the image, a refusal to "wear" the "photograph" through which one has been ratified as subject. This image of bodily dismemberment is evocative of some of the ways in which Frantz Fanon speaks about his rejection of the screen of "blackness."[14] A moment after introducing this metaphor, Lacan puts it to other interesting uses: the thrown-off skin can be deployed defensively, to cover a shield. It can, that is, not only be abjected, but also put between me and the world of others as a protective device.

But what precisely does it mean for Smithson to speak of a particular landscape as having assumed the attributes of a photograph before he had even trained his camera on it? More to the immediate point, what does it mean for a subject to invite the camera/gaze to apprehend him or her in a pregiven form? Through what mechanisms or strategies does the subject offer him- or herself as a "photograph"?

The Pose

It is first and foremost through the pose that the subject gives him- or herself to be apprehended in a particular way by the real or metaphoric camera. Much has been written in recent years on the topic of the pose, but only Craig Owens has fully grasped its essentially photographic nature, the fact that, in addition to being imitative of a preexisting image or visual trope, it is imitative of photography itself. "What do I do when I pose for a photograph?" Owens asks. "I freeze…as if anticipating the still I am about to become; mimicking its opacity, its stillness; inscribing, across the surface of my body, photography's 'mortification' of the flesh."[15] As Owens suggests, the pose not only arrests the body, hyperbolizing the devitalizing effects of all photographic representation, but it also approximates precisely that three-dimensional photography which Caillois associates with mimicry, assimilating proprioceptivity to exteroceptivity, corporeality to the image.

Like the stain, the pose puts the subject who assumes it "in the picture." In the caprella example, the picture might be said to preexist the act of stainlike mimicry, but here the representational logic is different. That picture need not already be in place, because the pose can conjure it into existence all by itself. The representational force which the pose exerts is so great that it radiates outward, and transforms the space around the body and everything which comes into contact with it into an imaginary photograph. Indeed, the pose includes in itself every other feature of the photographic image which is relevant within the domain of subjectivity.

The pose conjures into existence, first of all, that explicit or implicit frame which marks off all representation from the "real." We may not always know precisely where the frame resides; it may only be in place in a very general sense. However, lest we doubt for a moment that it is always there, we need only remember that the body has the capacity to designate the frame in a very precise and inexorable way. Simply through dramatic compression or expansion, the body can indicate its enclosure within a smaller- or larger-than-usual physical space.[16]

The pose is also generative of mise-en-scène. The pose always involves both the positioning of a representationally inflected body in space, and the consequent conversion of that space into a "place." This is as true when that body occupies an empty room as when it is positioned within a set as elaborate and cluttered as those found in a Sternberg film. The pose also includes within itself the category of "costume," since it is something "worn" or "assumed" by the body, which, in turn, transforms other worn or assumed things into costumes. When included in the pose, even a sensible winter coat ceases to be a source of protection against the cold, and becomes part of the larger "display."

Finally, the pose signifies "lit-upness" in a larger, metaphoric respect, and encourages us to make formal and conceptual sense of the actual play of light and shadows across the other components of the imaginary photograph. An oblique shadow cast across half of the face of a posed body is no longer random or insignificant; it becomes part of the "picture," and often connotes a photographic source of illumination (as in the Smithson passage, which characterizes the sun as a "monstrous light-bulb").

Although the pose is the most photographically resonant of all of the elements I have just listed, framing, mise-en-scène, costume, and lighting can also be deployed in ways that deepen the photographic qualities of a particular corporeal display. Alternately, they may provide the occasion for the production of a very different "picture" than that solicited by the pose. They must thus be identified not merely as extensions of the pose, but rather as themselves contributing to the photographic effect described by Smithson.

It is generally assumed that the pose is something deliberate and active. For instance, it is primarily through his account of mimicry, which represents the theoretical category to which we must subsume the pose, that Lacan factors agency into the field of vision. In *Four Fundamental Concepts,* he suggests that simple reproduction is the only possible relation of the animal to the image it imitates, but that in the human domain there is another option. "The human subject…is not, unlike the animal, entirely caught up in this imaginary capture," he writes. "He maps himself in it. How? In so far as he isolates the function of the screen and plays with it. Man, in effect, knows how to play with the mask as that beyond which there is the gaze" (107). Barthes advances a similar argument. In *Camera Lucida,* he writes: "I constitute myself in the process of 'posing,' I instantaneously make another body for myself, I transform myself in advance into an image. This transformation is an active one" (10).

However, even Barthes acknowledges almost immediately that this transformation often has little bearing upon how he is apprehended by the camera/gaze (11–12), so that his activity might be said to involve action without a corresponding result. And Bourdieu underscores the unconscious compliance with photographic stereotype which often overdetermines even the most conscious and willfully assumed pose. He also suggests that the specularized subject has at best only the barest modicum of control over how he or she is apprehended by the camera/gaze:

> it is always as if, by means of obeying the principle of frontality and adopting the most conventional posture, one were seeking as far as possible to control an objectification of one's own image. Axial composition, in accordance with the principle of frontality, provides an impression that is as clearly legible as possible, as if one were seeking to avoid any misunderstanding…. Looking at the person who is looking (or who is taking the photograph), correcting one's posture, one presents oneself to be looked at as one seeks to be looked at.[17]

How are we to reconcile these two very different accounts of what it means to offer oneself as a preexisting photograph to the camera/gaze?

By way of answering this question, I will suggest that the agency which Lacan imputes to mimicry—and, so, by extension, to the pose—is hemmed about with all kinds of constraints. It consequently does not always come into play, even in a limited way. To assume, in advance, the shape of a particular photograph represents at most an attempt to exercise some control over an unavoidable transaction; it is behavior in which the subject engages at the behest of the camera/gaze, and in response to the impossibility of avoiding specularity. Mimicry also proceeds in relation to a preexisting representation, which, in the case of the pose, derives from the cultural screen. It is thus limited to what is at a given moment representationally "possible." In both of these respects, to engage in mimicry is to be "inserted in a function whose exercise grasps us" (100).

Not only is the subject under the imperative to be within spectacle and to assume a guise there which makes some reference to the existing image-repertoire, but the form in which he or she gives him- or herself to be seen also must be symbolically ratified. We cannot simply choose from a kind of wardrobe of possible "photographs" what what we will "wear" on Monday as opposed to Wednesday. We must also be so apprehended.

As I emphasized in Chapter 1, the act of mimicry through which we attempt to assume a particular representational form may be doomed to failure because of certain bodily factors which provide the occasion for a dramatically other "photographic" transaction. The other inherently photographic elements which come into play when a body poses—frame, mise-en-scène, costume, lighting— also do not always conspire with that body to form the desired "picture"; they can often be the provocation for one which is not wanted. Most subjects understand this, at least partially, and attempt to exercise some control over the other features of the "photograph" they offer to the camera/gaze. However, economic and other constraints often drastically limit the success of such attempts. For all of these reasons, the "clicking" of the imaginary camera often does not produce the desired image.

As we will see, many of the poses in Cindy Sherman's *Untitled Film Stills* exhibit precisely this unfulfilled aspiration to be "photographed" in a particular way. Barthes confesses to having the same frustrated desire when confronted with an actual camera, in spite of his most refined and nuanced self-consciousness. "If only I could 'come out' on paper as on a classical canvas," he writes, "endowed with a noble expression—thoughtful, intelligent, etc.! In short, if I could be 'painted' (by Titian) or drawn (by Clouet)!" (11). Instead, the resulting image is "heavy, motionless, stubborn" (12).

Mimicry also does not always imply a resistant or even a conscious intentionality; on the contrary, it may bespeak a subject's completely unconscious compliance with the images to which he or she is accustomed to being apprehended by the camera/gaze. The pose needs to be more generally understood as the photographic imprinting of the body, and that imprinting is not always apparent to the subject in question. It may be the result of the projection of a particular image onto the body so repeatedly as to induce both a psychic and a corporeal identification with it. And the image in question may be generative not of pleasure, but unpleasure.

Perhaps most problematically, the pose may testify to a blind aspiration to approximate an image which represents a cultural ideal, without any thought as to what that ideal implies. Even the subject who arrives at some understanding of his or her specular dependency generally does not then call into question the authority of the images which conventionally represent the visual ideal. He or she merely seeks to be apprehended through them, thereby reaffirming the dominant fiction.

The aspiration to approximate the photographic ideal can also be incompatible with agency in those rare cases where it leads to success rather than failure. Mastery within the domain of mimicry does not imply only—or even primarily—that one successfully controls via the pose and various supplementary props how one is "photographed." The subject adopts an active role vis-à-vis the camera/gaze only insofar as he or she resists imaginary capture by the images through which he or she is voluntarily or involuntarily "photographed," and is consequently in a position to work transformatively with and upon them. However, remaining at a productive distance from the mirror is almost impossible when one simultaneously offers oneself to the camera/gaze in the guise of an ideal image, and has that self-identification "photographically" ratified.

As I stressed in the first chapter, the foreclosure of certain subjects from specular ideality renders further problematic the availability to others of idealizing self-images, no matter how fleeting the resulting *jouissance*. Indeed, the essentializing idealization of one group of subjects always entails the converse deidealization of another, not only at the cultural level but also at the psychic level. The attempt to sustain one's ever-failing identification with ideality requires both the constant projection onto designated others of everything within the self deemed inimical to that value, and the murderous repudiation of alterity.

Assuming even a limited agency with respect to the images through which one is seen thus necessitates more than a preliminary acknowledgment of the exteriority of the screen and the camera/gaze, and an attempt to control the circumstances under which one's self-constituting "photo" is taken. Adopting an active position in the field of vision entails, as well, a constant disruptive and transformative labor at the site of ideality. Such an effort requires the disjunction of the operations of idealization from both the self and the cultural ideal, as well as the subsequent identification at a distance with the newly and provisionally irradiated bodies for which I argued earlier in this book. However, it requires, as well, the exposure of our passionate and limitless desire to be the ideal, and, since that desire can never be definitely abolished, its continual deconstruction and displacement. Once again, I would maintain this as an ethical imperative (and as such a necessary impossibility) at the level of individual conscious subjectivity, and as a political imperative at the level of representational practice.

In order to indicate what such a representational practice might look like, I will now turn to Cindy Sherman's *Untitled Film Stills*. I will argue that these images permit us to see more clearly than usual that we conventionally offer ourselves to the gaze in the form of an imaginary photograph. They also demonstrate that our poses generally attest to the aspiration to conform as closely as possible to the cultural ideal, and that the camera/gaze is not often complicit with that aspiration. They thus dramatize that "long love affair/despair"[18] with the image about which I wrote in Chapter 2. But the *Untitled Film Stills* go even further: they promote our identificatory relation not with the ideal imago which the women they depict so dramatically fail to approximate, but rather with the women themselves, and they make this identification conducive of pleasure rather than unpleasure.

The Untitled Film Stills

The title of Cindy Sherman's *Untitled Film Stills* suggests that it is somehow about the arrest of movement—about the freezing of the flow of film into a single frame. We are seemingly encouraged to conceptualize this immobilization in ways that are primarily cinematic. However, because of the centrality which they give to the pose, with all of its hyperbolically photographic connotations, the *Untitled Film Stills* clearly make the film still metaphoric in some larger sense of the immobilization specific to the photograph. These images seem to be proposing, in other words, that since the film still is in relation to cinema what the photograph is to life, the two sets of terms can stand in for each other. The film still even provides a signifier through which to understand that cut inside the referent about which Metz speaks in his discussion of photography, since the simplest (if not the most typical or responsible) strategy for producing it is to slice a single frame out of the sequence of images which make up a film.

Arthur Danto has already suggested that the *Untitled Film Stills* are not only about conventional photography, but about that three-dimensional photography which Caillois associates with mimicry. Danto proposes, that is, that the images in Sherman's sequence reverse our usual way of thinking about the photograph, which is to assume that the photograph makes reference to the world. Sherman's images posit the world as somehow referential of the photograph. Danto argues that the profilmic event solicits the camera/gaze; it offers itself already as a photograph, or, rather (since actually "being" such an image necessitates the ratification of the camera/gaze), as a "would-be" photograph. Significantly, Danto also maintains that it is via the pose that the profilmic event gives itself to be seen in this way:

> The camera…does not now simply document the pose: the pose itself draws on the language of the still in such a way that even if it were never photographically recorded, the pose would be the photographic equivalent of a *tableau vivant*. Since the scene and the actors who compose the still do so for the sake of the still, the camera is internal to the work.[19]

In my own discussion of the *Untitled Film Stills*, I would like to elaborate on Danto's insight in ways that are more directly relevant to the present discussion.

In each of the black-and-white "film stills," a solitary white woman played by Sherman herself strikes a pose against a background which is either an extension of that pose, a contradiction of it, or something to which the pose lays claim. The pose indicates her desire to be seen in a particular, generally flattering way, by a real or imaginary look, which—because it is more formally than diegetically specified—comes to be symbolic of the camera/gaze.

The poses represented by the *Untitled Film Stills* are, as many critics have noted, extremely stereotypical in nature; they evoke normative ideals of one sort or another. These images thereby make evident not merely that one can only give oneself to be seen via an image drawn from the screen, but also that, for the most part, the subject gravitates for this purpose to those images which have been culturally valorized. However, Sherman's women are seldom "photographed" merely according to the preconditions they attempt to lay down in advance; a corporeal or environmental detail often provokes a very different photographic transaction. A number of the *Untitled Film Stills* also provide a commentary on the other elements of the implicitly photographic image which are imbricated with the pose, and will help us to arrive at a more precise understanding of what such an image involves.

Let us begin our analysis of the *Untitled Film Stills* with the second and third images in that series, images that are almost flamboyantly "about" the pose as a solicitation to be photographed in a certain way, but which dramatize just how unresponsive the camera/gaze can be to such an advance. In the first of these stills, a woman turns to look at herself in a bathroom mirror [figure 77]. The rest of her body still points in the other direction, as if she were about to walk out of the bathroom before she turned to look into the mirror. Because of this wracked posture, we see her face only in the reflecting surface: the image which it provides shows her head inclining langorously backward, the forefinger of her right hand just grazing her chin.

The mirror image in this still clearly represents its protagonist as she wants to be seen; as an embodiment of traditional female beauty. However, the camera/gaze does not cooperate with this wish. It photographs her not from the direction of the mirror, but from the other side. And although this position still affords us a view of the woman's framed and idealized self-portrait, it shows that self-portrait to be in striking contrast to the rest of her body. A bit chubby and undefined, the woman's body most definitely does not offer itself to be seen. Not only does her body lack the poised self-consciousness of her stylized head and right hand, but she also attempts to cover it with a large terry-cloth towel, as if to keep it out of the "picture." There is good reason for this, since its parameters are incommensurate with the specular reflection.

Although ostensibly more about a mirror than a photographic transaction, two features of this image demonstrate its reference to the camera/gaze. First,

figure 77

as Rosalind Krauss has recently pointed out, the grain of the image is unusually prominent, as if to suggest that photographic objectification of the body upon
which I have already repeatedly commented.[20] Second, the frame of the mirror
is contained within the larger frame of the doorway, which foregrounds the fact
that the image offers a perspective that is outside the dyadic exchange between
subject and mirror—a perspective which implies, precisely, the camera/gaze.
Together, these two details define the woman's pose more as an appeal to be
apprehended in pregiven ways by that apparatus than as a replay of the rapturous accession to ideality of the Lacanian mirror stage.

If *Still #2* proposes certain features of the body itself as counterindicative of
the wished-for "photographic" exchange, *Still #3* isolates more environmental
factors. In this image, a woman stands to the right, facing a sink with a dishrack,
a bottle of Ivory dishwashing liquid, an almost-empty juice bottle, and an opened
Morton's salt container [figure 78]. She wears a frilly apron and a sexy T-shirt.

figure 78

She looks seductively, with moistened lips, over her left shoulder at an unseen figure, presumably male. Because she leans with her left hand on the counter, her
shoulder is provocatively elevated, and her breasts sharply defined. Here, the
woman offers herself to be "photographed" as "vamp," as sexual tease, but the
mundane objects in her immediate vicinity contradict this self-definition, and
proclaim her instead to be a "Hausfrau."

The upper edge of the still crops the woman's face just above the left eye, cutting off her left eyebrow, forehead, and bangs, foregrounding both the frame
and the perspective from which the image has been shot. It is up to the observant
spectator to remark that the point toward which the woman looks is dramatically
different than the position from which she is photographed. This disjuncture
reminds us, once again, that the camera/gaze does not always apprehend us from
the vantage point to which we direct our self-imaging.

Still #34 provides yet another example of a woman aspiring to occupy a
desired "photograph" through a particular pose. However, it indicates more
clearly than *Still #2* or *Still #3* that a body may assume a pose more at the behest
of the unconscious than the conscious. This still also calls into question the
notion that the pose is unambiguously "active" by pointing to the discursive
source of the pose. It thereby suggests that mimicry means not only "to be inserted in a function whose exercise grasps" one, but, all too often, a passive compliance to a normative ideal.

figure 79

In this image, a dark-haired woman lies on a crumpled black sheet, wearing only a half-unbuttoned shirt and panties. Her head reclines voluptuously and her body assumes a typical "cheesecake" pose [figure 79]. In front of her is situated a pulp novel of the sort that by its very cover proclaims itself to be instigatory of traditional female fantasy. It is face down, presumably open at the page which inspired the dreamy, faraway look on the woman's face. Clearly, the woman seeks to project herself imaginarily into a mise-en-scène suggested by the novel, and her half-conscious pose represents her corporeal claim upon that position. It is as if she would be immediately transported there if she could only succeed in being "photographed" according to the logic of the pose.

However, the position adopted by the camera/gaze is, once again, poorly calculated to satisfy this desire: it shoots the woman from a position closer to her feet than her head, as a result of which the lower half of her body is disproportionately—and unflatteringly—distended in relation to the upper half. Indeed, her head is so small that it seems to belong to a completely other body, an effect which is compounded by the shading of her dark hair into the black sheets on which she lies.

The pose is not the only element of the profilmic event "captured" by this still which is inherently photographic. The black sheets showcase the woman's body in a way that connotes "erotic photograph," and, indeed, they are an extension of her pose. Significantly, the edges of the photograph also coincide almost seamlessly with the sides of the bed, as if to suggest that the bed determined in advance the image's frame-lines. The photograph is internal to *Still #34* in yet another way, as well. The half-buttoned shirt worn by the reclining woman is white, which serves to further accentuate the contrast between that pool of brightness which is her body and the shadowy folds of the sheets. Even prior to the installation of the lamp, which brightens the right side of the frame, and which presumably provided the primary source of illumination for the photograph, the woman in *Still #34* might be said to have been "lit up."

Still #50 represents another example of a woman posing in self-idealizing ways for an implied camera/gaze. However, it is to be distinguished in this respect from *Still #2,* where the woman seeks to transport herself out of her position in front of the sink and into one more commensurate with her fantasies merely by dint of her pose. Here, through her bodily configuration, the woman attempts to become the rightful occupant of the space she occupies, but to which she does not feel entirely equal. The room in which she sits, in other words, represents a kind of "dreamscape."

figure 80

That room is a study in 1960s interior decoration stereotypes; indeed, it could have been furnished through ideas drawn from magazine illustrations of the time [figure 80]. Both in this respect, and in the exaggerated neatness and precision with which its contents have been arranged, it is immanently "photographic." The room seems almost to solicit the camera/gaze—to say, much like Caillois's caprella: "This is how I want to be seen." It contains Indian rugs, a primitive carving, an abstract sculpture, and a rigorously symmetrical "conversational" grouping of contemporary chairs, couch, and coffee table, placed in front of a minimalist fireplace. The coffee table holds three ash trays.

On the couch sits a dark-haired woman in a low-cut black dress, with artificial leopard-skin collar and cuffs. One leg is folded with feigned casualness underneath her, and the other extends gracefully to the floor. However, the woman's upper body is hyperbolically erect, as if she is afraid of making a mistake, and she looks ahead of her with an equally intense attention. The woman holds a cocktail on her lap, again with an attitude of *savoir-faire,* but one has the impression that she is afraid to consume too much of its contents for fear of saying something gauche. The stiffness of her upper body indicates that she is overwhelmingly impressed by the contents and style of the room in which she sits, and that she yearns to be as sophisticated as its owner.

Here, it is again the body itself which works at the expense of the pose, and precipitates the production of a different photograph from the one the woman's artfully arranged legs and carefully selected costume solicit. To state the matter rather more precisely, certain anxieties and half-conscious desires manifest themselves corporeally in a way which disrupts the intended effect. The woman's hyperalertness leads to the involuntary assumption of a pose which is the very opposite of the one she means to produce, a pose which puts her tense torso in a relation of contradiction to the studied casualness of the lower half of her body. And, once again, the actual photograph signals the disparity between the desire and the end result by showing the woman looking toward a point other than that from which the camera shoots her.

However, it is not so much the woman's desire to be adequate to the room which is finally frustrated, but rather her aspiration to be photographed as the embodiment of sophistication. The first of these wishes is satisfied, albeit in a surprising way, because the room suffers the same fate as the woman. It also tries too hard to be "modern" and "cosmopolitan." Indeed, its three ash trays might be said to be the nonhuman equivalent of the woman's rigid torso, making it a very appropriate setting, finally, for its only visible inhabitant.

I have indicated that the pose is so representationally resonant that it can impart photographic significance to its surroundings and everything with which it comes into contact. Not only do the *Untitled Film Stills* provide us with an extended commentary on the pose as the primary mechanism through which

figure 81

the subject gives him- or herself to be "photographed" in a generally self-ideal-izing way by the camera/gaze, and the conditions under which this solicitation generally meets with failure, but, in addition, they offer a vivid dramatization of the reverberative qualities of the pose. *Still #35* is a case in point.

This image shows a blonde woman in a crumpled apron and cheap house dress standing in the center of the frame, her body facing a black coat hanging on a hook on the wall, but her head looking back toward an unspecified viewer [fig-ure 81]. Her arms are exaggeratedly "akimbo," and her legs robustly spread, as if to suggest that she stands on solid moral ground. Her facial expression is full of righteous indignation. All in all, she is the very image of virtuous and offended womanhood.

The corner where the woman stands is shabby. The door which partly frames her is badly scuffed at the bottom, and—like the woman's clothing—the room generally connotes poverty and neglect. Without the woman in it, these details would go unremarked, but her pose is so expressive that it works to inscribe meaning on everything in the frame. Because of the way she is positioned in front of the coat, we imagine that she has just searched or is about to search its pockets for evidence that the owner has drunk away his week's paycheck, or engaged in some form of sexual malfeasance. As further evidence of the coat owner's brutish character, we "see" that he habitually closes the door by kicking it with his dirty boots.

The woman addresses her pose not so much to this man, who would presumably be incapable of recognizing her suffering or force of character, as the gaze in the guise of the camera. I say "camera" rather than the "higher moral authority" to whom the woman might seem likelier to appeal because the attitude of her body is so evocative of cinematic melodrama, particularly of the silent variety, in which the body can often be congealed into a momentarily immobile pose, uncannily suggestive of the still photograph.

Interestingly, the woman's pose here makes a claim less on corporeal than moral ideality. The camera/gaze's position coincides with the point to which she addresses her pose, seemingly ratifying the latter. However, it is perhaps impossible to look at a photograph of a reasonably young woman without measuring her by the usual standards of feminine beauty, standards which have perhaps as much to do with erotic "self-presentation" as with corporeal features. The insistent centering of this figure in the frame and the slightly lower than usual viewing angle put her "on stage," as it were, and further specularize her. It is thus difficult not to notice that the woman wears clothes which are the very opposite of those in which most of us seek to be literally or metaphorically photographed: her stockings "bag" slightly and her hair is tied into a housewife's kerchief.

These details fade in significance only when the eye strays once again away from the "central exhibit" to the margins, when we glance for a second time at the scuff-marks on the door. These scuff-marks serve as a powerful reminder of the economic and other circumstances militating against the sublation of certain bodies into an idealizing frame. For the eye which has engaged in this revisionary act of looking, it is now also possible to see something which the baggy stockings and rumpled house dress and apron belie: the intelligence, intensity, and even beauty of the face with which the woman looks back over her shoulder.

As I intimated in passing in relation to *Stills #34* and *#50*, the *Untitled Film Stills* also provide us with a number of images in which not only the woman but also the pro-filmic event in its entirety might be said to solicit the camera/gaze, and so help to clarify further the nature of the "photographic." *Still #11* is one such image. In it, a woman lies diagonally across a made bed, her head in the

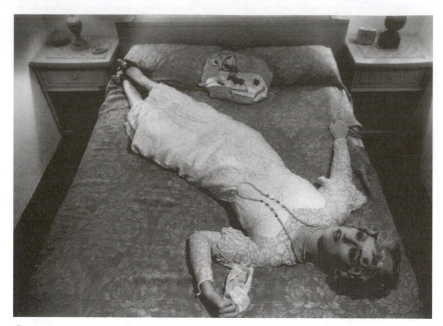

figure 82

lower right hand corner, her feet touching the left pillow. She wears a long white lace dress evocative of the 1930s, a matching coiffure, and a long strand of pearls [figure 82]. Her right hand clutches the bedspread, in a calculated gesture of despair, and her raised left hand elevates a lace handkerchief with studied grace. Her look is a bit out of focus, as if given over more to the mental than to the physical act of "seeing," and her expression is just melancholic enough to be evocative but not disfiguring. She lies at so precise a diagonal, and her dress and pearls are so artfully arranged, that one has the impression that the scene has already been carefully rehearsed. "Tragic Heroine" is the ideal image to which she aspires, and the clock on the night table conspires with her in articulating this trope: it reads 11:20, the time of night when one is likely to be alone in one's room in fancy dress only when the evening has ended badly and (hence) early.

But the carefully controlled conditions under which the woman expresses her grief—her general concern not only to look as attractive as possible while undergoing her "breakdown," but also to offer herself at this precise moment to the camera/gaze—results in a very different photograph than the one the woman solicits, as does the cushion with dog-appliqué which rests in the middle of the two pillows. Not only does the woman's body form a precise diagonal across the bed, but the bed is positioned exactly in the middle of the room, flanked on either side by identical night tables. And since, through a miracle of precision, the bedroom set fits exactly into the wall space into which it has been inserted, it is

The Threshold of the Visible World

216

framed on either side by a wall, a point which Sherman's camera underscores by matching its own edges to those of the room as a whole.

The light is as hyperbolically internal to *Still #11* as is the frame, since the two lamps resting on the night table provide a lavish source of illumination. Finally, although any item of clothing worn by a body assuming a pose automatically gains the status of a costume, and any hairstyle that of a "coiffure," that is doubly so here, since the woman wears a dress, necklace, and hairstyle which together connote "the thirties," while at the same time occupying a bedroom indicative of the 1950s. Unlike the fashion of the moment, retro always signifies "fancy dress," and—perhaps unavoidably, since that is primarily how we recognize it as such—"photography" and "cinema." "Insincerity" and "artificiality" are the values which come into play over and against the image which the woman offers to the camera/gaze.

Still #15 also provides an implicit commentary on how the photograph can come to be immanent within the profilmic event not only through the pose but also through framing and lighting. A dark-haired woman in shorts and a low-cut T-shirt with cinch belt, white socks, and high heels sits in the window of an exposed-brick room [figure 83]. One leg, bent at a right angle, reaches to the floor, while the other rests in a crooked position on the window sill. The woman's arms are strategically placed to afford the fullest and most idealized view possible of her breasts, waist, thighs, and legs. The three-dimensional photography which might be said to have preceded the actual photographic event sought out its own light and representational frame as well: illumination floods into the image through the uncurtained window before which the woman sits, and the wall surrounding the window encloses all of her body except for her dangling leg in a brick frame.

The woman looks through the window at an unspecified object. But, although she is ostensibly a spectator, she pointedly gives herself to be seen—not by some casual passerby, who would at best glimpse only a distant and partial view of her artfully displayed body, but by an imaginary gaze *inside the room.* I specify the viewer's location as being inside rather than outside because the woman's pose can only be fully apprehended from there. Surprisingly, Sherman's actual camera assumes that position. This is consequently one of the rare images in the *Untitled Film Stills* where the camera/gaze photographs, as it were, the flattering "photograph." (*Still #32* is another, where part of the face, neck, shoulders, and arms of a woman swim out of darkness toward the illumination of a single match, with which she is about to light her cigarette. There, however, ideality is so fully an effect of the lighting that it would be dispelled with a single switch of the light.) Only the inappropriate placement of a gold cross between the woman's partly exposed breasts sets up a slight disturbance in the image.

figure 83

I will briefly mention only two more stills in which Sherman makes the frame internal to the image before raising the question of where, precisely, the screen might be said to reside in the readings I have just performed. The first of these is *Still #37*, in which a woman images herself as "Nature Girl." The figure in question stands in front of a rustic brick fireplace, her right arm reclining at a ninety-degree angle on the mantel, a cigarette in her hand [figure 84]. One leg rests in an elevated position on the hearth, and her left arm hangs at her side. She wears a black sweater, pants, and walking shoes. Above the mantel hangs a stereotypical painting of rocks, mountains, and water, and to its left stands a piece of petrified wood. The photograph is here immanent within the image because the painting depicts the landscape of the woman's desire—the frame into which she seeks to project herself through the studied "naturalness" of her pose and costume. It is, in fact, doubly so, since the scene is all in all evocative not so much of the natural world as of that highly stylized troping of it familiar to us through a film like Douglas Sirk's *All that Heaven Allows,* with its Thoreau quotes and wood-paneled station wagon.

figure 84

In *Still #43*, a woman with a '60s-style bouffant haircut and cotton sundress sits decoratively on a large, sprawling tree [figure 85]. She gazes dreamily into space. What she "sees" is shown in backdrop through what I take to be an astonishing photographic compilation: the famous vertical rock formations of Monument Valley. This is an imaginary landscape, made famous through the films of John Ford, which the woman has chosen as the scene for an unspecified fantasy, perhaps of the "white woman kidnapped by Indians" variety. Its inclusion here divests the profilmic referent of actuality, making the photograph in its entirety more a representation of a representation than a sublation from actuality to art. Both the seeming unself-consciousness of the woman's pose and her vague look into a fantasmatic "elsewhere" once again call into question the notion that such bodily display always operates at the best of a willed agency, and point to the origin of the pose in a prior textual instance.

figure 85

The "Good Enough"

Many of the readings I have produced of selected *Untitled Film Stills* have involved my isolation of details in those photographs that activate certain almost impossible to avoid meanings, meanings which often collide with a character's desire to be "photographed" in a particular way—details of body, clothing, decor, etc. (Examples of such details include the slight chubbiness of the woman in *Still #2*, the seemingly inappropriate gold cross situated between the breasts of the woman in *Still #15*, the crumpled apron worn by the woman in *Still #35*, and the exaggerated erectness of the woman's posture in *Still #50*). There are unquestionably ways in which my look has intervened here in idiosyncratic and transformative ways, but most of the pictorial elements to which I have attributed the opening up of an unflattering distance between the actual stills and the photographs Sherman's women solicit would be capable of generating the same meaning within any reader from the same culture. This meaning is so readily available because it is so frequently reiterated—because it comprises what, in the previous chapter, I called the "given-to-be-seen."

In her own discussion of the *Untitled Film Stills*, Judith Williamson suggests that the stills themselves are "innocent"; it is the viewer who "suppl[ies] the femininity" in question "through social and cultural knowledge." Thus, "the stereotypes and assumptions necessary to 'get' each picture are found in our own heads."[21] I am, in effect, elaborating here upon Williamson's insight through another vocabulary. The screen is finally not only "on" the bodies of the women Sherman's *Untitled Film Stills* showcase, but also "inside" us. Moreover, although the look is not the gaze, nevertheless, we must collectively assume at least partial responsibility for the terms under which the latter "photographs" the world.

By way of clarifying the first of these points, I will suggest that the screen or cultural image-repertoire inhabits each of us, much as language does. What this means is that when we apprehend another person or an object, we necessarily do so via that large, diverse, but ultimately finite range of representational coordinates which determine what and how the members of our culture see—how they process visual detail, and what meaning they give it. And just as certain words suggest themselves to us more readily than others, because they are the currency of daily use in our society, so certain representational coordinates propose themselves as more appropriate frames through which to apprehend the world than others, simply because they are subject within our society to a more frequent and emphatic articulation. The full range of representational coordinates which are culturally available at a particular moment in time constitute what I have been calling the "screen," and those which propose themselves with a certain inevitability the "given-to-be-seen."

By way of explaining how we might collectively be at least partially responsible for the way the gaze photographs the world, I want to return once again to the diagrams with which Lacan clarifies the field of vision in *Four Fundamental Concepts*. In *Male Subjectivity at the Margins*, I wrote that the third of these diagrams accounts only for the placement of an individual subject within the field of vision. When another subject occupies the place of "object" in relation to this subject, and returns the look, a second, inverted diagram has to be superimposed upon the first in order to schematize his or her simultaneous status as "eye" and "spectacle."[22] This double diagram shows that each of these two subject's looks occupies the position of the gaze for the other. It thereby makes apparent that although the gaze is always external to every subject in his or her capacity as spectacle, and always radically in excess of every eye, nevertheless the subject's look is often a provisional signifier of the gaze for that other who occupies the position of the object in relation to him or her:

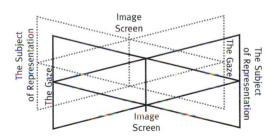

To state the matter in a way less likely to lead to a reactivation of the Cartesian fantasy, the look is a "functionary" of the camera/gaze.[23] This means not only that that imaginary apparatus "uses" the eye, much as a machine does the worker, but that it depends upon the latter for its operation. The look helps to determine how and what the gaze "photographs." It turns the imaginary view-finder.

As I suggested in Chapter 4, the optical apparatus which presently provides the primary trope for the gaze is simultaneously a representational logic and a series of material practices, in complex interaction with each other. In this metaphoric capacity, as in its capacity as illumination, the gaze clearly stands to one side of any human eye. Indeed, in many respects—its mortifying and memorial functions, its "objectivity"[24]—it is antipathetic to the look, which is on the side of flux, memory, and subjectivity. However, the camera/gaze is only a local elaboration of something much more fundamental and durable: what Lacan calls "the presence of others as such" (84). It is the inscription in the field of vision of the symbolic, of the necessity for every subject to be seen in order to "be." And although this scopic transaction is in every sense much "bigger" than the look, the look nonetheless plays a key role in bringing it about.

To paraphrase Marx, the look finally "makes" the "photograph," although not just as it pleases.[25] The look's agency is limited by the representational logic and material practices which organize the visual field at any moment in time, and which influence its ways of seeing in all kinds of perceptible and imperceptible ways. Its agency is further circumscribed by the imperative placed upon it to apprehend the world via the screen. But although impinged upon in both of these crucial ways, the look nonetheless helps to determine the precise parameters through which the world is "pictured."

When one scrutinizes the above diagram, the subject-as-look can be seen to occupy the geometral point, which is the site from which the given-to-be-seen comes into focus. This diagram would thus seem to suggest that the geometral point is the viewing position from which the subject inevitably apprehends its objects. It seems to suggest, that is, that the given-to-be-seen is so deep "inside" us that we almost automatically register certain normative meanings when we perceive, for instance, a black skin, a female morphology, or the tattered clothes of a homeless person. And even in the event we could apprehend the world through another representational grid, the given-to-be-seen would prevail within the larger socius, and so at the unlocatable site of the camera/gaze.

I want to distance myself from such a totalizing account of the look, while at the same time acknowledging once again the force of normative representation. As I suggested in the previous chapter, although the given-to-be-seen imposes itself with a great deal of insistence upon the eye, the eye is nevertheless capable of seeing productively—of occupying a viewing position other than that assigned in advance, and, so, of apprehending its object under radically different terms. However, it is often only retroactively, through a *Nachträglichkeit,* or deferred action, that it manages to assume this "deviant" viewing position.

The normative aspects of the screen may indeed be so deeply rooted within our psyches, and so tightly imbricated with our desires and identifications, that they generally determine what we see at the first moment of looking at a particular object. Fortunately, however, no look ever takes place once and for all. Rather, each act of spectation is subject to a complex series of conscious and unconscious "vicissitudes," which can completely transform the value of what is originally seen, and which cannot be easily predicted in advance. Subsequently, the eye may invest libidinally in the given-to-be-seen, or pursue a radically other itinerary, one which works to derealize rather than to affirm the visual standard.

Alone our look can only make a difference within the ethical domain of inter-subjective relations. This difference is not inconsequential: those subjects who are accustomed to having an unflattering set of visual coordinates projected onto them depend for their psychic survival upon the loving look of their inti-mates, which (as Barthes suggests) can at least temporarily erase the terrible effect of that projection (12). But if the look acts in concert with enough other looks, it can reterritorialize the screen, bringing new elements into cultural prominence, and casting into darkness those which presently constitute nor-mative representation. Under such necessarily collective conditions, the look could significantly change how the camera/gaze "photographs" the world.

In the previous chapter, I explored memory as a crucial vehicle for revisionary looking. I want to suggest by way of concluding both this chapter and the book as a whole that Sherman's *Untitled Film Stills* make available another kind of *Nachträglichkeit,* one engaging us in the first instance more as conscious than as unconscious viewers, but with important unconscious implications. And since these images are so hyperbolically "about" the gaze as camera, their solicitation of us to look again, differently, can perhaps best be understood as an invitation to "rephotograph" the women in them through a different representational frame.

As Judith Williamson suggests, the *Untitled Film Stills* dramatize over and over again the seemingly mechanical way in which visual detail precipitates the generation of stereotypical meaning in us. The the bottle of Ivory dishwashing liquid and opened container of Morton's salt immediately prompt the assign-ment of the value "housewife" (and, by implication, "drudge") to the woman in *Still #3,* just as the lace handkerchief imparts "artificiality" and "insincerity" to the woman in *Still #11.* However, these images subsequently open up to us the pos-sibility of looking again, from a new vantage point, and so of both subjecting the initial act of perception to critical scrutiny, and apprehending the object via different representational parameters.

Other critics have also sensed that the *Untitled Film Stills* make available to us more than one viewing position, but this alternative viewing position is generally assumed to involve an ironic detachment from the women and their poses. Gerald Marzorati, for instance, writes that in these photographs Sherman "has sought to capture the look and feel of stills from '50's films, and at the same time has sought to deny it all." He goes on to say that there is a "tension in these pictures" between the stereotypes they portray, and "Sherman's own feelings about the stereotype."[26] Similarly, Michael Danoff speaks about the pleasure which comes when one no longer passively absorbs the stereotypes, but actively "gets" them, a "getting" which once again implies a distanciation from the women who ostensibly embody them.[27]

However, I would myself agree with Peter Schjeldahl that there is "an absence of any reassuring, campy wink or nudge" in these images.[28] We are not invited to laugh, either about the aspiration of the figures in them to be apprehended in idealizing ways, or about the generally doomed nature of that undertaking. Rather, we are encouraged to recognize ourselves in the *Untitled Film Stills*. The tenderness with which Sherman details her protagonists' narcissistic ambitions, and the fact that she literally puts herself in their place, not only gives us a position to one side of the geometral point from which to look at them, but encourages us to identify with them.

Significantly, it is not these women's ideal imagos with which we identify. That identification is for the most part foreclosed by the repeated exposure in the *Untitled Film Stills* of the aspiration to ideality. It is rather with the women themselves, in all their manifest distance from the mirror, that we are encouraged to form this psychic alignment. The case needs to be stated even more forcefully: it is *because* the protagonists of the *Untitled Film Stills* are shown to fall so far short of approximating their ideal imagos that we identify with them.

This psychic relation is to be distinguished from that discussed in the first half of this book. The latter still involves an identification with ideality, but only provisionally, and in the image of another. The relation which the *Untitled Film Stills* finally make possible, on the other hand, has less to do with maintaining as exterior an image which we would like to incorporate, than with recognizing as our own something we would normally abject as "other." It involves acknowledging through identification with Sherman's women the abyss that separates us and always will separate us from ideality.

It might be assumed, from what I have just said, that this alternative viewing position would necessarily involve our psychic alignment with values, such as lack and insufficiency, which are the very opposite of ideality—that it would promote feelings of unpleasure and self-loathing. But although much of Sherman's subsequent work, from the fashion photographs through the "sex pictures," can be seen to constitute an ever-more virulent attack on the notion of the ideal image, and a commitment to a directly contrary aesthetic, the *Untitled Film Stills* are in my opinion very much to one side of this project.

I believe that these photographs do not withhold pleasure from us, but induct us into a new kind of pleasure. This pleasure follows from a more improvisatory relation to the ideal—"improvisatory" in the sense that one grasps the latter as a series of finally unrealizable tropes, tropes which can only ever be provisionally activated through pose, costume, make-up, mise-en-scène, lighting, and other fundamentally extrinsic "props." I am not invoking masquerade under a different name. It is quite possible to sustain an identification with ideality under the pretext that one is only theatrically rendering it. The emphasis falls here upon ideality not only as something one accesses only through "tropes" and "extrinsic props," but as something which can only ever be partially approximated.

The *Untitled Film Stills* propose something like the principle of the "good enough" over and against the binarisms "sufficiency/insufficiency" or "ideal/failure." I borrow this notion from D. W. Winnicott, who maintains that the mother need not be ideal, only "good enough." Indeed, he argues that the "good enough mother" is to be preferred to her ideal counterpart, since she does not attempt to fill the void upon which desire is predicated.[29] Similarly, the *Untitled Film Stills* make available for corporeal identification not the ideal wife, nature girl, or femme fatale, but the "good enough" equivalents of each of these.

Implicit in this principle is the knowledge (which Sherman's stills keep ever-present in the viewer's consciousness) that since no one can ever *become* the ideal, there is no such thing as either "natural entitlement" or "organic insufficiency" in relation to it. All that is available to us is the possibility of effecting a "good enough" approximation, and—through it—of shaking a little stardust onto the otherwise quotidian expanse of human existence. Also implicit in Sherman's articulation of this principle is the sense that it is triumphant in exact proportion to the adversity it overcomes—that it counts most when circumstances most conspire against it, when it is, from a social standpoint, most *impossible*.

There is one photograph in particular upon which I base this reading—*Still #3*. As soon as one steps out of the geometral point, one can see that in spite of her Ivory detergent and Morton's salt container the woman in this still nevertheless *is* sexy; she is what might be called a "good enough vamp." We don't forget about the objects on the kitchen sink in affirming her as such. On the contrary, we impute value to her pose over and against those objects. Indeed, we come to admire her for triumphing over her environment—or (more precisely) what normative meaning makes of that environment—through the artistry of her self-presentation, and, in a retroactive way, we affirm the three dimensional "photograph" into which she has transformed herself.

Although the concept I have appropriated from Winnicott is for me most fully instanciated by this image, I suggested earlier some of the ways in which it comes into play in relation to a second image from *Untitled Film Stills*. I proposed, that is, that when the viewer looks more closely at the room in which the woman sits in *Still #50,* he or she can see that it is no more successful than she is in achieving the exalted norm to which it aspires. If this were the limit of what this still could teach us about looking, it would be only condescendingly that we would acknowledge its protagonist to be "good enough" for the room full of '60s artifacts. However, Sherman gives us no vantage point from which to maintain our own superiority to the woman and the room. Rather, it encourages us radically to relativize values like "sophistication" and "cosmopolitanism"—it teaches us that they do not exist in any absolute sense, only in elegant partial gestures and half-approximations. In this sense, the woman in *Still #50* is not only a worthy inhabitant of the room she so admires, but a "good enough sophisticate."

An inexorable logic has led me back, once again, to the topic with which I began this book: ideality. If the mirror image is indeed "the threshold of the visible world," one can never talk for very long about the last of these categories without invoking the first—without confronting, in one guise or another, the ideal imago and its opposite, the body in pieces. It is also difficult to explore in any detail the metaphoric connection of camera and gaze without arriving at the issue of the ideal imago, since that metaphoric connection has clearly worked in all kinds of ways to consolidate the powerful hold which ideality must always have had upon the human psyche. The first of those apparatuses is responsible, after all, for the unceasing mass production of highly idealized bodily representations, representations to which only a small percentage of subjects have even a delusory identificatory access. And those literal photographs provide, in turn, the primary mimetic models for that three-dimensional photography through which the contemporary human subject attempts to control the terms under which he or she is apprehended by the gaze.

In most of her work since the *Untitled Film Stills,* Sherman has attempted to counter the idealizing function of much of photography by putting her own deployment of that textual form to a directly contrary purpose. Indeed, from the fashion photos to the "sex pictures," that work could be grouped together under the rubrics "Dehiscence," "Decomposition," or even "Bodies in Pieces." However, it is my opinion that the *Untitled Film Stills* represent her most important intervention within this psychically and politically fraught terrain, since the notion of the "good enough" displaces altogether not only the idea of an intrinsic ideal, but also the fantasy of the fragmented body. In so doing, it deconstructs two of the primary psychic supports for "difference." As it is elaborated in the *Untitled Film Stills,* the notion of the "good enough" also produces in us a conscious understanding of the tropological nature of the images through which we see and are seen. It thus represents a crucial device for putting us at a productive distance from the screen, and for teaching us how to "play" with it.

I hasten to add that since these are not lessons that we can ever unconsciously learn, they must be taught to us over and over again at that only site at which knowledge is possible—at the site, that is, of consciousness. I also want to caution the reader against too rapid an assimilation of the concept of the "good enough" to an untroubled agency. Merely by converting our aspiration to embody a particular form of corporeal ideality into a more improvisatory and approximate rendition of some of its elements, we do not circumvent the imperative to be "photographed" by the camera/gaze. To perform an ideal in the "good enough" mode, it must also be apprehended as such, and not simply as a failed attempt to approximate what our corporeal and environmental coordinates render impossible. And this returns us once again to the primary mechanism we have for steering the camera/gaze, our collective look.

The reader may have remarked that it was only with the greatest difficulty that I found some basis in the previous chapter for maintaining the possibility of productive vision—of an eye capable of seeing something other than what is given to be seen, and over which the self does not hold absolute sway. It is, nonetheless, with an assertion of the look's potentially transformative powers that I end this book. The eye can confer the active gift of love upon bodies which have long been accustomed to neglect and disdain. It can also put what is alien or inconsequential into contact with what is most personal and psychically significant. Finally, it can apprehend in the guise of the "good enough" not only the knowing performance by a sophisticated drag queen of an exemplary femininity, but also the naive and unpracticed poses with which some of Sherman's women lay claim to the ideals which haunt them.

I mention only those powers which are accessed in the spectator through an encounter with the visual works discussed in this book. No doubt others lie dormant, awaiting the textual conjurer's wand. Although Chapter 3 proposed a possible model for a political cinema of the 1990s, I do not mean in any way to circumscribe the range of what is possible or important in film, video, and photography today. I utter only one short but passionate appeal to those now working in such areas: help us to see differently.

Notes

Introduction

(1)   I will follow the practice throughout this book of putting the word "difference" in quotation marks when referring to that more overarching set of effects which follows from the principle of the "self-same body," which will be elaborated in Chapter 1. I will put "other" in quotation marks when designating what results when the subject projects onto an object what he or she cannot accept in him or herself.

(2)   Jacques Lacan, "The Mirror Stage as Formative of the Function of the 'I' as Revealed in Psychoanalytic Experience," in *Ecrits: A Selection*, trans. Alan Sheridan (New York: Norton, 1977), p. 3.

Chapter One: The Bodily Ego

(1)   Sigmund Freud, *The Ego and the Id*, in *The Standard Edition of the Complete Psychological Works*, trans. James Strachey (London: Hogarth, 1961), vol. 19, p. 27. All subsequent Freud quotations will be taken from this volume.

(2)   Sigmund Freud, "Instincts and their Vicissitudes," in *The Standard Edition*, vol. 14, pp. 121–22.

(3)   Sigmund Freud, *The Interpretation of Dreams*, in *The Standard Edition*, vol. 5, p. 536.

(4)   This is perhaps the single most important overarching argument advanced in Sigmund Freud and Joseph Breuer, *Studies in Hysteria*, in *The Standard Edition*,

vol. 2, although the word "signifier" is of course a term whose inception post-dates that text. Hypochondria is another disorder involving a certain "somatic compliance," as Freud suggests in "On Narcissism" (*The Standard Edition*, vol. 14, p. 83)—another disorder in which the psyche speaks through the body.

(5)   Lacan returns again and again to this premise in his writings and seminars. For a particularly schematic formulation of it, see his *Four Fundamental Concepts of Psycho-Analysis*, trans. Alan Sheridan (New York: Norton, 1978), pp. 203–229.

(6)   See Jacques Lacan, "The Mirror Stage as Formative of the Function of the 'I' as Revealed in Psychoanalytic Experience," in *Écrits: A Selection*, trans. Alan Sheridan (New York: Norton, 1977), pp. 1–7.

(7)   Jacques Lacan, "Some Reflections on the Ego," *International Journal of Psychoanalysis* 34 (1953): 13.

(8)   Jean Laplanche, *Life and Death in Psychoanalysis*, trans. Jeffrey Mehlman (Baltimore: Johns Hopkins University Press, 1976), p. 81. I also proposed a broadly metaphoric account of the Lacanian mirror in *The Subject of Semiotics* (New York: Oxford University Press, 1983), p. 160.

(9)   In *The Seminar of Jacques Lacan, Book I: Freud's Papers on Technique, 1953–54*, trans. John Forrester (Cambridge: Cambridge University Press, 1988), p. 138, Lacan remarks that whereas "the animal makes a real object coincide with the image within him," and this image "strengthens" the real object, giving it "substance" and "embodiment," an "eminent disorder characterizes the manifestations of the sexual function" in man. "Nothing in it adapts," he goes on to say; "This image, around which we, we psychoanalysts, revolve, presents, whether in the neuroses or in the perversions, a sort of fragmentation, of rupture, of breaking up, of lack of adequation, of inadequation." Lacan attributes this "inadequation" to the ideal-ego.

(10) Jacques Lacan, *The Seminar of Jacques Lacan, Book VII: The Ethics of Psychoanalysis, 1959–1960*, trans. Dennis Porter (New York: Norton, 1992), p. 151.

(11) For an excellent discussion of the role of physical pain in defining the outlines of the body, see Judith Butler, *Bodies that Matter* (New York: Routledge, 1993), pp. 57–64.

(12) For a fuller discussion of the postural model of the body, see Elizabeth Grosz, *Volatile Bodies: Toward a Corporeal Feminism* (Bloomington: Indiana University Press, 1994), pp. 67–85.

(13) Paul Schilder, *The Image and Appearance of the Human Body: Studies in the Constructive Energies of the Psyche* (New York: International Universities Press, 1950), p. 11.

(14) Sigmund Freud, *Three Essays on a Theory of Sexuality*, in *The Standard Edition*, vol. 7, pp. 135–243.

(15) Lacan, "The Mirror Stage," pp. 1–2.

(16) Henri Wallon, *Les Origines du caractère chez l'enfant: les préludes du sentiment de*

personnalité (Paris: Boivin & Cie, 1934), p. 204. See also Maurice Merleau-Ponty's essay on this text, *Les Relations avec autrui chez l'enfant* (Paris: Centre de Documentation Universitaire, 1958).

(17) Wallon also adduces a third category, the interoceptive ego, which is formed through the psychic registration of activity internal to the body. However, it does not play as central a role in his account of the mirror stage, which is my primary concern here, as do the proprioceptive and exteroceptive egos.

(18) Henri Wallon, "Kinesthesia and the Visual Body Image in the Child," in *The World of Henri Wallon,* ed. Gilbert Voyat (New York: Jason Aronson, 1984), p. 129.

(19) Michel Foucault, *Discipline and Punish: The Birth of the Prison,* trans. Alan Sheridan (New York: Random House, 1979).

(20) This is how Grosz describes the bodily ego in *Volatile Bodies,* p. 37.

(21) I spoke earlier about the values which can be inscribed on the infant body by the parental touch, values which help to determine a subject's subsequent gender and sexual preference. The way in which the body is touched (or, for that matter, not touched) can also communicate love for, or revulsion against, its color. Similarly, the body can be coerced into assuming a postural configuration implying sexual, racial, or economic superiority or subordination.

(22) For a lengthy discussion of the part played by cutaneous sensation in the production of the bodily ego, see Didier Anzieu, *The Skin Ego,* trans. Chris Turner (New Haven: Yale University Press, 1989).

(23) What Grosz says of the "body image" is thus also true of the sensational ego—it "does not map a biological body onto a psychosocial domain," but rather "attests to the necessary interconstituency of each for the other" (*Volatile Bodies,* p. 85).

(24) Lacan, *Four Fundamental Concepts,* p. 83.

(25) For an extended discussion of the metaphorization of the gaze as a camera, and an interrogation of what, precisely, that metaphor implies, see Chapter 4 of this volume.

(26) Lacan's presentation of the gaze and the screen is contained in his *Four Fundamental Concepts,* pp. 67–119. For a more detailed commentary on this account of the visual field, see my *Male Subjectivity at the Margins* (New York: Routledge, 1992), pp. 125–56.

(27) The concepts of indexicality and iconicity derive from Charles Sanders Peirce, *Collected Papers,* eds. Charles Hartshorne and Paul Weiss (Cambridge: Harvard University Press, 1931), vol. 2.

(28) In "The Mirror Stage," Lacan writes that "the total form of the body by which the subject anticipates in a mirage the maturation of his power is given to him only as *Gestalt,* that is to say, in an exteriority in which this form is certainly more constituent than constituted, but in which it appears to him above all as a contrasting size (*un relief de stature*) that fixes it and in a symmetry that inverts it, in contrast with the turbulent movements that the subject feels are animating him" (2).

(29) Lacan, "Some Reflections on the Ego," p. 15.

(30) Wallon, "Kinesthesia and the Visual Body Image in the Child," pp. 129–30.

(31) Lacan, "The Mirror Stage," pp. 4, 6. I will discuss the aggressivity which under-pins the relation to those others who occupy the position of the ideal imago in Chapter 2.

(32) Sigmund Freud, *Group Psychology and the Analysis of the Ego,* in *The Standard Edition,* vol. 18, p. 105.

(33) Sigmund Freud, *Totem and Taboo,* in *The Standard Edition,* vol. 13, pp. 1–161.

(34) Sigmund Freud, "Mourning and Melancholia," in *The Standard Edition,* vol. 14, pp. 243–58. A fascinating recent discussion of melancholia as an "irretrievable loss of unity" might be said to undo the incorporation assumed to be at the heart of the normative ego. See Mieke Bal, *Reading Rembrandt: Beyond the Word-Image Opposition* (Cambridge: Cambridge University Press, 1991), p. 354.

(35) Max Scheler, *The Nature of Sympathy,* trans. Peter Heath (Hamden, Conn.: Archon, 1970), p. 18. For a discussion of the murderous logic of (idiopathic) identifica-tion, see Mikkel Borch-Jacobsen, *The Freudian Subject,* trans. Catherine Porter (Palo Alto, Calif.: Stanford University Press, 1988). I discuss heteropathic identi-fication at much greater length in *Male Subjectivity at the Margins,* pp. 214–96.

(36) I do not mean in any way to propose the heteropath and idiopath as each other's complements. Also, I mean by heteropathic identification a much more capacious psychic transaction than that proposed in Chapter 6 of *Male Subjectivity at the Margins.*

(37) Jacques Lacan, *The Seminar of Jacques Lacan, Book II: The Ego in Freud's Theory and in the Technique of Psychoanalysis, 1954–55,* trans. Sylvana Tomaselli (Cambridge: Cambridge University Press, 1988), p. 167.

(38) Lacan, *Seminar II,* p. 166.

(39) Sigmund Freud, "Some Psychical Consequences of the Anatomical Distinction Between the Sexes," in *The Standard Edition,* vol. 19, p. 152.

(40) Sigmund Freud, "Fetishism," in *The Standard Edition,* vol. 21, pp. 149–57.

(41) Luce Irigaray, *Speculum of the Other Woman,* trans. Gillian C. Gill (Ithaca: Cornell University Press, 1985), pp. 25–27.

(42) Frantz Fanon, *Black Skin, White Masks,* trans. Charles Lamm Markmann (London: Pluto Press, 1986), p. 14.

(43) The notion of the look as a functionary of the camera derives from Vilem Flusser, *Towards a Philosophy of Photography* (Gottingen, West Germany: European Photography, 1984), p. 19. For an elaboration of the metaphoric relation of cam-era and gaze, see Chapter 4.

(44) Mary Ann Doane, *Femmes Fatales: Feminism, Film Theory, Psychoanalysis* (New York: Routledge, 1991), p. 225.

(45) Jean-Joseph Goux, "The Phallus: Masculine Identity and the 'Exchange of Women,'" *differences* vol. 4, no. 1 (1992): 49.

(46) Freud, "Some Psychical Consequences," p. 252.

(47) See in particular Michèlle Montrelay, "Inquiry into Femininity," *m/f*, no. 1 (1978): 83–101, and Doane, *Femmes Fatales*, pp. 165–77.

(48) This argument is most fully associated with Mary Ann Doane. See her *The Desire to Desire: The Woman's Film of the 1940's* (Bloomington: Indiana University Press, 1987), and *Femmes Fatales*, pp. 17–32.

(49) For a much fuller discussion of the Oedipus complex in the terms proposed here, see Chapter 1 of *Male Subjectivity at the Margins*.

(50) See Sigmund Freud, "Female Sexuality," in *The Standard Edition*, vol. 21, pp. 225–43, and "Femininity," in *The Standard Edition*, vol. 22, pp. 112–35.

(51) In "Femininity," Freud writes: "The discovery that she is castrated is a turning-point in a girl's growth. Three possible lines of development start from it: one leads to sexual inhibition or to neurosis, the second to change of character in the sense of a masculinity complex, the third, finally, to normal femininity" (126).

(52) Freud, "Female Sexuality," pp. 236, 237; and "Femininity," p. 134. For a fuller discussion of both this early, pleasurable identification with the mother, and with the later, unpleasurable one which is installed through the female castration crisis and the positive Oedipus complex, see my *The Acoustic Mirror: The Female Voice in Psychoanalysis and Cinema* (Bloomington: Indiana University Press, 1988), pp. 141–59.

(53) I say "original" maternal imago because Freud suggests that there are two maternal identifications available to the female subject, one specific to the negative Oedipus complex, and one to the positive Oedipus complex. Significantly, the latter is so radically devaluating that it renders the female subject an impossible love-object not only for herself but also for the male subject. In "Femininity," Freud suggests that it is only via the earlier of these identifications that the male subject makes his libidinal approach to his female counterpart (p. 134).

(54) Freud, "On Narcissism," pp. 88–89.

(55) "On Narcissism" finally shows all object-choice, whether on the part of the male or female subject, to take place under the sign of narcissism.

(56) Freud, "Femininity," pp. 132–33.

(57) Sigmund Freud, "'A Child Is Being Beaten,'" in *The Standard Edition*, vol. 17, pp. 184–186.

(58) Laura Mulvey's "Visual Pleasure and Narrative Cinema" is most easily accessed in *Visual and Other Pleasures* (Bloomington: Indiana University Press, 1989), pp. 14–26.

(59) Laura Mulvey, "Afterthoughts on 'Visual Pleasure and Narrative Cinema' inspired by King Vidor's *Duel in the Sun* (1946)," in *Visual and Other Pleasures*, pp. 32–33.

(60) Teresa de Lauretis, *Alice Doesn't: Feminism, Semiotics, Cinema* (Bloomington: Indiana University Press, 1984), p. 123. This formulation turns more upon the notion of a narrative than a corporeal transvestism. It is thus not entirely assimi-

lable to my own argument. Mary Ann Doane also argues for the greater spectatorial mobility of the female spectator in "Film and the Masquerade," in *Femmes Fatales*, pp. 24–25.

(61)   This would seem to be the moment to indicate that within the context of a particular subculture, the gaze might be capable of producing a different "photograph" than that which comes into play at the larger cultural level, and so of sometimes sustaining an identification which would be at other times impossible.

(62)   For a discussion of such a pathologization, see Judith Butler, "Melancholy Gender/Refused Identification," in *Constructing Masculinities*, ed. Simon Watson (New York: Routledge, 1995), pp. 21–36.

(63)   Once again, a subcultural gaze might provide more support for this identification than that provided by the larger culture.

Chapter Two: From the Ideal-Ego to the Active Gift of Love

(1)   Jacques Lacan, "The Mirror Stage as Formative of the Function of the 'I' as Revealed in Psychoanalytic Experience," in *Écrits: A Selection*, trans. Alan Sheridan (New York: Norton, 1977), pp. 2–3.

(2)   As will become evident later, I am echoing here the formulation with which Lacan defines sublimation in *Seminar VII*: the elevation of a thing to the status of *das Ding*. I will be arguing that sublimation and idealization are even more intimately linked in Lacan than they are in Freud, and that the first of those operations does not necessarily involve a desexualization.

(3)   Marx discusses commodity fetishism in *Capital*, vol. 1, trans. Ben Fowkes (New York: Vintage Books, 1977), pp. 163–69.

(4)   Jacques Lacan, *Le Séminaire, Livre XX: Encore* (Paris: Éditions du Seuil, 1975), p. 67.

(5)   Jacques Lacan, *The Seminar of Jacques Lacan, Book II: The Ego in Freud's Theory and in the Technique of Psychoanalysis, 1954–55*, trans. Sylvana Tomaselli (Cambridge: Cambridge University Press, 1988), 169.

(6)   Jacques Lacan, *The Seminar of Jacques Lacan, Book I: Freud's Papers on Technique, 1953–54*, trans. John Forrester (Cambridge: Cambridge University Press, 1988), 145.

(7)   Ibid., p. 223.

(8)   In "The Freudian Thing," Lacan writes that the "identification precipitated from the ego to the other in the subject" classically "has the effect that this apportionment of functions never constitutes even a kinetic harmony, but is established on the permanent 'you or I' of a war" (*Écrits*, 138). For a discussion of this binary logic, see also *The Seminar, Book II*, p. 169; and Chapter 6 of my *Male Subjectivity at the Margins* (New York: Routledge, 1992).

(9)   In *Seminar I*, for instance, Lacan observes, "The subject originally locates and recognizes desire through the intermediary, not only of his own image, but of the body of his fellow being. It's exactly at that moment that the human being's con-

sciousness, in the form of consciousness of self, distinguishes itself. It is in so far as his desire has gone over to the other side that he assimilates himself to the body of the other and recognizes himself as body" (147).

(10) Jacques Lacan, *The Seminar of Jacques Lacan, Book VII: The Ethics of Psychoanalysis, 1959–1960,* trans. Dennis Porter (New York: Norton, 1992), p. 298.

(11) Paul Schilder, *The Image and Appearance of the Human Body* (New York: International Universities Press, 1950), p. 273.

(12) I do not mean to suggest that the formulations advanced by these two theorists are in all respects commensurate. Laura Mulvey's concern is with the positioning of woman as spectacle within classic cinema (see "Visual Pleasure and Narrative Cinema," in *Visual and Other Pleasures* [Bloomington: Indiana University Press, 1989], pp. 14–26). Mary Ann Doane addresses rather what she sees as the psychic proximity of the female subject, particularly of the female spectator, to the image—her lack of symbolic differentiation from it (see *The Desire To Desire: The Woman's Film of the 1940's* [Bloomington: Indiana University Press, 1987]; and "Film and the Masquerade: Theorizing the Female Spectator," in *Femmes Fatales: Feminism, Film Theory, Psychoanalysis* [New York: Routledge, 1991], pp. 33–43).

(13) This argument derives primarily from Doane's "Film and the Masquerade," pp. 24–26. But Mulvey also talks about female transvestism in her "Afterthoughts on 'Visual Pleasure and Narrative Cinema' inspired by King Vidor's *Duel in the Sun,*" in *Visual and Other Pleasures,* pp. 29–38. For an engagement with the second of these formulations, see Chapter 1.

(14) Again, within film studies, it is primarily Doane who has articulated the argument that woman stands outside lack. See, in addition to the texts cited above, "Woman's Stake: Filming the Female Body," in *Femmes Fatales,* pp. 165–177.

(15) Lacan there observes that "*Bilder* [images] means imaginary" (137).

(16) I am arguing in some crucial respects against Doane's formulation. However, it would seem important to acknowledge that whatever the differences in our models with respect to how we account for the dilemmas of normative femininity, we are agreed in arguing that they can only be overcome if the female subject accepts her distance from the representations which define her. See Doane, "Film and the Masquerade," pp. 22–26.

(17) For a discussion of the cinematic conventions surrounding the male look, see Mulvey, "Visual Pleasure and Narrative Cinema."

(18) Although *Bildnis* does not seem to me to be a film primarily about lesbian desire, it clearly contains many lesbian tropes and locations, and even a number of manifestly lesbian characters. Judith Mayne offers an excellent formulation of this apparent contradiction in *The Woman at the Keyhole* (Bloomington: Indiana University Press, 1990). Mayne suggests that although Madame is herself narcissistic rather than lesbian, she circulates primarily within a world of women, one which is often transected by lesbian desire: "The woman drinker appears to live

entirely and exclusively within the narcissistic world of her own regressive fantasies, but female figures of social marginality function, however briefly and tangentially, as marks of otherness and signs of fascination. On the other end of the social spectrum, the film is equally taken up with how Blumenschein's woman drinker tantalizes and even challenges the less obviously narcissistic but equally self-enclosed world of the three houndstooth ladies. Lutze fascinates the woman drinker in some of the same ways that the woman drinker fascinates the three houndstooth ladies, with the significant difference that the woman drinker, located on the brink between subject and object, is much more susceptible to crossing over those boundaries than the houndstooth trio" (141). Lutze, as Mayne suggests, is clearly a figure who is able to step over the threshold of the mirror stage and into a relational visual field. She thus remains a key player within the lesbian "thematic" of the film. Madame, on the other hand, remains for the most part on the far side of that threshold.

(19) For a discussion of the woman who takes as her ego-ideal the man she would like to have been, see Chapter 1 of this book.

(20) See Sigmund Freud, "Femininity," in *The Standard Edition of the Complete Psychological Works,* trans. James Strachey (London: Hogarth Press, 1964), vol. 22, pp. 132–33.

(21) See Jacques Lacan, *Four Fundamental Concepts of Psycho-Analysis,* trans. Alan Sheridan (New York: Norton, 1978), p. 106. For a general discussion of the gaze, see not only this text, but Chapter 3 of my *Male Subjectivity at the Margins,* and Chapter 4 of the present volume. In the latter, I provide a fuller discussion of the metaphorization of the gaze as a camera.

(22) See Lacan, *Four Fundamental Concepts,* pp. 91–107; *Male Subjectivity,* Chapter 3; and Chapters 1, 4, and 6 of the present volume for an account of the screen.

(23) Miriam Hansen, "Visual Pleasure, Fetishism and the Problem of Feminine/ Feminist Discourse: Ulrike Ottinger's *Ticket of No Return,*" *New German Critique,* no. 31 (1984): 100.

(24) Jacques Lacan, "The Function and Field of Speech and Language in Psychoanalysis, in *Écrits,*" p. 104.

(25) *Four Fundamental Concepts,* pp. 210–11.

(26) Synchronization implies above all else a unified subject. Its absence here attests yet again to the heterogeneity of Madame's bodily ego, as well as to her dependence upon the Other. For an analysis of the cinematic norm of synchronization, and its implications for sexual difference, see my *The Acoustic Mirror: The Female Voice in Psychoanalysis and Cinema* (Bloomington: University of Indiana Press, 1988), Chapter 2.

(27) Freud's "On Narcissism," in *The Standard Edition,* vol. 14, pp. 73–102, and *Group Psychology and the Analysis of the Ego,* in *The Standard Edition,* vol. 18, pp. 105–16, also establish the fundamentally narcissistic nature of all love; the first through its

examples, the second through its explicit argument. See below for a discussion of these texts.

(28)   See Alexandre Kojève, *Introduction to the Reading of Hegel: Lectures on the Phenomonology of Spirit,* trans. James N. Nichols, Jr. (Ithaca: Cornell University Press, 1980).

(29)   I want to stress once again that I deviate here from the model of heteropathic identification proposed in *Male Subjectivity at the Margins* (New York: Routledge, 1992), pp. 214–96. Although I still stand by that discussion as an accurate account of how such an identification can function within masochism or sado-masochism, I am concerned here to provide a much more general account of the role of heteropathic identification in love. I will ultimately be proposing the conditions under which it can effected from a position of *activity* rather than *passivity.*

(30)   Subsequently, Freud expresses discomfort with this formulation and substitutes for it the following two sentences: "In the [first] case…the object has been lost or given up; it is then set up again inside the ego, and the ego makes a partial alteration in itself after the model of the lost object. In the other case the object is retained, and there is a hypercathexis of it by the ego and at the ego's expense" (114). Once again, he emphasizes that love involves a certain "shrinking" or diminution of the ego.

(31)   Lacan here closely follows Freud, for whom—as I indicated above—love always involves such an exteriorization.

(32)   This is a point upon which I will lay great stress in Chapter 3, when discussing Isaac Julien's film *Looking for Langston.*

(33)   See Jacques Lacan, "Kant avec Sade," in *Écrits* (Paris: Éditions du Seuil, 1971), vol. 2, p. 129.

(34)   "Vacillation" would here seem to mean "hesitancy to accede to the loss of being," or "the inability to make a clean break with what has been lost through language."

(35)   I want to make clear here that while I find Lacan's characterization of courtly love extremely suggestive, I do not at all points agree with that characterization. I also wish that I had access in this discussion to an example of the gift of love which is less problematic with respect to gender. However, as I will indicate below, courtly love is politically exemplary in at least in one respect: it confers ideality upon socially subordinate bodies.

(36)   In quoting this passage from *Seminar VII,* I of course do not mean to propose stereotype as an exemplary strategy through which to open up a distance between the loved other and the images through which the subject idealizes him or her. On the contrary, such a strategy is for me completely inimical to the project of loving the other in his or her "particularity" urged by *Seminar I.*

(37)   Lacan's account of the gift of love owes much to Stendhal's *On Love,* trans. Vyvyan Beresford Holland (New York: Grosset & Dunlap, 1967), particularly to the passage which compares the lover's idealization of the love-object to salt-crystallization: "In

the salt mines of Salzburg a bough stripped of its leaves by winter is thrown into the depths of the disused workings; two or three months later it is pulled out again, covered with brilliant crystals: even the tiniest twigs, no bigger than a tomtit's claw, are spangled with a vast number of shimmering, glittering diamonds, so that the original bough is no longer recognizable" (6).

(38)   Sigmund Freud, *The Ego and the Id,* in *The Standard Edition*, vol. 19, p. 19.

Chapter Three: Political Ecstasy

(1)   Laura Mulvey, "Visual Pleasure and Narrative Cinema," *Screen*, vol. 16, no. 3 (1975): 6–18; Christian Metz, "The Imaginary Signifier," *Screen*, vol. 16, no. 2 (1975): 14–76; Jacqueline Rose, "Paranoia and the Film System," *Screen*, vol. 17, no. 4 (1976/1977): 85–104; Stephen Heath, "Anata Mo," *Screen*, vol. 17, no. 4 (1976/77): 49–66.

(2)   See *Screen*, vol. 15, no. 2 (1974), and *Screen*, vol. 16, no. 4 (1975/76).

(3)   Stephen, Heath, "Lessons from Brecht," *Screen*, vol. 15, no. 2 (1974): 103–128.

(4)   Sylvia Harvey, "Whose Brecht? Memories for the Eighties," *Screen*, vol. 23, no. 1 (1982): 58.

(5)   Bertolt Brecht, "Conversation with Ben Brecht," in *Brecht on Theatre: The Development of an Aesthetic,* ed. and trans. by John Willett (New York: Hill and Wang, 1964), p. 14.

(6)   Brecht, "Alienation Effects in Chinese Acting," in *Brecht on Theatre*, p. 91.

(7)   Brecht, "The Modern Theatre is the Epic Theatre," in *Brecht on Theatre*, p. 38.

(8)   Ibid., pp. 37–38.

(9)   Brecht, "Theatre for Pleasure or Theatre for Instruction," in *Brecht on Theatre*, p. 70.

(10)   Peter Wollen, "Godard and Counter Cinema: *Vent d'Est,*" in *Readings and Writings: Semiotic Counter-Strategies* (London: Verso, 1982), pp. 79–91. It is a mark of the complexity of Wollen's thinking that although he seemingly subscribes to the necessity of at least disrupting identification within political cinema, he also goes on in this essay to argue that "desire, and its representation in fantasy, far from being necessary enemies of revolutionary politics—and its cinematic auxiliary— are necessary conditions" (88).

(11)   Stephen Heath, "Narrative Space," in *Questions of Cinema* (Bloomington: Indiana University Press, 1981), pp. 19–75. Significantly, Heath does not call for the end of narrative, which—as he makes clearer elsewhere in the same volume (170) is for him inseparable from identification—but for a cinema which might be said to stage "an action at the limits of narrative within the narrative film, at the limits of its fictions of unity" (64).

(12)   Claire Johnston, "Towards a Feminist Film Practice: Some Theses," *Edinburgh Magazine*, no. 1 (1976): 56. As can be seen from the passage quoted in the body of my text, Johnston does not go so far as to call for the complete suspension of the

operation of identification in political cinema, although she—like Wollen and Heath—sees it as something which in its conventional deployment is antipathetic to the notion of such a cinema.

(13) "Dominant fiction" is the category I have recently used to retheorize the operation of what most often passes ideologically as "reality." See *Male Subjectivity at the Margins* (New York: Routledge, 1992), Chapter 1.

(14) Kaja Silverman, *The Subject of Semiotics* (New York: Oxford University Press, 1983), pp. 194–222.

(15) Anne Friedberg, "A Denial of Difference: Theories of Cinematic Identification," in *Psychoanalysis and Cinema,* ed. E. Ann Kaplan (New York: Routledge 1990), p. 45.

(16) Brecht, "Indirect Impact of the Epic Theatre," in *Brecht on Theatre*, p. 58; and "On the Use of Music in an Epic Theatre," in *Brecht on Theatre*, p. 87.

(17) See Heath, "Lessons from Brecht," for an extended discussion of the dependence of identification upon the fourth wall. Although Heath does not specify that the identification of which he speaks is heteropathic rather than idiopathic, it seems to me that it must be understood as such.

(18) Walter Benjamin, "What is Epic Theatre?" in *Understanding Brecht*, trans. Anna Bostock (London: New Left Books, 1977), p. 1.

(19) "*Fremd*" means "strange," or "unfamiliar" in German.

(20) Brecht, "The Literarization of the Theatre," in *Brecht on Theatre*, p. 44.

(21) See Ben Brewster, "The Fundamental Reproach (Brecht)," *Ciné-Tracts*, vol. 1, no. 2 (1977): 44–53, for a fuller discussion of Brecht's objections to cinema.

(22) Christian Metz, *The Imaginary signifier: Psychoanalysis and the Cinema,* trans. Celia Britton et al. (Bloomington: Indiana University Press, 1988), p. 63.

(23) Friedberg, "A Denial of Difference," p. 39.

(24) Mary Ann Doane, "Misrecognition and Identity," *Ciné-Tracts*, vol. 3, no. 3 (1980): 29.

(25) Mary Ann Doane, *The Desire to Desire: The Woman's Film of the 1940s* (Bloomington: Indiana University Press, 1987), pp. 22–37.

(26) Béla Balázs, *Theory of the Film: Character and Growth of a New Art* (New York: Dover, 1970), p. 48.

(27) Balázs is not the only early film theorist to illustrate cinematic identification with this anecdote. See also Siegfried Kracauer, *Theory of Film: The Redemption of Physical Reality* (New York: Oxford University Press, 1960), pp. 164–65.

(28) Wallon offers his account of the mirror stage in *Les Origines du caractère chez l'infant: les préludes du sentiment de personalité* (Paris: Boivin & Cie, 1934). For a discussion of the differences between this model and that elaborated by Lacan, see Chapter 1 of the present volume.

(29) Henri Wallon, "L'Acte perceptif et le cinéma," in *Lecture d'Henri Wallon: Choix de textes* (Paris: Éditions Sociales, 1976), p. 295.

(30) For a discussion of *Les Origines du caractère chez l'enfant*, see Chapter 1 of this volume.

(31) Kracauer, *Theory of Film*, pp. 164–65.

(32) Sergei Eisenstein, "Film Form: New Problems," in *Film Form, Essays in Film Theory*, trans. Jay Leyda (New York: Harcourt, Brace and Jovanovich, 1977), pp. 122–23.

(33) Eisenstein, "The Structure of the Film," in *Film Form*, pp. 167.

(34) As will become clear later, I derive from Eisenstein more the notion of a leap into opposition—a notion which in my own model implies above all self-opposition—than that of the dialectic.

(35) Eisenstein, "The Structure of the Film," p. 172.

(36) Eisenstein, "The Structure of the Film," p. 160.

(37) Eisenstein, "The Filmic Fourth Dimension," in *Film Form*, p. 69.

(38) Eisenstein, "Methods of Montage," in *Film Form*, p. 80.

(39) Fredric Jameson, *The Political Unconscious: Narrative as a Socially Symbolic Act* (Ithaca: Cornell University Press, 1981), p. 73.

(40) Two important essays which have engaged "On Some Motifs in Baudelaire" are Miriam Hansen, "Benjamin, Cinema and Experience: 'The Blue Flower in the Land of Technology,' *New German Critique*, no. 40 (1987): 179–224; and Richard Allen, "The Aesthetic Experience of Modernity: Benjamin, Adorno, and Contemporary Film Theory," *New German Critique*, no. 40 (1987): 225–40.

(41) Jacques Lacan, "Aggressivity in Psychoanalysis," in *Écrits: A Selection*, trans. Alan Sheridan (New York: Norton, 1977), p. 23.

(42) Walter Benjamin, "The Work of Art in the Age of Mechanical Reproduction," in *Illuminations*, trans. Harry Zohn (New York: Harcourt, 1969), p. 220.

(43) Benjamin, "Some Motifs in Baudelaire," in *Illuminations*, p. 200 n17.

(44) Birgit Recki, *Aura und Autonomie: Zur Subjektivität der Kunst bei Walter Benjamin und Theodor Wiesengrund Adorno* (Wurzburg: Königshausen & Neumann, 1988), p. 24.

(45) I mean to invoke here the discussion of the "looping" of the drive around the *objet a* in Chapter 2. In both cases, the relation to the object is nonacquisitive.

(46) Jacques Lacan, *Four Fundamental Concepts of Psycho-Analysis*, trans. Alan Sheridan (New York: Norton, 1978), pp. 194–96. The English translation of the passage involving what I have called the "look" reads: "Does it not seem that the drive, in this turning inside out represented by the pocket, invaginating through the erogenous zone, is given the task of seeking something that, each time, responds in the Other?... Let us say that at the level of the *Schaulust*, it is the gaze" (196). Although Sheridan translates "*le regard*" as "gaze," it would be better translated as "look." The relation of subject-to-subject can only be established in the visual field through the look, which is one of the primary signifiers of lack and desire. To introduce the gaze into this relation, as Terry Eagleton also does in *Walter Benjamin, or Towards a Revolutionary Criticism* (London: Verso, 1981), p. 38, is

immediately to precipitate that inequality which Lacan associates with the master/slave dialectic, a dialectic to which the active gift of love is radically opposed.

(47) Jacques Lacan, *The Seminar of Jacques Lacan, Book VII: The Ethics of Psychoanalysis, 1959–60,* trans. Dennis Porter (New York: Norton, 1992), p. 59.

(48) Ibid.

(49) Walter Benjamin associates light with the aura, and hence with ideality, in "A Short History of Photography," trans. Stanley Mitchell, *Screen,* vol. 13, no. 1 (1972): 18–20. Mieke Bal also at times links illumination with ideality in *Reading Rembrandt: Beyond the Word-Image Opposition* (Cambridge: Cambridge University Press, 1991). For instance, she accounts for the gleam on Rembrandt's nose in his *Self-Portrait* (1629) with the "shine" on the nose of Freud's fetishist (309), and the light in *The Blinding of Samson* (1636) with the promise of "subjective wholeness" (343).

(50) Benjamin, "The Work of Art in the Age of Mechanical Reproduction," p. 238.

(51) I say "analogue" because in *A la recherche du temps perdu,* Proust, by his own admission, does not "recollect" so much as "create." See *Remembrance of Things Past,* trans. C. K. Scott Moncrieff and Terence Kilmartin (New York: Vintage Books, 1982), vol. 1, p. 49. Strictly speaking, the *mémoire involontaire,* like the *correspondance,* can be equated with unconscious memory only in its weaving of associative networks. The Proustian category is otherwise discrepant, since it includes preconscious as well as unconscious memories, and many other elements which are in excess of Freud's account of the latter. This asymmetry is even more marked with the Baudelairean *correspondance,* which is not in a conventional sense a mnemonic category. However, Bejamin not only uses the *mémoire involontaire* as a signifier for the textual correlative of unconscious memory, but sometimes as a synonym *tout court* for unconscious memory

(52) Roland Barthes, "Rhetoric of the Image," in *Image/Music/Text,* trans. Stephen Heath (New York: Hill and Wang, 1977), p. 44.

(53) Andre Bazin, "Theater and Cinema—Part Two," in *What Is Cinema?,* trans. Hugh Gray (Berkeley: University of California Press, 1967), vol. 1, pp. 108–9.

(54) Thus, white masculinity might be later assimilated to the ego of the white male subject and to the ego-ideal of the white female subject.

(55) Sigmund Freud, "A Child Is Being Beaten," in *The Standard Edition of the Complete Psychological Works,* trans. James Strachey (Hogarth: London, 1955), vol. 17, pp. 185–86.

(56) See Freud, "On Narcissism," in *The Standard Edition,* vol. 14, pp. 100–101; and *Group Psychology and the Analysis of the Ego, The Standard Edition,* vol. 18, pp. 111–14.

(57) Freud's *Interpretation of Dreams* provides an extended discussion of both of these representative principles (*The Standard Edition,* vols. 4 and 5).

(58) For an early discussion of cinema's illusory three-dimensionality, see Hugo

Munsterberg, *The Film: A Psychological Study* (New York: Dover, 1970), pp. 18–30.

(59) Freud, "Some Psychical Consequences of the Anatomical Distinction Between the Sexes," *The Standard Edition,* vol. 19, p. 252.

(60) Things are obviously rather complex here, since at the same time that the film withholds from our look that part of Beauty's body which is most associated with black masculinity, it provides us with an image of that part which is most associated with homosexuality: the buttocks.

(61) This text is read in the original, British version of *Looking for Langston,* but not in the censored, American version. The Hughes estate refused to give Julien the right to include it and several other Langston poems in the latter.

(62) Émile Benveniste, *Problems in General Linguistics,* trans. Mary Elizabeth Meek (Coral Gables: University of Miami Press, 1971), p. 224.

(63) Mieke Bal writes very suggestively about the second-person pronoun in terms which underscore the potential of that pronoun to undermine the notion of an autonomous self: "The concept of second personhood…indicates the derivative status of personhood; the fundamental impossibility to be, both psychologically and socially, a person without the traces of the person's grafted being. Second, as presented by Benveniste and subsequent theorists in his vein, it indicates the reversible relationship of complementarity between first and second-person pronouns whose use produces subjectivity and constitutes the essence of language." See her "Third Person, Second Person, Same Person," *New Literary History,* vol. 24, no. 2 (1993): 307.

Chapter Four: The Gaze

(1) Christian Metz, *The Imaginary Signifier: Psychoanalysis and the Cinema,* trans. Celia Britton, Annwyl Williams, Ben Brewster, and Alfred Guzzetti (Bloomington: Indiana University Press, 1982), pp. 49, 97.

(2) Jean-Louis Baudry, "Ideological Effects of the Basic Cinematographic Apparatus," trans. Alan Williams, in *Narrative, Apparatus, Ideology,* ed. Philip Rosen (New York: Columbia University Press, 1986), p. 295.

(3) Stephen Heath, *Questions of Cinema* (Bloomington: Indiana University Press, 1981), p. 30.

(4) Laura Mulvey, *Visual and Other Pleasures* (Bloomington: Indiana University Press, 1989), pp. 3–26. See also Teresa de Lauretis, *Alice Doesn't: Feminism, Semiotics, Cinema* (Bloomington: Indiana University Press, 1984), pp. 1–36; Linda Williams, "Film Body: An Implantation of Perversions," *Ciné-Tracts,* vol. 3, no. 4 (1981): 19–35; Lucy Fischer, "The Image of Woman as Image: The Optical Politics of *Dames,*" in *Genre: The Musical,* ed. Rick Altman (London: Routledge and Kegan Paul, 1981), pp. 70–84; Sandy Flitterman, "Woman, Desire, and the Look: Feminism and the Enunciative Apparatus in Cinema," *Ciné-Tracts,* vol. 2, no. 1 (1978), pp. 63–68; and Kaja Silverman, *The Subject of Semiotics* (New York: Oxford

University Press, 1983), pp. 222–36.

(5) The theorists of suture are Jacques-Alain Miller, "Suture (elements of the logic of the signifier)," *Screen,* vol. 18, no. 4 (1977/78): 29–34; Jean-Pierre Oudart, "Notes on Suture," *Screen,* vol. 18, no. 4 (1977/78): 35–47; Stephen Heath, "Notes on Suture," *Screen,* vol. 18, no. 4 (1977/78): 48–76, and "Anato Mo," *Screen,* vol. 17, no 4 (1976/77): 49–66; Daniel Dayan, "The Tutor-Code of Classical Cinema," *Movies and Methods,* ed. Bill Nichols (Berkeley: University of California Press, 1976), pp. 438–51; and Kaja Silverman, *The Subject of Semiotics,* pp. 194–236.

(6) This is how Scotty/Johnny characterizes himself after he discovers that he has been "framed."

(7) Mary Ann Doane, *Femmes Fatales: Feminism, Film Theory, Psychoanalysis* (New York: Routledge, 1991), p. 85.

(8) Jean-Louis Baudry, "The Apparatus," in *Narrative, Apparatus, Ideology,* p. 311.

(9) Geoffrey Nowell-Smith, "A Note on History/Discourse," *Edinburgh 76 Magazine: Psychoanalysis/Cinema/Avant-Garde,* no. 1 (1976): 31.

(10) Jean-Louis Comolli, "Machines of the Visible," in *The Cinematic Apparatus,* ed. Teresa de Lauretis and Stephen Heath (New York: St. Martin's Press, 1980), p. 123.

(11) Comolli also stresses that the camera exceeds the eye in "Technique and Ideology: Camera, Perspective, Depth of Field," *Film Reader 2* (1977): 135–36.

(12) Jonathan Crary, *Techniques of the Observer: On Vision and Modernity in the Nineteenth Century* (Cambridge: MIT Press, 1990), pp. 14–16.

(13) André Bazin, *What Is Cinema?* trans. Hugh Gray (Berkeley: University of California Press, 1967), vol. 1, p. 13.

(14) For an interesting discussion of Muybridge's photographs and their bearing on the issue of photography's ostensible "realism," see Linda Williams, *Hard Core: Power, Pleasure, and the Frenzy of the Visible* (Berkeley: University of California Press, 1989), pp. 34–48. Mieke Bal launches a fascinating argument against the continuity of Muybridge and cinema in "The Gaze in the Closet," in *Vision in Context,* ed. Teresa Brennan and Martin Jay (forthcoming, Routledge, 1996), although she, too, stresses that Muybridge's photographs show what the eye cannot see.

(15) Vilem Flusser, *Towards a Philosophy of Photography* (Gottingen, West Germany: European Photography, 1984), p. 19.

(16) Jacques Lacan, *Four Fundamental Concepts of Psycho-Analysis,* trans. Alan Sheridan (New York: Norton, 1978), p. 106.

(17) Kaja Silverman, *Male Subjectivity at the Margins* (New York: Routledge, 1992), pp. 125–56.

(18) In the next chapter, I will suggest that the screen performs the same function with respect to the relation between the object and the subject-as-look.

(19) The Dürer drawing is used, in other words, in ways which are rather different from those implied by the text from which it is taken. In its original content, it would

seem primarily to serve a didactic function with respect to the articulation of perspective.

(20) For a discussion of mechanically reproduced images, see Walter Benjamin, "The Work of Art in the Age of Mechanical Reproduction," in *Illuminations,* trans. Harry Zohn (New York: Harcourt, 1969), pp. 217–51.

(21) Christian Metz, "Photography and Fetish," in *The Critical Image: Essays on Contemporary Photography,* ed. Carol Squiers (Seattle: Bay Press, 1990), p. 158.

(22) The screen to which I refer is of course that intervening between the camera/gaze, and the subject-as-spectacle. I still stand by my original definition of this particular screen as that repertoire of ideologically marked representations through which the members of a particular culture are visually defined and differentiated from one another.

(23) Roland Barthes, *Camera Lucida: Reflections on Photography,* trans. Richard Howard (New York: Hill and Wang, 1981), pp. 10–12.

(24) Here, I am proposing that the discussion of the field of vision provided in the section of *Four Fundamental Concepts* which is entitled "Of the Gaze as *Objet Petit a*" needs to be thought of in relation to that entitled "The Field of the Other and Back to the Transference." I am suggesting, that is, that the screen, like language, constitutes one of those agencies whereby the subject is installed within signification, and isolated from being. It should be evident by now that I am imputing to the relation of subject, screen, and gaze a logic which is in excess of the imaginary. As I suggested earlier, the gaze exercises a symbolic function; it represents "Otherness" within the field of vision. The screen, moreover, not only provides the subject with a specular but a *meaningful* body, one marked by all kinds of differential values. Thus, although the relation of subject, screen, and gaze should not be confused with the relation of the subject to language, nevertheless, it too— as Barthes suggests—induces not only the subject's alienation in the image but a certain existential "fading."

(25) In "Mimicry and Legendary Psychasthenia," trans. John Shepley, *October,* no. 31 (1984), Roger Caillois speaks about mimicry as "a reproduction in three-dimensional space with solids and voids: sculpture-photography or better *teleplasty*" (23). For a discussion of the uses to which Lacan puts this essay in *Four Fundamental Concepts,* see my *Male Subjectivity at the Margins,* (148–49), and Chapter 6 of this book.

(26) This is, as I will claim at the end of the next chapter, a camera not of the gaze, but the look. *Bilder der Welt und Inschrift des Krieges* shows that the camera is not invariably wed to the gaze, even within the present social regime, but may be at times subordinated to the eye.

(27) For a discussion of this text, see the next chapter.

(28) This passage is quoted by Martin Jay in *Downcast Eyes: The Denigration of Vision in Twentieth-Century French Thought* (Berkeley: University of California Press,

1993), p. 166.

(29)   Sigmund Freud, *The Interpretation of Dreams,* in *The Standard Edition of the Complete Psychological Works,* trans. James Strachey (London: Hogarth, 1953), vol. 5, pp. 536–41.

Chapter Five: The Look

(1)   When referring to this voyeur, I will consistently deploy the male pronoun, since the fantasy of mastery which this figure sustains is so hyperbolically masculine.

(2)   Jean-Paul Sartre, *Being and Nothingness: An Essay on Phenomenological Ontology,* trans. Hazel E. Barnes (London: Methuen, 1957), pp. 259–60.

(3)   For a fine discussion of this notion of specularity, particularly as it is elaborated in the writings of Barthes and Bakhtin and the paintings of Francis Bacon, see Ernst van Alphen, *Francis Bacon and the Loss of Self* (London: Reaktion Books, 1992), pp. 114–63.

(4)   Clearly, there is much overlap between these three categories of oppositions, but because Sartre's account of the field of vision differs so much from Lacan's with respect to the subject/object opposition, I want to deal with that opposition separately from those of God/sinner and master/slave.

(5)   Jacques Lacan, *The Four Fundamental Concepts of Psycho-Analysis,* trans. Alan Sheridan (New York: Norton, 1978), p. 83.

(6)   Lacan breaks here not only with Sartre, but with Merleau-Ponty, for whom there is an absolute symmetry and reciprocity of seer and seen. Merleau-Ponty writes in *The Visible and the Invisible,* trans. Alphonso Lingis (Evanston: Northwestern University Press, 1968): "He who looks must not himself be foreign to the world that he looks at. As soon as I see, it is necessary that the vision...be doubled with a complementary vision or with another vision: myself seen from without, such as another would see me, installed in the midst of the visible.... he who sees cannot possess the visible unless he is possessed by it, unless he *is of it,* unless...he is one of the visibles, capable by a singular reversal, of seeing them—he who is one of them" (134–35). But at the same time that Lacan insists upon the incommensurability of look and gaze, it is clear that he derives his notion that the look is also within spectacle at least in part from Merleau-Ponty.

(7)   In the next chapter, I will argue that, since the gaze represents above all else "the presence of others as such," we must also impute some agency in this respect to the collective look. I will suggest that this look turns the imaginary view finder of the camera/gaze in one direction or another, thereby determining which aspect of the cultural screen is mobilized in a given "photographic" transaction.

(8)   These texts consist primarily of "The Mirror Stage," in *Écrits: A Selection,* trans. Alan Sheridan (New York: Norton, 1977), pp. 1–7; *The Seminar of Jacques Lacan, Book I: Freud's Papers on Technique, 1953–1954,* trans. John Forrester (Cambridge: Cambridge University Press, 1988); *The Seminar of Jacques Lacan, Book II: The Ego*

in *Freud's Theory and in the Technique of Psychoanalysis, 1954–1955,* trans. Sylvana Tomaselli (Cambridge: Cambridge University Press, 1988); and "Some Reflections on the Ego," *International Journal of Psychoanalysis,* vol. 34 (1953): 259–60.

(9)   The classic discussion of fetishism is to be found in Sigmund Freud, "Fetishism," in *The Standard Edition of the Complete Psychological Works,* trans. James Strachey (London: Hogarth, 1961), vol. 21, pp. 152–57.

(10)   Lacan, *Four Fundamental Concepts,* p. 81.

(11)   Rosalind Krauss, *The Optical Unconscious* (Cambridge: MIT Press, 1993), pp. 112–13.

(12)   Jean-Francois Lyotard, *Les TRANSformateurs DUchamp* (Paris: Galilee, 1977), pp. 137–38. Quoted and translated by Krauss in *The Optical Unconscious,* p. 113. "*Con*" means "cunt" in French, but is also used as a standard scolding term for men, equivalent to "prick." The French text is thus not entirely translatable.

(13)   For a discussion of *Nachträglichkeit,* see Sigmund Freud, *Project for a Scientific Psychology,* in *The Standard Edition,* vol. 1, pp. 347–59, and *Studies in Hysteria,* in *The Standard Edition,* vol. 2, pp. 125–34; and Jean Laplanche, *Life and Death in Psychoanalysis,* trans. Jeffrey Mehlman (Baltimore: Johns Hopkins Press, 1976), pp. 25–47.

(14)   The "given-to-be-seen" is a translation of "*le donne-à-voir.*"

(15)   Each of us is "the subject of representation" in all three senses. It is through representation that we are "photographed," and that we apprehend both the object and the gaze.

(16)   For readings of the Holbein painting, see Jurgis Baltrusaitis, *Anamorphic Art* (New York: Harry N. Adams: 1977), pp. 91–130; Mary F. S. Hervey, *Holbein's "Ambassadors": The Picture and the Men* (London: George Bell and Sons, 1900); Stephen Greenblatt, *Renaissance Self-Fashioning: From Moore to Shakespeare* (Chicago: University of Chicago Press, 1980), pp. 17–25; and Mieke Bal, "Un ou deux choses…," *Protee,* vol. 19, no. 1 (1991): 51–60.

(17)   The figure standing on the left side of the table wears a small death's head on his cap, suggesting a less absolute opposition between the two portions of the painting than I have proposed. *The Ambassadors* also represents in part an allegory about the exemplary relation between nationalism and religious reform and tolerance. However, the sumptuousness of fabric and floor tiles, and the many signifiers of human achievement within the domains of knowledge, politics, and the arts give a solidity and substance to the earthly domain depicted in the upper part of the painting which is negated by the death's head below. Greenblatt makes a similar point in *Renaissance Self-Fashioning,* pp. 18–20.

(18)   Again, I find myself in fundamental agreement with Greenblatt, who writes: "The skull expresses the death that the viewer has, in effect, himself brought about by changing his perspective, by withdrawing his gaze from the figures of the painting. For that gaze is, the skull implies, reality-conferring; without it, the objects so lov-

ingly represented in their seeming substantiality vanish. To move a few feet away from the frontal contemplation of the painting is to efface everything within it, to bring death into the world" (Ibid., p. 20).

(19) *Male Subjectivity at the Margins* (New York: Routledge, 1992), Chapter 1.

(20) For an extended discussion of the necessity for something to be constantly iterated as the possibility for its resignification, see Judith Butler, *Bodies that Matter* (London: Routledge, 1993), especially Chapters 1 and 2.

(21) For an account of some of these libidinal transactions, see *Male Subjectivity at the Margins*, Chapters 4, 5, and 8.

(22) Sigmund Freud, *The Interpretation of Dreams*, in *The Standard Edition*, vol. 5, pp. 533–621. The following discussion of memory draws extensively from this text, but also from three other Freud texts: *Studies in Hysteria;* "The Mystic Writing Pad," in *The Standard Edition*, vol. 19, pp. 227–32; and "Screen Memories," in *The Standard Edition*, vol. 3, pp. 303–22.

(23) For a definition of the stereotype plate, see Sigmund Freud, "The Dynamics of Transference," in *The Standard Edition*, vol. 12, pp. 99–100. For an account of the closely related notion of the fantasmatic, see Jean Laplanche and J.-B. Pontalis, *The Language of Psycho-Analysis*, trans. Donald Nicholson-Smith (New York: Norton, 1973), pp. 314–19. I elaborate on the meaning of the stereotype plate or fantasmatic at great length in *Male Subjectivity at the Margins*.

(24) Sigmund Freud, *Beyond the Pleasure Principle*, in *The Standard Edition*, vol. 18, p. 42.

(25) Roland Barthes, *Camera Lucida: Reflections on Photography*, trans. Richard Howard (New York: Hill and Wang, 1981), p. 51.

(26) For an excellent discussion of the punctum in relation to Proust, see Mieke Bal, "The Gaze in the Closet," in *Vision in Contexts*, ed. Teresa Brennan and Martin Jay (forthcoming, Routledge, 1996).

(27) I am once again indebted to Walter Benjamin for this formulation. See *Illuminations*, trans. Harry Zohn (New York: Harcourt, 1969), p. 160.

(28) For a discussion of the primary process, see Freud, *Interpretation of Dreams*, vol. 5, pp. 588–609. In Chapters 2 and 3 of *The Subject of Semiotics* (New York: Oxford University Press, 1983), I argue that the primary process plays an important part in artistic production.

(29) See Fredric Jameson, *The Political Unconscious: Narrative as a Socially Symbolic Act* (Ithaca: Cornell University Press, 1981), p. 102.

(30) Michael Renov suggests that in some larger sense *Sans Soleil* approximates the operations of memory, a point with which, I hope it is clear, I am in fundamental agreement: "It is my sense that the film, in its intricately textured mounting of visual and acoustic elements, constitutes itself as a kind of simulacrum for the psychic processes, memory in particular" ("Documentary/Technology/Immediacy: Strategies of Resistance" [unpublished manuscript], pp. 5–6).

(31)   Michael Walsh also comes close to characterizing *Sans Soleil* as a cinema of the look. "The film's fascination with the eye is openly thematized by the voice-over," he writes, "recurring in everything from the redeployment of the credit sequence of *Vertigo* to the documentation of a Japanese ritual in which a victorious politician paints out the eye of a totemic figure." Walsh, "Around the World, Across all Frontiers: *Sans Soleil* as *Depays*," *CinéAction* (Fall 1989): 32.

Chapter Six: The Screen

(1)   Guy Debord, *The Society of the Spectacle,* trans. Fredy Perlman (London: Practical Paradise Publications, 1977), p. 1.

(2)   Jacques Lacan, *Four Fundamental Concepts of Psycho-Analysis,* trans. Alan Sheridan (New York: Norton, 1978), p. 75.

(3)   Ibid., pp. 74, 99, 117.

(4)   Vilem Flusser, *Towards a Philosophy of Photography* (Gottingen, West Germany: European Photography, 1984), p. 7.

(5)   Flusser characterizes the camera as a "black box," to whose program most photographers are blindly subservient, and to the extension of which the most gifted and original photographers work. Scarcely a second intervenes between the production of a "new" image and the expansion of the program to include it. Within this model, it is difficult to imagine any genuinely contestatory gesture.

(6)   Susan Sontag, *On Photography* (New York: Farrar, Straus & Giroux, 1977), p. 85.

(7)   Roland Barthes, *Camera Lucida: Reflections on Photography,* trans. Richard Howard (New York: Hill and Wang, 1981), p. 12.

(8)   Christian Metz, "Photography and Fetish," in *The Critical Image: Essays on Contemporary Photography,* ed. Carol Squiers (Seattle: Bay Press, 1990), p. 158.

(9)   Barthes, *Camera Lucida,* p. 15.

(10)   Pierre Bourdieu, "The Cult of Unity and Cultivated Differences," in *Photography: A Middle-brow Art,* trans. Shaun Whiteside (Stanford: University Press, 1990), p. 19.

(11)   Siegfried Kracauer, "Photography," *Critical Inquiry,* vol. 19, no. 3 (1993): 433.

(12)   From "The Monuments of Passaic," quoted in Craig Owens, *Beyond Recognition: Representation, Power, and Culture,* ed. Scott Bryson, Barbara Kruger, Lynne Tillman, and Jane Weinstock (Berkeley: University of California Press, 1992), p. 27.

(13)   Roger Caillois, "Mimicry and Legendary Psychasthenia," trans. John Shepley, *October,* no. 31 (1984): 17–32.

(14)   Frantz Fanon, *Black Skin, White Masks,* trans. Charles Lamm Markmann (London: Pluto Press, 1986), p. 112.

(15)   Owens, *Beyond Recognition,* p. 210.

(16)   The still photographs Cindy Sherman produced using a "centerfold" format could be said to offer a sustained dramatization of this principle. The unnatural poses

assumed by the women in an attempt to fit into a much shallower than usual frame—and, in some cases, one which is generally too constrained—would imply the frame even if it were not there.

(17) Pierre Bourdieu, "The Social Definition of Photography," in *Photography: A Middle-Brow Art,* p. 83.

(18) Once again I would like to indicate that this felicitous phrase derives from Laura Mulvey's *Visual and Other Pleasures* (Bloomington: Indiana University Press, 1989), p. 18.

(19) Arthur Danto, "Photography and Performance: Cindy Sherman's Stills," in Cindy Sherman, *Untitled Film Stills* (London: Jonathan Cape, 1990), p. 13.

(20) Rosalind Krauss, "Cindy Sherman Untitled," in *Cindy Sherman, 1975–1993* (New York: Rizzoli, 1993), p. 56.

(21) Judith Williamson, "Images of 'Woman'—the Photographs of Cindy Sherman," *Screen,* vol. 24, no. 6 (1983): 103.

(22) *Male Subjectivity at the Margins* (New York: Routledge, 1992), p. 152.

(23) Again, this is Flusser's notion (*Toward a Philosophy of Photography,* p. 19).

(24) By "objectivity," I mean both the camera's traditional claim to see things as they actually are, and its isolation from subjectivity.

(25) In *The Eighteenth Brumaire of Louis Bonaparte,* Marx writes: "Men make their own history, but they do not make it just as they please, but under circumstances directly encountered, given, and transmitted from the past" (*Selected Writings,* ed. David McLellan [Oxford: Oxford University Press, 1977], p. 300).

(26) Gerald Marzorati, "Imitation of Life," *ARTnews* (September 1983): 85–86.

(27) Michael Danoff, "Cindy Sherman: Guises and Revelations," *Cindy Sherman* (New York: Pantheon Books, 1984), p. 194.

(28) Peter Schjeldahl, "The Oracle of Images," in *Cindy Sherman* (New York: Whitney Museum of American Art, 1987), p. 8.

(29) See, for instance, D. W. Winnicott, *Playing and Reality* (London: Penguin, 1974), p. 163, where the author differentiates the notion of the "good enough mother" from that of the "perfect mother," and endorses the former, and pp. 11–12, where he associates good enough caretaking with the opening up of the child to lack.

Index